The
LAST FRONTIER

The
LAST FRONTIER

Edited by Jill Shepherd

THE LYONS PRESS

Guilford, Connecticut

An Imprint of The Globe Pequot Press

The Lyons Press is an imprint of The Globe Pequot Press.
10 9 8 7 6 5 4 3 2 1

Printed in the United States of America.

Library of Congress Cataloging-in-Publication Data is available on file.

Contents

Preface

One of the benefits of working for *Alaska* magazine is having access to a complete collection of past issues. On slow afternoons I sometimes slip into the conference room, pull a volume of *The Alaska Sportsman* off of the shelf and lose myself in the lives and experiences of past Alaskans.

After years of random browsing, I began to realize that *Alaska* magazine and its predecessor, *The Alaska Sportsman*, are unique chronicles of the ever-changing face of Alaska. Though founded to promote hunting and fishing opportunities to the Outside reader, it also reflected beliefs and attitudes of the day.

While the first issue is dedicated almost completely to hunting and fishing there also was poetry; From Ketchikan to Barrow, a news department that survives to this day in *Alaska* magazine and is a surprisingly accurate prediction of what the future held in store for Alaska.

In an essay titled, *Alaska Wonderland*, Dr. Will H. Chase of Cordova writes, *Alaska is destined to be America's playground and, in my opinion, the tourist traffic will be so vast in the not so far distant future that we of today can form no adequate conception of the number of people it will bring to see our wonders and the increased development which will come in their wake.*

How prophetic his words were.

Early issues lived up to the founders' intent to promote Alaska's world-class fishing and hunting. In *Every Inch a King* (June 1936) a young Bob Henning described a battle of more than two hours to land a 62-pound king salmon near Juneau. Twenty-two years after this piece was published Henning bought the magazine. He owned it for 28 years.

Wolf control, still a contentious issue in 2002, is addressed in the first issue in an article titled *The Wolf Pack* by F.W. Gabler. The article portrays the wolf as a vicious predator that should be eradicated from the territory. Through the 1930s and 40s, the magazine routinely favored this popular viewpoint common in the territory and the Lower 48.

Many early pieces tell of fantastic challenges experienced while wresting a living from the land. In *Polar Fury* (April 1936) by Charles Madsen, the author sets out with his chief Eskimo hunter, Anoyak, to fill an order for 100,000 pounds of green, salted walrus skins at seven cents a pound. During the hunt they learn that a wounded, 2,000-pound walrus can be a dangerous adversary. In *Bush Madnes* (November 1939) by S. A. Camp, a fur trapper explains just how much tougher life can get when your only companion is gripped with cabin fever and the nearest neighbor is forty miles away on the other side of the mountains.

Flipping through magazines of the 1940s, one can trace changes brought by war construction and improved access via the Alaska Highway and many new airfields built around the territory. By the 1950s, writers were beginning to reminisce about the simpler days before the war and first person recollections of the Gold Rush all but disappear. In the 1960s editorials begin to grapple with the influx of people and the effect of development on the state's wild places.

And through those decades right up to the present there are stories of ordinary people living extraordinary lives here in the North. I could go on but soon you'd be crowding into the conference room to look through the old magazines yourself and I'd have to find work to do on slow afternoons.

This book is the next best thing.

To create *The Last Frontier*, Senior Editor Jill Shepherd spent months reading every issue from January 1935 to the present. Jill's fifty years in Alaska and twenty years at the magazine made her ideal for the job. Over the winter she methodically read her way through sixty-seven bound volumes of *The Alaska Sportsman* and *Alaska* magazine, flagging stories with sticky notes and ferrying stacks of the heavy books between the conference room and her office on a wheeled chair. She enlisted our long-time editorial assistant, Donna Rae Thompson, to copy the stories selected for the book and tapped Assistant Art Director Mishelle Kennedy to scan old covers for the color insert. When Jill wavered on whether or not to include a story she asked managing editor Tim Woody or me for our opinions. The book project became a labor of love and at times it seemed that work on current issues of *Alaska* magazine took a back seat to work on the book. But the result was worth it, fifty-nine stories representing sixty-seven years of the best writing in Alaska. We hope you enjoy reading it as much as we enjoyed creating it.

—ANDY HALL, EDITOR
ALASKA MAGAZINE
JUNE 2002

Introduction

More than sixty-five years ago, a band of Ketchikan businessmen pooled their resources and talents to create *The Alaska Sportsman*, a 15-cent, glossy hunting and fishing magazine that made its debut in January 1935.

These men not only founded one of the nation's first regional magazines, they also founded what is considered a founding icon of today's trends toward adventure journalism. It is also the only national magazine exclusively dedicated to life in Alaska, edited and written by people who have lived, worked, loved and, yes, died in the Great Land.

During its 67 years, *Alaska* magazine has grown from little more than a sportsman's black and white newsletter into a full-color award-winning national magazine with a circulation of almost 200,000, most of it in the Lower 48, also known in Alaska as "Outside." The magazine has also "grown up" with Alaska, covering every important issue to face the state, from managing wildlife to the throes of statehood, from the building of the pipeline to the environmental tragedy of the Exxon Valdez, from the emergence of Native land trusts and corporations to the continuing legacy of the gold-panning sourdough. For many years, the only contact many bush Alaskans had with outside news, other than short wave radio, was their monthly issue of *Alaska* magazine. Even today, around the middle of the month, bush-bound mail pouches carry thousands of *Alaska* magazines to readers in remote villages and settlements. No other magazine in America has a more geographically diverse readership.

The founders of *Alaska Sportsman*, however, were among other things, just trying to bring more attention from people Outside to the sporting paradise of Alaska. It was, one could argue, the beginning of Alaska's promotion of itself as a visitor destination. Still today, hunters and fishers comprise almost half of the leisure-time visitors to Alaska. Each of the magazine's founders was a member of the Alaska Sportsman's Association, a budding trade association looking to build more interest in Alaska hunting and fishing.

"It is a mission of relating some of the adventures of the out-of-doors men in this great northern territory," wrote editor Tom Smith in Volume 1, No. 1," . . . of picturing its scenic grandeur, its romance, its fauna and flora. Of relating facts which will give a true idea of the country and of advising intelligent conservation of its great natural wildlife resources against wasteful despoilers."

The association contracted with the Journal Printing Co. of Ketchikan, which printed *The Ketchikan Chronicle*. Tom Smith, editor of the *Chronicle*, was appointed editor of *The Sportsman*.

F.W. Bill Gabler of the Gilmore Clothing Store was named advertising manager, and Emery Tobin, who worked as linotype operator for the *Chronicle*, was named business manager.

Vol. 1, No. 1, hit the stands in January 1935. It was a slick-paper magazine of thirty pages that sold for 15 cents a copy; subscriptions cost $1.50 per year. Printing costs were about $600 per issue for 1,000 copies.

"I still retain a very graphic memory of our collating operation, circa 1940," wrote Ray Roady, in an unpublished manuscript in 1989. "Eight or 10 women, mostly Norwegian housewives, sat around the diameter of a 12-foot revolving round table powered by a washing machine motor. On the table were stacks of newly printed pages of the magazine arranged in numerical piles around the outer edges. The table rotated and the seated women gathered the sheets as they came by. . . . Each of these accumulated bundles was then passed on to a stitcher, a person with a crude foot-operated treadle machine who stapled the pages into a complete magazine ready to go to the manually operated trimmer." Producing a thirty-page magazine proved to be a challenging task for the original ten staffers. They scrounged from other association members as well as friends for articles, photographs, and advertisements, wielding whatever influence they could muster to get material. Stanley Adams, manager of Tongass Hardware, put pressure on salesmen from whom he bought, to get their companies to buy ad space. Gabler, an accomplished commercial artist, contributed numerous illustrations and a number of articles. According to Roady, every member of the association (records show fifty-eight people paid $1 each to join the association in 1935) was enthusiastically interested in contributing time and materials.

Articles also were solicited from readers: "You need not be an expert at story writing! Write the story in your own style and we will gladly edit it for you, but be sure you include pictures for illustration purposes," urged a February 1935 advertisement. The ad even suggested topics: "Have you ever had an unusual experience while hunting or fishing? Have you ever bagged an unusually fine trophy or caught an unusually fine fish? Have you ever had a narrow escape from death while hunting or fishing?"

Although twelve issues were planned for 1935, the association ran into financial problems and published only six. With the December issue, Emery F. Tobin emerged as the magazine's third editor that year, a position he held until May 1958. The magazine never skipped another issue.

Through its two monthly editorials, one by the editor and one by The Alaska Sportsmen's Association, the magazine portrayed Alaska as a hunting and fishing paradise. The association acted as a clearinghouse for hunting and fishing guides, and urged other communities in the territory to join. Alaska was touted as a winter playground, with the Dog Derby and Ice Carnival in Fairbanks presented as examples of "natural attractions."

Keeping in mind that Alaska was a territory, early editorials took a strong stand on gaining more local control of fish and game. The magazine urged abolishment of the federally controlled Alaska Game Commission; it opposed the $1 hunting license fee imposed only on residents in the Southeast; and it supported a move to make Admiralty Island a preserve for brown bears. Editorials also called for a reclassification of black bears from furbearers to game animals. An editorial from the association's president urged the Territorial Legislature to "protect wild life by increasing the wolf bounty, sufficient to warrant "trappers to devote their time to wolf destruction, a debate that rages to this day."

In 1958 Alaskans Robert A. Henning and Robert DeArmond bought the magazine, which in all its previous years of operation had never made a profit. "It was a handy deduction for tax purposes," wrote Roady who along with Emery and Clara Tobin was one of the last two shareholders.

The June 1958 issue was published by Henning's newly formed company, Alaska-Northwest Publishing Co. He operated out of Juneau and Seattle until June 1959, when he moved most of the operation to Edmonds, Washington, retaining an editorial office in Juneau. In March 1969 he opened an editorial office in Anchorage and changed the magazine's name to *Alaska*.

Henning and DeArmond bought the 23-year-old magazine for $15,000; DeArmond provided the cash. Four years later DeArmond sold his shares to Henning and stayed on as managing editor for a number of years.

Henning continued to focus the magazine mostly on hunting and fishing, which he felt were among the most important activities in Alaskan life.

"We don't fool around with society, traffic accidents, and politics," he said in a 1981 newspaper interview. "Those things are of passing interest. What's really important is what stage the clam tides are, and how the clams are doing. Whether or not the fish come each year means life or death to a lot of people." He didn't report on suicide or alcoholism, and told staffers that they were not to report on Anchorage — the largest city in Alaska, which held half the state's population. Why? Because readers wanted the "real" Alaska.

Manuscripts published during Henning's 28-year-ownership often arrived untyped and unsolicited. A former editor said one of the best manuscripts he ever received was about life on a tugboat. The story was handwritten and an accompanying note stated, "There are no dictionaries on *The Seaflyer*, so we all got together and voted on the hard words."

The last handwritten manuscript purchased was in 1991. Titled "The Simple Gifts of the Bush," it was a recollection of Christmases past by Interior resident Caroline Geisler-Schlentner.

By the time Henning sold *Alaska*, he had greatly expanded Alaska Northwest Books, publishing, among others, *The Milepost*, *Alaska Geographic*, and more than 100 book titles. *Alaska*, however, remained his flagship publication. "I always knew the magazine would be popular," he said.

In 1986 Henning sold *Alaska* to Yankee Publishing Co., of Dublin, New Hampshire. The family-owned company also publishes *Yankee* magazine and the venerable *Old Farmers Almanac*, which is the oldest continuously published periodical in America. A purchase price was not disclosed, but Rob Trowbridge, president and publisher of Yankee Publishing Co., reportedly paid several million dollars for the magazine.

"We see a lot of similarities between *Yankee* and *Alaska* magazine," Trowbridge told the *Anchorage Times*. He said both magazines are regional publications that appeal to the readers' sense of history and culture. Both magazines celebrated their 50th birthdays in 1985.

During the almost 10 years that Yankee owned *Alaska*, all editorial, advertising sales, and pre-production operations were moved from Edmonds, Washington, to the Anchorage office. Once *Alaska* had reached a circulation in excess of 50,000, printing in and mailing from Alaska was no longer practical. Since that time the magazine has been printed by companies located in the center of the U.S. mailing zones, a reflection of the publication's national footprint." Alaska Publishing Properties Inc. was formed to manage the new property, which included Tom Brennan, owner of the public relations firm of Brennan & Brennan Inc.; Tom Gresham, *Alaska* magazine editor; Barrie White, an Anchorage businessman; and Eric Wohlforth, an Anchorage attorney and Princeton University classmate of Trowbridge. Peter W. Sykas, vice president of operations for *Yankee* magazine, served as general manager of *Alaska*.

In July 1995, Morris Communications Company, LLC (MCC) acquired the magazine, its third publishing acquisition in the Alaska market, following the *Juneau Empire* (1968) and Kenai-based *The Peninsula Clarion* (1990), both daily newspapers. For MCC Chairman William S. (Billy) Morris III the acquisition of *Alaska* magazine fulfilled a long-time goal.

"I fell in love with Alaska in 1968, the year we acquired the *Juneau Empire*, and the ardor of that love affair has not diminished an iota since. Alaska is not only a place of seldom-equaled beauty for the eye, but also a never-ending source of replenishment for the soul. It is here that land and water, man and spirit *do* live in concert. Once one tastes Alaska, he must taste more. And no other publication sums up the Alaska experience better than *Alaska* magazine."

Since acquiring the magazine, Morris has added other media properties to its Alaska mix, including the *Alaska Journal of Commerce*, the *Anchorage Media Group*, which operates six radio stations, the *Homer News*, the *Alaska Star* of Eagle River and *Destination Alaska*, a shipping and cultural guide used annually by more than 450,000 cruise passengers. In 1998, Morris also acquired *The Milepost*, the 53-year-old mile-by-mile guide to the Alcan Highway system, one of the best selling travel guides in the world.

For current editor Andy Hall and his staff, the job remains much the same as that faced by the amateur magazine journalists who started the magazine: bring the 200,000 *Alaska* magazine readers the essence of life on the Last Frontier in an exciting, authoritative, and intimate fashion ten times each year. To accomplish that mission the magazine continues to seek first-person stories from Alaskans and Alaska adventurers, still ferrets out the most interesting and unusual stuff from an interesting and unusual land, and continues to chronicle the slow changes on the face of Alaska geology and the ever-quickening changes in the faces of its people and their march into the future.

—JILL SHEPHERD, EDITOR

Chapter 1

THE WOLF PACK

January 1935

By F. W. Gabler

The howl of the wolf pack, year after year, is becoming a more familiar note to the ear of the Alaska woodsman and he listens today with foreboding, as the chorus reaches crescendo. For, all over Alaska, and Southeastern Alaska especially, fear is felt for the harmless denizens of the woods as this marauder takes his toll.

So bold has the outlaw become that stories are told of his encounters even with man, and though no case has yet been proved wherein he actually killed a human, there are those who will relate instances, with proof, that he does attack and threaten.

It is the wolf's effect on wildlife with which the woodsman most concerns himself, and he vows vengeance as he views the remains of each fresh kill. Alaska has for years had a bounty on the wolf, but he works with such cunning and stealth that in spite of a kill of 1,000 wolves in 1933, his tribe increases. The wolf seems to sense the presence of traps and firearms and is therefore the most difficult of all of Alaska's animals to take.

There is a growing sentiment in the territory for an increase in the wolf bounty from $15 to a sum sufficient to serve as a greater incentive for woodsmen to trap them as a livelihood. Some advocate the employment of paid hunters. The situation has become so grave during the past few years that the Alaska Sportsmen's Association, among others, is seeking ways and means for wolf extermination as one of its major objectives.

A wolf's selection of food depends largely upon the territory in which he ranges. Goat, sheep, deer, caribou, moose and reindeer fall victims to his fangs annually in large numbers.

Wolves have been known to pass up winter quarters where deer are plentiful, easy prey, to take to the deep snow and make their way to a beaver colony, there going from den to den, until the entire population has been annihilated. Leaving the desolate scene, they proceed in their relentless search for more and more quarry. When their appetites have been appeased they kill for sport.

In summer months, with food plentiful, the wolf will hunt by himself , or in small bands, depending upon the variety of game he seeks. They are clever hunters, these wolves, and they apparently plan their hunt with the skill of experienced rangers.

While on a deer hunting expedition in the vicinity of Traitors Cove near Ketchikan, members of the Alaska Sportsmen's Association, last fall, experienced considerable difficulty, for a time, in even sighting a possible shot. Whereas game had been plentiful in this locality, on this hunt, three days were spent in fruitless effort.

Eventually, however, an opportunity presented itself in the form of a fleeing deer, and a well-placed bullet dropped the four-point buck.

The pulse of the sportsmen quickened and they listened intently as the howling of wolves in the direction from which the buck had come, reached their ears.

The hunters were quick to grasp the significance. "That explains the big buck's flight, and the scarcity of deer in these woods!" they decided. "Mr. Wolf is hunting, too, and protesting the interruption of his chase!"

After the hunters reached their boat, other members of the party told of having seen two wolves patroling the sand, apparently waiting for their cohorts to chase the quarry out of the woods into their ambush, a cleverly planned trap!

Further testimony of the wolf's cunning is given by a woodsman of Kenai peninsula. His observations were made from a bluff, commanding a view of a wide expanse of country. The level land below was covered only with a short brush. It was fairly open, only slightly timbered. Objects could be seen for a considerable distance against the background of the snow.

As the hunter surveyed the country below him, his eyes came upon the forms of four wolves, making their way through the snow. Two of the wolves had separated from the group, taking a stand on the knoll. Their heads moved from side to side as they sampled the air, keeping a close watch in the direction which they had come. The others went on and took up a similar position about a quarter of a mile from the first pair. This position was also a vantage point, about half-way up a hillside, nearer the bluff from which the woodsman was watching.

They, like the first two, appeared interested in the distant timber, as if anticipating excitement.

Twice the woodsman leveled his rifle at the nearest pair, but, on second thought, decided to lie low and perhaps learn the reason for the wolves' actions.

As he watched, the hunter suddenly saw all four turn their heads to the right. Something had attracted their attention. In a moment there was an uproar from the timber as the voice of a pack broke the stillness.

A moose, his speeding form eloquent of fright, emerged from the timber, with five wolves in hot pursuit. From a far side of the clearing three more wolves made their appearance. Running straight for the head of the approaching bull, the four which had taken their positions in ambush now sped forward—a total of twelve—all leaping to the attack, fangs bared, tearing at the moose from all sides.

The strategy displayed by the four wolves he had first seen was now disclosed. The atrocity had been planned, apparently, with the cleverness which comes from knowledge of the habits of the quarry and experience!

The bull was making a mighty fight for his life. Again and again he struck out with his forefeet. Again and again he swung his mighty antlers as he endeavored to toss the attackers aside. A wolf fell. He lay writhing on the ground, beneath the long forelegs of the mighty animal. Another wolf was down, wounded in his hind quarters.

The time had come for intervention on the part of the woodsman. He sprang into action; started firing at the wolves. The first two shots claimed one of the brutes, but so engrossed were his fellows that they did not notice he had fallen.

A third shot sent a second wolf writhing in the snow. By this time the others appeared to realize that they were in danger from some unknown quarter. They drew away, gradually, while the bull kept swinging his massive head. Reluctantly, they left the scene of battle and scattered into the brush, leaving four of their number lying limply in the snow, never to howl again, and a fifth in the brush, badly wounded.

As the hunter approached the scene of battle, he felt pity for the torn giant, slashed by the wolves' fangs. The moose, freed from his enemy, but mortally wounded, made his way out of the clearing. The snow was scarlet from the blood of both moose and wolf and a bloody trail marked the path of the moose's retreat.

One of the attackers had been disemboweled when the bull had struck a blow with his massive antlers.

Tracking and finding the moose was an easy matter. He was rapidly losing blood. His strength was spent. Great pieces of flesh had been torn from the bull by the powerful jaws of the wolves. They were now registering their disapproval in long, dismal wails, but from a safe distance. One bullet, through the brain, put the moose out of misery.

There are stories to the effect that wolves have killed men, tired on the trail, but no proof has been produced to that effect. There is the story, for instance, that a man by the name of LaBrande was attacked and killed by wolves, many years ago, near Kasaan, on Prince of Wales Island. All that remained, by which to identify the man, was his rifle, a knife and a few tattered bits of clothing and bones scattered about the ground.

Whenever it is said that wolves will not attack a person there it at least one man who will rise and challenge the statement. He is Frank Steiner.

Frank has lived at Herring Cove, on George Inlet, Revillagigedo Island, for thirteen years, and in his spare time from work as an operator at the hydro-electric plant there he has hunted and trapped the animals.

On a frosty November morning two years ago, Frank had no thought of wolves as he ascended the precipitous trestle to Lake Whitman, from which the hydro-electric plant receives its water supply. He was on the mission of ascertaining whether or not the lake had frozen over.

A new fall of snow covered the trestle, and the going was slippery. Upon reaching the lake, and finding that only a thin coating of ice covered the water, he proceeded to retrace his steps.

The single plank, which formed the foot path beside the pipeline, was so treacherous with snow and ice that he chose a course along the snow-covered ground which led across a large, open muskeg.

He had hardly reached the middle of the muskeg when he detected a movement in the brush to the right. Again he noticed a movement in the brush, this time in a different spot, to the left. At the same instant the howl of a wolf echoed across the flat.

It was the signal of the leader of a pack. Wolves emerged here and there all around. A large pack had him completely surrounded!

The pack closed in. They howled and they barked. Frank shivered as he realized he was their quarry!

He was unarmed except for a hunting knife. A futile weapon against the powerful jaws and brutal fangs of a pack of wolves! His only hope lay in reaching a tree.

He ran for the nearest tree, pulled himself up into the branches. It was a small one. He soon learned that he had chosen a very flimsy sanctuary, but now, with the ambush closing in, he had to make the best of it.

The tree was a scant five inches through at the base. The frail branches were strained to the limit with his weight and he easily encircled the trunk with his fingers.

Frank was hardly out of reach when the pack reached the tree. There were about twenty or thirty of them in the circle and others could be seen or heard howling at a distance, at least forty wolves in the vicinity.

The wolves nearest the tree leaped into the air to reach him. One nipped the heel of his boot. He wanted to ascend to the next branch, but dared not. The tree was already swaying dangerously as he made frantic efforts to avoid the fangs that snapped under his feet. Should the tree break, he would fall among the vicious besiegers and be torn to shreds.

Shouting at the top of his voice, he called for help, in hopes that his friends at the power house would hear and come to his rescue. He knew that the cry of wolves on this muskeg was often heard at the plant, possibly when they were rallying to attack a deer.

Again, he felt a tug at his boot and instinctively raised his foot. The motion threw his entire weight on the opposite limb. Without warning, the limb broke. He fell with a sickening crash! His hands frantically grasped the slender trunk. For a moment the wolves appeared almost awed, and using that moment to advantage, he raised himself to the remaining lowest branch.

As he pulled himself up, one wolf, the largest of the pack, leaped and sunk his fangs, but the teeth barely grazed his leg. There was a rip, and at the same time he felt a draft as the pant-leg was severed from his trousers. The weight of the wolf almost dislodged his new foothold.

Wrapping a leg around the trunk, he seized his knife and threw it angrily at the wolf which had almost downed him. It struck the animal squarely on the head and bounced into the now well-packed snow. The wolf seized it, carried it a few feet, dropped it again, and returned to the tree.

It seemed hours and weeks passed. His heart was pounding, his throat burned and his arms and legs ached as he endeavored to retain his hold on the tree. His head whirled, he felt faint.

Eventually the howling diminished. He noticed that the pack grew smaller. Part of the pack headed toward the lake, those remaining either circling the tree or sitting on their haunches, watching with hungry eyes.

Another group of besiegers headed toward the lake. Possibly all would give up and seek game which could not climb trees. Eight were left, apparently reluctant to leave. Then they, too, gave a final howl and left to join the pack.

He watched them go with relief, but waited to make sure that their departure was not a ruse to entice him from his perch. At last he dropped to the ground and raced for the timber. He was weak and stiff, but felt that once in the timber he would have bigger trees to climb.

Finally he made his way to the power house, nervous and tired, with new ideas regarding the wolves he formerly trapped and shot. His advice is: "Take it from me and never go into the woods in the winter without a gun!" He feels that had he carried a gun the wolves would never have dared approach him, and in any event, the story would have been very different.

The wolf's sense of smell is acknowledged so strong that he can detect firearms at a distance and experience has taught him to fear guns, traps and even poison.

Another story wherein wolves, in a large band, showed no fear of a man even when he had a gun, was related by Henry Fawcett, a native, who, when he hunted with a partner, was surrounded for a time by over fifty wolves. It occurred on Duke Island, Southeastern Alaska, late in 1933, he says.

The wolves snapped at him, came almost to the muzzle of his gun. It was not until he had killed two wolves and his partner had rushed to his aid from a distance, and killed another, that the band dispersed. One of the wolves killed was the leader, they believe, for the pack dragged it off the field of battle and into the woods. They brought the forelegs of two of the wolves to Ketchikan and collected the bounty.

Evidence is plain that wolves travel a definite route, taking in a large area of game country. They often remain in one district to hunt for ten to fifteen days, depending upon the extent of their circuit and the game supply.

The prolific nature of the wolf accounts for his rapid increase in numbers. The female will produce from three to thirteen pups in one litter and it has been shown that she gives birth to young at the early age of two to three years.

Seven pups a year may be considered the average increase of the wolf family. Observers say that they mate for life and often live ten to twelve years.

Throughout the winter months, when food is more difficult to obtain, the wolves band together in packs of from four to forty or fifty in number, with a powerful fellow as their leader who commands the respect of his band through qualifications of brawn and brain.

Disregarding the fact that a portion of the wolf's kill is purely for sport, it has been estimated that he destroys annually a total of 730 pounds of flesh for food. The average human family will not consume a like amount in the same time.

While there are comparatively few livestock farms in Southeastern Alaska, ranchers have complained that wolves killed considerable domesticated stock in the past year. Certain farmers at Point Aggassiz, near Petersburg, are reported to be considering killing off their herds of sheep before the wolves do.

Whenever a movement is started to reduce the quantity of any animal, be it rat or rattlesnake, some champion of the outcast arises to protest, stating, that however unnecessary the villain may appear, he keeps in check a still greater evil. Suffice it to say, that in districts where the wolf is extinct, such as east of the Mississippi River, there has never been felt the need for re-stocking the land with his kind.

Chapter 2

TUNDRA TERROR

December 1935

By Victor Shaw

Strange things happen in the Land of the Midnight Sun. Every Alaskan has heard tales of White and Indian murderers, men who killed in camp and on trail, stole gold or outfits from prospectors and hunters and continued on in the solitudes, going their mysterious ways.

Then, there are the stories of madmen, men who killed in the madness which Arctic hardships and loneliness sometimes do bring on. Such a breed was Klutuk, a known killer as long ago as 1919. For years he had the whole Nushagak region terrorized. Then, about 1929, the following report appeared in Alaska newspapers:

Klutuk, alleged native murderer to the westward, is now more of a mystery than ever, for he seems to have vanished from off the face of the earth.

Last fall a trapper discovered what he thought was Klutuk's cabin on the Hoholitna River, a tributary of the Kuskokwim, but since then there has been no sign of him anywhere so far as the inhabitants of that remote region are concerned.

The following weird story is based, to a considerable extent, on fact. The locale is farther to the south than the place where Klutuk spread his reign of terror but it occurred at the time the news report appeared. Does it contain an explanation of what happened to Klutuk?

A wild screech exploded Ken Strong's deep sleep one night in camp. He was on his first spring bear hunt, among the foothills of the bleak Aleutian Range. Only half awake, he stared drowsily into the inky shadows of the lava cave, vaguely aware of a queer, fetid odor.

He heard a muffled oath, then a snuffling snarl, and detected the quick pad-pad-pad of retreating feet. The rattle of a rifle-bolt throwing a shell into the chamber, jerked him back to full consciousness.

"Pete?" he queried. The answer was a warning hiss.

Sitting up in his sleeping bag, Ken fumbled for the flashlight, found it, snapped it on.

Near the cave entrance, his sourdough guide, Kobuk Pete, crouched, rifle in hand, peering tensely into the Alaskan night. Pete blinked in the glare, motioned for quiet.

"Have a nightmare?" Ken grinned at him.

Pete arose, tiptoed across the cave.

"Nightmare, hell," he whispered. "Gimme that flash."

Handing it over, Ken crawled from the bag with a slight sensation of unease. Come to think, there had been a weird note in the howl that waked him—something almost inhuman. Not what one would expect from close-mouthed, hard-boiled Peter Conley.

"Did you do that yelling?" Ken asked, pulling on his boots.

"Not me. It was the damn thing that had me by the throat."

"The devil-you-say!"

"The devil, it was! Close call, too. Let's scout around."

The most careful search of the starlit tundra failed to disclose a trace of their midnight visitor. On the return, being still weary from yesterday's tough, back-pack trip Ken was moved to voice his skepticism regarding Pete's experience.

"Don't I know when human thumbs sink in my windpipe and a couple knees dig into my guts? . . . Stunk like some kinda polecat, too. Betcha my neck's all red. Look and see." It was, but Ken remained unimpressed.

"Nonsense," he chuckled. "It was your blanket got twisted and wound around your Adam's apple. You've just been thinking about those wild tales Bill McKay told us, at Egegik cannery, and it resulted in a bad dream, that's all. Forget it."

"Mebbe," Peter muttered. They re-entered the cave.

But Ken realized that the guide was unconvinced when he saw, before dropping off to sleep, that Pete kept the loaded rifle handy, as if planning to remain awake and watchful until daybreak.

Pete was out scouting as soon as it was light. He returned, baffled and morose, when Ken called him to breakfast. Pete reported numerous tracks of caribou, gathering for the great spring migration northward, also wolf sign and the deep spoor of giant brown bears, just out from their winter dens. Nothing else. His fingers were shaky as he rolled a smoke beside the dying breakfast fire.

"What," Ken chucked, "did you expect to find?"

"Laugh and be danged! There's something in what McKay told. I've heard before that men have come in here and never been heard of again. There's been trappers quit good fur country because they was scared stiff, and prospectors come back telling of being nearly choked to death in their bunks. Besides, you can't drag an Indian in here on a bet. They claim it's haunted, and after last night I sure don't blame 'em for thinking so." He waved gloomily at the desolate country westward.

The elevation here gave Ken his first good view of the region. Across the rolling tundra lay blue Lake Becherof, where they had left their boat, with ice-choked Bering Sea rimming the far horizon. It was a dreary expanse of land and water which they had crossed after days of back-breaking toil.

Behind and to the eastward, the gray reek of numerous somnolent volcanoes stained the sky; Kugak, Mageik, Trident and treacherous Katmai, rearing hoary, snow-crowned heads around the strange Valley of Ten Thousand Smokes.

A raw, dead land, still in the making. An arid waste, shrouded with pumice, that whispered eerily underfoot. Truly, anything might happen here and Ken rather hoped it would. He had counted on possible adventure, mixed with bear hunting. Yet, he still groped for some plausible explanation of the night's disturbance.

"If it was no dream, how do you explain it?" he demanded.

"Search me. Let's snag your brownie and beat it, quick."

Days of strenuous hunting followed. Pete grew more silent and preoccupied. He halted often to peer and listen.

He formed a habit of darting a swift glance over his shoulder. At last, even Ken began to sense that they were being watched from ambush—that an invisible Something dogged each step.

Camp was shifted often. They pressed into the hills, yet never did they succeed in shaking off the feel of a stalking menace. Ken continued to deride Pete's thinly veiled hint at the supernatural. Nor was this lessened by the wild outcries, seemingly from nowhere, which frequently halted them in their tracks.

Never could they detect the source of the howling, or explain it. Possibly, Ken suggested, it was a strange species of bird. Or the coyotes from the eastward. But at such times Pete merely favored him with an oddly silent stare.

Could it be a maniacal human?

Once, when they knocked over a caribou for meat and packed in the heavy hind quarters, they returned for the rest to find only the head, hide, and bones, stripped of meat. Ken pointed to some fresh bear tracks nearby, but the guide shook his head.

"It's no bear's work," he asserted, with grim significance.

Late one afternoon, after a long, exciting stalk, Ken secured his bear. It was a monster, so big that just the green hide was far too heavy to pack out and it had to be scraped and dried to lighten weight. With obvious reluctance, Pete agreed to camp and prepare the trophy.

It looked as though it would be a dry camp. As luck would have it, the area appeared wholly arid and waterless. So, when the pelt had been well scraped and pegged out to dry, both set out on a hunt for water to boil the pot. At first the quest seemed hopeless. Repeated quakes had so shaken and rent the earth that even snow seep, from the slopes above, had been absorbed by the parched soil.

They searched the country for miles around, found depressions and cracks in the ground, but no water.

Finally, just as they began to fear a complete failure, they encountered a great, dark crevasse in the ground, so deep and extensive that Ken's hopes soared. If, he argued, all water here ran underground, it was possible that this earth-crack was deep enough to tap its level. Anyway, it was worth trying.

Following a game trail that paralleled the rim of the crevasse, they came, at last, to a place where an earth slide, formed by the caving of the side walls, gave access to the depths. Ken pointed eagerly to the beaten pathway down the steep incline.

"It's a game trail to water!" he exclaimed. "I'm so dry my throat is plugged with dust. Come on, Pete."

"Don't like the looks of it," the guide demurred.

"Nerts," Ken gibed. "Spooks don't make tracks like those."

Kobuk Pete's tanned face turned a dull red.

"Brownies do," he said quietly. "I'll tackle one anywhere in the open, but I wouldn't corner a brownie in a hole like that."

Ken hesitated an instant, but thirst made him reckless.

"Tracks look old," he argued. "Ten to one there's no bear now."

"Hop to it," Pete shrugged. "I'll mosey over yonder and prospect up them draws. If you get in a jam—yell."

Nor did he return Ken's bantering grin. He stood slit-eyed and thoughtful as Ken plunged down the slide, canteen in hand.

Descending rapidly, Ken discovered presently that the surface soil changed suddenly to rock; rock identical with the lava sheet that blanketed the whole region, seamed and pitted by cavities, large and small, caused, perhaps, by exploding gas bubbles. Daylight faded and was replaced by impenetrable gloom. The dark path he followed became more level, easier to travel. The air seemed fresher, too.

Groping blindly forward, he soon became aware of the sound of water gurgling somewhere ahead. He pressed on thirstily, feeling the way with outstretched hands.

Suddenly, he recoiled. His fingers touched something furry. Close at hand he sensed movement and a filthy stench.

His scalp crawling with excitement, he ducked swiftly to one side, fumbled for a match with shaking fingers. He thumbed one into flame.

Looming over him was a pair of fiery eyes. A snarling, foam-flecked mouth that snapped viciously, with fierce animal whimperings that swelled into inhuman shrieking:

"Wh-e-e-e-e-!"

Then the match flame died, winked out. The Thing leaped at him.

Limp with horror, Ken stumbled backward. He tripped as The Thing struck him, clawing savagely. His brain seemed to explode . . .

Outside, in the cheerful sunlight, Ken came to his senses, wet and dripping with icy water from a canteen held by Kobuk Pete, who bent solicitously, his face twisted by an odd mixture of sheepishness and relief. Ken sat up dizzily and felt, with tender fingers, at a throbbing lump at the back of his head.

"What h-h-happened?" he demanded, weakly.

"Must've bumped your head on the rock wall," Pete said. In a few words he related what he had found below.

"Lucky you heard that screetch 'way over in those draws."

"Didn't go. Thought I better trail you into that water hole."

"Thanks, Pete, but how did you—"

Ken paused with a little shiver, as Pete drew his hunting knife and passed a thoughtful thumb along its keen edge. Then—

"What did you do with The—"

"Let it lay. Better so. Least said, soonest mended."

"My Lord, it's amazing! Ever see, or hear of him before?"

"Damn near everybody in Alaska knows about him I reckon."

"A native?"

"Klutuk was a breed, part white. He was a murderer and a thief, said to have come from the Hohlitna, though he ranged clear down across the Mulchatna into Nushagak country, north of here. He's been wanted for a whole bunch of killings, the last five—six years. Disappeared suddenly a while back and it's been a big mystery where he's gone. We stumbled on his hideout, that's all."

"Sort of queer, his attacking us."

"Figgered we was out to get him and bring him in, likely."

"Well, he looks to me like he was crazy as a coot."

"Crazy like a fox, you mean," Pete grinned.

At Ken's questioning stare, the guide added, pithily:

"I mean—that 'bird' wore bear-paw mukluks, with the claws on!"

Chapter 3

POLAR FURY

April 1936

By Charles Madsen

Although the Pacific walrus is a huge and in some respects a formidable looking animal and I had many times encountered him while a guide for large hunting expeditions and moving picture companies, I had never had much respect for his fighting qualities until a certain Fourth of July that I shall long remember . . .

We had an order for one hundred thousand pounds of green salted walrus skins at seven cents a pound. An order this size was a most desirable one. We outfitted the Sea Wolf, at Nome and, in the spring of 1909, set sail for the ever-shifting polar icepack of the Siberian coast.

At King Island, we stopped to pick up eight Eskimo hunters and three umiaks, which are skin-covered boats, and other hunting paraphernalia. Anoyak, a capable Eskimo, was our chief hunter and he had his own little skin covered canoe, known as a kayak.

I knew, from previous experience, where we were most likely to find the biggest herds of the grotesque animals and after proceeding through Bering Strait for the Siberian Arctic we were not long in encountering the ice fields and found a number of leads through the ice, which we followed.

After several hours, on the morning of July 4th, we got into open water again and here found the scattered floe and pan ice stretching for great distances. This, we knew, was a walrus paradise and here we might find the herds we were seeking, lazily sleeping on the floes or flopping into the water and pulling themselves back on the ice with the air of their long, ivory tusks.

The hunters became a band of happy, bustling men as they prepared for the battle and anticipated the feast they would later have on the flesh of the animals after the first kill. The umiaks were prepared, and the ivory harpoons, floaters and other hunting equipment was placed in them. All except the engineer and cook had a loaded rifle ready for the fray.

It was shortly after noon that we sighted a few scattered walrus, asleep on the ice, far in the distance. These sentinels were what we had been seeking. We knew them to be the outposts of the big herds. Indications were for a good day.

The westerly breeze kept the wind in our faces and we made the Sea Wolf fast to a large ice-floe about a mile from the nearest slumbering group. Two of the umiaks were sent to the largest herd, to the left and the third umiak to an adjoining floe to the right. Anoyak, my chief Eskimo hunter, followed the umiaks in his little kayak so as to be prepared to chase any wounded walrus.

Late that afternoon we had fifty-nine walrus, representing about eighteen thousand pounds of hides. The strategy had been to creep up to the herd, then all twelve rifles fire at once. The roar of the bulls ceased with the first volley. Then there were intermittent shots as the wounded animals were dispatched as they tried to clamber over their dead comrades.

After taking one herd we proceeded to another, always farther to the west. In order to take advantage of the favorable wind, we left our kills on the floes. When we had all the walrus possible within easy distance, the Eskimos had their feast and they started the skinning process. Each animal represented about three hundred pounds of hide.

The twenty-four hours of summer daylight came in handy. The huge animals weigh a ton or more and it takes several men and ship's tackle to turn them over. After skinning, the hides were left on the ice to allow the animal heat to escape. Salt is then applied to preserve them. They are rolled and tied up like a beef hide and placed in the hold of the vessel.

While the natives and our crew were busy skinning, I paddled leisurely along from floe to floe in the stern of one of the umiaks, to see if all the animals were dead. My ivory harpoon lay ready in the bow and attached to it was the long skin rope with the "seal poke," or floater, filled with air, which has enough buoyancy to float a dead walrus that otherwise would sink like a rock.

As I did not anticipate an encounter with any more walrus, I thought the two cartridges which were still in my .30–40 rifle and the three in my .41 revolver would be sufficient to finish any wounded animal which might still be alive. Much to my surprise, however, I discovered five walrus on the floe farthest to the west, where we had originally killed only three, according to my recollection. It did not take me long to realize that the two "extras" were live walrus which evidently had not heard the shots and had clambered up on the floe and were now sleeping peacefully beside their dead comrades.

In a few moments I was crawling along the ice toward the dead animals. They afforded excellent cover for a stalk. The nearest live walrus was sound asleep, but the other seemed disturbed and had probably got the scent. Immediate action was necessary. I aimed and fired at the first one, killing him instantly. As I turned to shoot at the other, however, my foot slipped, and in my hurry and excitement I missed the vital spot. I say "vital spot" because there are only two chances of killing a walrus instantly: By the brain shot, either through the eye or through the cavity in the back of the skull; or by breaking one of the neck vertebrae.

The walrus went scrambling for the water at breakneck speed, and as my .30–40 was empty, he reached it in safety. I noticed, however, that he stayed very close to the ice and though he would dive occasionally for a few seconds, he always came up again nearby, roaring like a mad bull and blowing a stream of blood into the air. This was sufficient evidence that he was mortally wounded and it would be only a matter of minutes before he would die and sink unless I could get the harpoon into him and throw out the floater or, if necessary, give him the finishing shot with the .41.

All this seemed very easy, as I had done it many times before with wounded walrus. Getting into the umiak, I paddled quite close to him. He was floating along with half of his head and parts of his back above water. I drove the harpoon with full force at the center of the back, but was very much astonished to see it glance off as if it had been a rubber ball. This, I discovered later, was due to the fact that the ivory spearhead was broken.

The blow seemed to arouse the walrus afresh and with a terrific splash and a plunge he turned and charged the umiak. He made several attempts to get his big tusks over the gunwale, but as soon as I realized his intentions I jumped to the opposite side, thereby raising the boat so much that he could do nothing but bump his head against the outside. I tried the harpoon again, but this seemed to increase his fury. Presently, with a roar, he turned a half-somersault and dived under the boat, coming up again on the other side. Here, after blowing several gallons of blood and water into my face, he tried the same thing over again.

After several attempts, I finally succeeded in getting the harpoon into him, but as soon as he felt it was fast he started rolling around in the water and in a few seconds had the whole harpoon line wrapped around his body and the floater overboard. Then, in a frenzy of rage, he dashed at the umiak again, butting his head savagely against the side. Although I worked hard with the paddle, it was impossible to avoid his blows, which several times nearly upset the boat.

Again and again he repeated the attacks. He was apparently growing stronger instead of weaker. He tried frantically to get his tusks over the stern, where I was sitting with the paddle. I tried to swing the boat out of the way at each renewed attack. In the excitement, I had forgotten all about the three cartridges in my .41, but just as he was about to take another dive I remembered them and decided to be ready for him when he again came up.

As I was sitting there, revolver in hand, waiting patiently for a sign of his reappearance, I felt a bump and was thrown from the seat. The revolver went off with a bang and the bullet crashed into the stern. I was certain my umiak was smashed, but found, to my surprise, that it was still intact. A few feet from the stern was the walrus, floating along lazily. Quick as a flash I fired for his eye. By the commotion in the water I thought I had hit my mark as he again disappeared.

While I was sitting astern, waiting for him to reappear, a peculiar feeling seemed to take possession of me. I felt sure, somehow, that the walrus was about to tear the bottom of the skin boat with his enormous tusks. I glued my eyes on the bottom, and in another second or two, I felt an odd motion. Then, very slowly, two white tusks appeared through the heavy skin, like two great, white knives. Curiously, enough, however, they went out again as slowly as they had come in, leaving two gaping holes. I speedily plugged them with my fur cap and a piece of old canvas which happened to be handy.

Quite a lot of water had got into the boat and as my improvised plugs did not fit well I decided to make for the nearest floe in order to keep the boat from filling. Still followed by the walrus, I started for the ice. When I was almost alongside I heard a voice calling me. It was Anoyak. He had evidently heard the shots and had hurried out in his little kayak in search of me.

In a few words, I explained the situation to him, and with a smile he took his .30–40 and fired at the walrus, now swimming directly toward the oncoming kayak. I am sure he hit the brute's skull, but the bullet merely glanced off. With a roar and a splash the animal disappeared. Anoyak sat still, waiting for its reappearance. In the meantime I busied myself with fixing the holes in my umiak which I finally plugged by cutting two pieces of skin and blubber from one of the dead walrus on the floe. I was just ready to bail the water out when I heard a shriek from Anoyak.

I really don't know how to describe what I saw during the next few moments. All I know is that I stood as if nailed to the ice-floe. Picture the Arctic ocean now calm as a mill-pond—filled with masses of floating ice of all sizes. Away to one side and about a mile distant were the masts and part of the hull of the *Sea Wolf*. On the other side, the bleak blue mountain ranges and undulating tundra land of the northeast coast of Siberia. Directly in front of you a combat to the death is raging between man and beast.

A walrus is tearing at an overturned kayak, his immense tusks goring the yellow skin and splintering the frail frame at every stab. An Eskimo hunter is hanging on for dear life to his pitching, rolling canoe.

The next moment the scene changes. A large umiak is madly rushing to the rescue of the distressed hunter, and in the stern, paddling frantically, you see the former antagonist of the fighting bull. The roar of the frenzied walrus and the cries of the helpless Eskimo are the only sounds that break up the stillness of the Arctic air.

Now the umiak is almost up to them, but the Eskimo, no swimmer, is splashing and scrambling around in the wreckage, trying to get hold of something—anything—that will keep his head above water! Swiftly the walrus swims toward him, and in another moment you see the immense white tusks rise in the air, then down they come with the intention of goring the enemy. He misses. In another moment the Eskimo, in desperation, makes a grab for one of the tusks, seizes them and holds on. While you watch, amazed, he swings himself around on the brute's neck and in another moment the pair of them disappear below the surface, only to come up again immediately.

Now the umiak is turning toward them, and in another second two strong arms embrace the distressed hunter and lift him safely into the boat. The midnight sun, in a blaze of glory, is smiling in approval at the outcome of another near tragedy in the "friendly Arctic."

A few minutes later the *Sea Wolf* came along. After we reloaded our rifles, accounts were soon settled with our big friend, which was still swimming around looking for a fight. After that experience, however, I always believed the Eskimos' stories about the pluck and tenacity of the fighting bull walrus.

Chapter 4

NOME CAFÉ

June 1936

By A. F. Raynor

At the time the exciting news of the discovery of the beach diggings at Nome began spreading like wildfire from camp to camp in 1900, I was stationed just across Norton Sound, at St. Michael, as port steward for the Blue Star Navigation Company.

The stampede got me, too. Not to dig gold did I join the crowd, but to make the "easy money" that was reported to be had in serving the thousands of gold-mad prospectors. I resigned, and as soon as affairs could be arranged for me to leave, I accumulated a stock of groceries, obtained the large range and an assortment of crockery that were lying idle in the warehouse and a thirty by forty tent. The range and kitchenware were originally intended for a hotel up the Yukon River, but had never been claimed.

A kitchen range that size was as good as a gold mine at that stage of affairs at Nome. One of the navigation company's freighters, the schooner *Hera*, took me and my freight. I was landed the only way there was of putting freight and passengers ashore—by ship's boats. I was fortunate in landing safely with all my equipment. The surf often breaks there with considerable force.

I found that one individual had a monopoly of the lumber business. He had landed a schooner load on the beach by simply dumping it over the side and towing it ashore. That lumber sold for one thousand dollars a thousand feet— one dollar a board foot!

On landing, I got to work hauling my outfit to a safe place. I was at once offered one hundred twenty-five dollars for my case of eggs, but refused it, for how is a man to start a restaurant without eggs? I soon found that I had the only eggs in camp, the only range and the only ambition to start a café.

There was only one frame building in the entire camp; the tents housed no less than twenty-five hundred people. Every steamer arrival swelled the population. Things were booming!

I purchased enough lumber from the lumberman to build a lunch counter and some stools of the crudest kind. I added my tent to those that were continually going up and opened it for business right opposite "Tex" Rickard's saloon and gambling house—the largest of its kind in the camp.

I arranged my simple menu. Beans, $1.00 per plate. Ham and eggs, $2.50. Black coffee, 25 cents per cup; with cream, 50 cents. Evaporated potatoes, 50 cents per order. No fresh ones were to be had. Also, there was no fresh milk at that time—just evaporated milk or cream. Pie was 50 cents per cut—and the filling was of dried fruits, at that. Canned fruit, at 75 cents per order, was too expensive to put in pies. The natives occasionally brought in fresh grayling, caught in the streams, and fresh ptarmigan from the tundra. These were snapped up at any price one might put on them.

Meantime, Tex Rickard had nothing on me. Drinks were $1.00. No mixed drinks were to be had. Champagne, which I doubt very much was genuine, was $30.00 a pint. Later on, as the boats began to arrive with further supplies, drinks dropped to 50 cents; beer to $2.50 a quart bottle.

At that time, the medium of exchange was principally gold dust, fresh from the ground. Very little currency was in circulation and that was usually Canadian as miners from Dawson were well represented. The mouth of the Yukon River, near St. Michael, when I left, was lined with boats, scows, and even rafts by the hundreds. On these the prospectors had made their way down the river to St. Michael. There they abandoned their craft and came over to Nome by regular steamer.

Gold dust was accepted and weighed in at sixteen dollars an ounce. When it was refined at the Seattle assay office it brought eighteen dollars and thirty cents an ounce and in some cases even more. One can imagine the profit there was to those fortunate enough to exchange any great amount of goods for gold!

My business was exceptional from the very hour I opened the wooden door of my canvas tent. Miners must eat! My usual working hours were five o'clock in the morning until one the next morning. To get help at any price was an undertaking that almost drove me frantic! It was just as difficult to keep the help. I was fortunate in being able to get a man who, though only a fair cook, was an exceptionally steady worker. He put in a twelve-hour day and I paid him $17.50 a day. We never closed.

Two weeks after I opened my café, a man with a cow arrived on the steamer *Centennial*. The owner at once called and solicited the delivery of fresh milk at one dollar a quart. I ordered what I thought was all the cow could produce—planning a monopoly on it. My first delivery arrived in a bright, new, tin milk can—one gallon. By comparing notes, I discovered later in the day that the man had contracted to deliver and was delivering fifty gallons of alleged fresh milk a day—all from one remarkable cow! It was soon evident that the cow's ability to produce milk was limited only by the owner's ability to produce orders.

After testing the milk, I cancelled my order. I do not know by what process he manufactured his milk, but I took down the counter sign which advertised fresh milk at one dollar per glass and advised the dairyman that I felt I could make just as good if not better milk by simply mixing water with the canned, evaporated product.

A few days later the owner of the cow appeared again. This time he informed me that because of the practical impossibility of procuring feed, he had decided to slaughter the cow. Did I wish to purchase any fresh beef?

Did I . . ?

Visions of having the only fresh meat in camp at once arose. Would that give my place prestige . . ? Did I want any part of the cow . . ? I wanted all of it!

I had bargained for delivery the next day, but he made delivery of the cow, skinned and dressed, the same evening. I at once went to work on the carcass and soon had it cut into steaks, roasts, and soup bones.

Cards went up. Plain steaks, $2.50. Sirloins and T-bones, $4.00. Stews, $2.00. Soup, $1.00 per bowl.

I will always believe that the cow never met her death at the hands of a butcher, but just laid down and died from malnutrition. Such a scrawny array of bones I had to work with I never saw before and never expect to see again.

The first morning that I proudly displayed the array of fresh steaks and stews, the door opened and a short, stocky, very blond man weaved up to the counter. Spying the steaks, he exclaimed, "A-h-h-h, fresh meat! Dot is vot I vant! Gif me dot vun!" He pointed at a family porterhouse, the largest steak in sight. There are only two to a loin. It is cut all the way across the loin and there is usually enough for four to six portions in one porterhouse. My card read, $8.50.

I noticed he had been drinking and suggested a smaller cut. I knew he could not possibly consume all that meat. At once becoming very indignant and abusive, he cried, "I know vot I vant and I haf der pay to buy it!" Reaching under his shirt, he pulled out a buckskin poke and started hammering on the counter with it.

To silence him, I took the steak back into the kitchen and cooked it. It had to be cut in four pieces to lie on the plate. We had no platters. As soon as I placed the pile of meat in front of him, with his coffee, he proceeded to attack the steak.

Unfortunately for my customer, the tail end of the steak, always the toughest part, was on top. He sawed and stabbed at it with his knife and fork, but made no more impression than if it had been leather. Throwing it down, he picked up the meat with both hands and tried to gnaw on it with his teeth, all the time complaining about "Der tam meat!"

Grunting disgustedly, he climbed down from the stool, stumbled to the door and threw plate and all to the group of malamutes which invariably were crowded around outside. It at once created a free-for-all fight in the pack.

Calling for some beans and a whole pie, he downed them easily enough and, as was customary, handed me his poke. His bill, with the cigar he bought, amounted to thirteen dollars. As I weighed this out, I estimated that his poke contained three thousand dollars. I learned afterward he had about thirty-eight hundred in it. Leaving my place, the fellow made a bee-line for Tex Rickard's.

Later in the day, I found that other customers encountered the same difficulty with my steaks, so I put nearly the whole carcass through a meat grinder and thereafter served hamburger and stew.

As I prepared to retire that night at one a.m., as usual without disrobing, I heard the door open and a man cry out in a cracked, hoarse voice, "Can you gif a feller a kup of kaffee?"

To my surprise, I discovered my German friend of the morning before. He was in a pitiful condition, shaking and trembling like a leaf. As the season was fall, the nights were chilly and dark. He explained that he had a ten-mile walk up the beach to where his tent was, ahead of him, and needed something to warm him up.

I could not help but express surprise at his already being "broke."

"Vell, you see, der 'fluezeys' and der 'craps,' they cleaned me oud. But dot is noddings. I haf plendy more vare I am!"

After I had persuaded him to drink three cups of strong black coffee, he thanked me and went out into the bleak, dark morning.

It appears he had run on to a rich spot on the beach the first or second day after erecting his tent. He immediately took out about five thousand dollars from a beach "pocket." In high spirits, determined to make up for his former self-denial, he hit it out for Nome.

On returning after the spending spree, he worked feverishly for three or four days in the same spot . . . found nothing!

He arose one morning soon thereafter and, taking out his revolver, blew out his brains.

Chapter 5

EVERY INCH A KING

October 1936

By Robert A. Henning

Three o'clock in the morning. I dreamed deliciously. Great fish leaped to prodigious heights and shook the water as they fell back in crashing crescendo. Hungry fish glared at me from their watery retreats. I fought at least a dozen to gaff. Fish were swimming all about, now and then bumping the boat, rocking it dangerously. Suddenly—a great brute of a salmon, longer than the boat, let out a villainous chuckle and bore down on me, eyes flashing! I shuddered and covered my eyes.

Then I awoke with a start. Someone was shaking me. It was Walt Gerwels.

"Huh?" I rubbed the sleep from my eyes. "Oh, yeah," I yawned. "We're going fishing, aren't we? Be right up."

Gray dawn and gray water. The camp was still sleeping soundly as we tiptoed out of the tent and down to the boat. Two pairs of oars, grub, sail, fishing gear, bait, anchor—everything seemed to be there.

It was a chill Alaska morning and we shivered. Was it going to be worth it? Bits of spray salted our cheeks and the sail rounded satisfyingly. Once well under way, we forgot the shivers. We were going fishing . . .

We began to take stock of the day's prospects. Gulls were in evidence everywhere and here and there a school of herring splattered on the surface, agitating the water like flurries of rain would do. A good sign! There were surely bigger fish, underneath.

A half-hour passed. We neared our favorite spot. It is just off a little island in Lynn Canal, about halfway between Juneau and Skagway. Here the tide boils and eddies past the outer reef, only to come back again in a great circle. Here in this eddy is a wonderful place for feed to collect and, of course, where there is feed there are salmon.

It was toward this feeding ground we were headed, but someone was there before us. Was it a power troller? God forbid.

However, it proved to be a boatload of townsfolk, bent on strip-fishing, as we were. A bit peeved, and inwardly cursing them for interlopers, we made our way to an anchorage. Had we known what the morning had in store for us, we would have probably welcomed the sight of that other boat.

The anchor hit bottom. I hurriedly picked up my tackle and, putting on a side of herring, cast. No luck. I cast again. Again no sale. The next cast had the right English. There was a mighty slap and a flash of silver at the end of my line. The fish went down, boring steadily for the bottom. Down, down—steadily down. It could mean only one thing. The kings were in!

And it was a king. He wasn't terribly large, but he was a real battler. Twice he came half out of water and circled the boat viciously, his black dorsal fin ripping through the water, only to sound again and resort to the tackle-punishing habit of headsnapping, common to salmon of the king tribe.

Walt had about two hundred feet of line out over the stern, soaking, when I connected. He took it back now in long strokes so we would not foul each other, but the fates had decreed otherwise. I heard a "whunk!" from Walt's rod, and a muffled swearing from Walt, himself. His rod bent almost double and yard after yard of precious gut scorched through the guides. This was a real fish!

But I had an armload of trouble, myself. The little king I had hooked was cutting all sorts of capers. They made it hard to keep the two lines apart. I horsed him up to the boat and kept him churning white water until he rolled over on his side, quite spent. I slipped my fingers in his gills and lifted him into the boat. A sound rap behind the head dispatched him to fish heaven.

When I looked up from my gory mess, I saw that Walt's fish was still taking out line. Frantically, Walt tried to slow the flight of the gut, but it was "no go." That fish had a destination and he was rapidly going there!

Three hundred feet of line was nearly gone and there was no sign of any slackening in speed. The knot where the gut joined the cuttyhunk backing was dangerously close and we prayed fervently that the knot would pass through the guides intact. It did! With half a dozen nerve-shattering jerks, it squeezed through and fled after the gut.

Still no slackening of speed. Would he ever stop? Bits of felt began to show on the reel can and our prayers were renewed. The reel can was jumping crazily up and down as the line uncoiled, rattling from gunwale to gunwale with a sound like a stick on a picket fence.

Then, again our prayers were answered! The salmon slowed his downward plunge to a stop with nearly six hundred feet of line trailing behind him. For a few minutes he sulked. Then, with new tactics in mind, he rushed for the surface. All thumbs, Walt strove to take up the slack. Three hundred feet of line came back and once more there was gut in the guides.

A good two hundred feet from the boat, the big king showed himself for the first time. A heavy swirl, and again he sounded.

"Holy cats!" yelled Walt. "Did you see that tail?"

When I had gotten back my breath, I said I had. Why, that darn fish must have been first cousin to a whale, the way he raised his broad rear structure out of water and plunged down on a straight course for Yakasaki!

Walt was sweating and I was doing a bit of the same in sympathy.

Another run and two hundred feet more of line went out. Again the king broached, and again that great tail was raised in ponderous salute before he went down.

It was the same thing for the next hour. Up and down. I felt sorry for Walt. Often it would take ten minutes of honest-to-goodness labor to get in a precious hundred feet of line, only to have it fly out in one determined rush. He cursed roundly and shook his rod arm frequently to renew the circulation.

We had cut adrift at the beginning of the fight and we were now drifting at the will of the current and friend fish. In a short while, the rushes became shorter and slower, but no less heavy. Putting on all the strain that the light stripping gear would stand, Walt was just able to hold him. Behind the boat was a good wake. We were being towed at about a knot and a half!

Now and then the king would circle the boat, rolling slowly like a porpoise, leaving a trail of bubbles when he sounded. Whenever he poked that black snout out of the water and spat out a mouthful of bubbles, it seemed as though he were saying in a deep and husky voice, "Bottle of beer, Bud, bottle of beer."

Slowly, but surely, Walt was gaining line, and I prepared to end the argument with the gaff. Then came the crushing shock! We had no gaff!

Fishing trips, I suppose, are failures unless one manages to forget something at home, but why—with a "once-in-a-lifetime" fish "on"—did we have to leave such an indispensible piece of equipment as a gaff at home?

If we only had a few big halibut hooks! Or a gun! Anything, just to get that fish into the boat . .

I bent a nail and ran it though a piece of broken thwart. On another such stick I lashed a big bass plug—but these implements looked so pitifully weak whenever that big king showed his broad sides.

Could we beach him? He might get afoul of the rocks.

Could we grab him by the gills? That was out of the question. He would permit himself to be raised just so far, and there, about fifteen feet below the boat, he would hold firm as a rock.

There was but one hope. The stripping party on the boat! They would have a gaff, or something. I rowed fifty feet in that direction as Walt grudgingly gave line. I stopped. He regained as much as possible, and we repeated the process. Slowly we neared the boat, though sometimes we lost more to the big fish than we gained. Soon we came within hailing distance and we assumed our most pitiful expressions.

"Can we borrow a gaff?" we yelled. More shouts. More explanations. A flurry of excitement on the gasboat. Ah, Doc Williams, bless his soul, had brought a landing net from Juneau. A last struggle for line, a cautious pass of the net, and willing hands laid the lordly fish on the deck! His great fins fluttered weakly, his big jaws opened and shut spasmodically—a king among kings, of shimmering silver and glowing bronze, beautiful and proud in death.

Two hours and thirty-five minutes of fighting that nerve-fraying fish had left us tired and weak—Walt from exertion and I from plain excitement. Walt was grinning. The women "Oh'd and ah'd." We males just cussed. He was so blessed big we submittd him to the care of our new-found friends in order that they might ascertain his true dimensions in Juneau.

We got his measure over the radio the next night. He was the biggest salmon of the 1935 season, weighing sixty-two ornery fighting pounds, fourteen hours after catching. He was forty-seven inches long, seven and a half inches thick and—get this—had a waistline of thirty-one inches. Truly, he was every inch a King!

Chapter 6

ARCTIC TRAPPER

November 1939

By Frank North

In 1925, on the north coast of Alaska, I spent the summer with Alexander Malcolm (Sandy) Smith surveying a group of oil claims back of Cape Simpson. After we finished the job and were on the way back to Point Barrow, we met some Eskimos going east. They were bound for Pitt Point, near Cape Halkett. And, as they were going to try their luck in the region where I had decided to conduct trapping activities the next winter, I said good-bye to Sandy and his men and went along with the natives in their whaleboat.

The party consisted of old Annakhay, his wife, their son Angashak, and two young girls, besides his aged mother. She, it turned out, was making the last boat journey of her long and honorable career. There was also the customary assortment of duffle, dogs, sleds, provisions and household equipment, which, when increased by my own camping outfit and two more dogs, made the boat quite crowded.

But the weather was favorable and, after camping overnight at Cape Simpson, we squared off before a nice breeze the following morning and headed out through the drifting ice across Smith Bay, arriving at Pitt Point late that evening.

Pitt Point is a small promontory at the eastern end of a dry lagoon behind a series of high sand dunes that have been pushed up by the ice. It is situated approximately 125 miles east of Point Barrow. The rest of the country, for miles around and on either side and behind, is low and flat and marshy, as is commonly the case along the Arctic shore.

Passing by Pitt Point the winter before, I had noted on the beach a considerable collection of driftwood logs suitable for building material. That was its main attraction, and the deciding factor in my choice of this place for my coming winter's trapping operations. Wherefore, before leaving on the surveying expedition with Sandy Smith, I had instructed the Liebe's Company's trading vessel from San Francisco to land my outfit at that point.

I had had some misgivings that they might not find the place. I knew the water thereabouts to be very shallow a long way out. A ship the size of the *Chas. D. Brower* could not hope to get within five or six miles of the beach. But the Captain and the Purser had both assured me that the supplies would be landed exactly where I wanted them. And in this they had been as good as their word. For my grub pile was there, on the small sandspit, where it had been landed in longboats from the ship and securely covered with heavy canvas nearly two months before. No polar bears had come ashore to disturb it. It was a welcome sight.

My Eskimo friends were as pleased as I. We lost no time setting up the tents, breaking out the cache, and having a good feed. But as it was getting late in the season—the geese were bunching up for their trip south and the snow would soon be flying—our first and foremost thought was of getting our huts built before the ground froze. So, for the next three weeks, Annakhay and I were as busy as they make 'em, each putting up our own igloo. We made these by setting up a framework of split driftwood logs, then banking the walls and roof with sod. That made a warm and windproof shelter.

To Angashak who, like all Eskimo boys, loved to hunt ducks, fell the task of skirmishing for what remaining birds were yet available for the pot. The grandmother and Annakhay's wife were occupied with making new, as well as patching old fur clothes for all of us. The two girls, though they were big enough to be of some help, being eleven and thirteen years of age respectively, were excused from all work and spent the time just sitting around twiddling their thumbs or playing. The overworked mother had to do all the chores about the camp, though the old man and I often stopped our own work to help her by chopping wood for the cooking which was of no elaborate nature, because practically all the Eskimos ever cook besides meat are baking powder bannocks and teas. They gorge themselves on that three times a day, and between meals. How they manage to maintain vitality on such a lopsided diet is beyond me. But they do, and for long periods. If meat happens to be scarce, they live entirely on half-baked baking powder bannocks straight, sometimes even without decent seal oil in which to dunk them.

I staged a real old-fashioned housewarming when my hut was finished, at last, and I could move in and get myself a mess of hotcakes for breakfast. Just baking powder bread and seal oil never did set well with me. Up there in the cold, I craved more than that, especially if I had to work hard or hit the trail all day.

A couple of mornings after I moved in, I woke up to the first real cold and wintry day. It was further distinguished by the surprise of seeing the Hudson's Bay Company's steamer *Baychimo* come piling out from the east where, we later learned, she had been held up in the ice. The ice had fortunately broken up again and set her free. It was a unique sight, the lonely steamer, like a lost soul in search of its heritage, belching smoke and racing under forced draft through a snowstorm against time and tide and the closing Arctic pack.

Being a sailor myself, my heart went out to those on board the *Baychimo* and I prayed she would get safely through. And whether my prayers had anything to do with it or not, I learned she made it without difficulty and probably set a record by clearing Point Barrow well along in October, which I believe is the latest that a ship has rounded the tip of the North American Continent. But the pack closed in right behind her, and a week later the country was in the grip of winter, with zero weather prevailing.

Our own life settled down to the monotonous routine that is the outstanding feature of an Arctic trapper's existence. But, as ever so many things remained to be done before we could be comfortably set for the long winter ahead, there was no chance for time to hang heavy on my hands.

The next, and most important thing after the igloos were built, was to scour the nearby beaches and gather driftwood for fuel, and to stack it up so we would be able to find it during the short days when, for two months, the sun disappears and the land is shrouded in almost continual darkness.

Nor was that all there remained to do. As soon as sledding on the accumulating snow was good, there was fish to be hauled home. These we caught by stringing nets under the ice in a lake ten miles west of us. And lastly, before trapping for foxes began, we ran out a line for owls—big Arctic owls, fat and insolent, of which there seemed to be an unusually large number that year. The Eskimos esteem them highly as food.

The best way to catch these birds, I found, is to stand a stout stick upright in the snow and place a trap on top of it. Owls like to perch off the ground so they can scan the surroundings for lemming. They never pass up such an invitation to sit down on a high perch. Thus, as we set out a goodly number of these resting places, we often gathered in twenty fowl of a morning, and lived like kings. Being fat as hogs, the owls, with whitish meat closely resembling chicken, proved to be wholesome and palatable. In this connection, the story is told of a roadhouse keeper near Nome who regularly served owls for turkeys. His guests rarely discovered the substitution.

Besides being excellent eating, the owls are a nuisance on the trapline. I discovered this when we started out after foxes on the first of December. By that time the country looked like a choppy sea of wind-propelled snow. Shifting drifts formed and reformed in the perpetual winter twilight. The only place to set traps in that endless white expanse was on protruding tussocks where they would not drift in. But these, being few and far between, were as eagerly sought by the owls as by the trappers, with the result that, until they became thinned out, far more owls than foxes were caught.

It still rankles me to recall when I caught what I thought was my first fox. In the empty white space I could see something a long distance away, but as I neared it, mirage steadily increased its size, until at last I was wondering if it could be a reindeer I had in the trap. When I got there, however, it proved to my dismay to be one of those big-eyed owls vainly flapping its wings. My disgust knew no bounds.

But that was only the beginning of my exasperation, for nearly every trap I visited that day had been sprung by owls. When I returned to camp, long after dark, and threw down the pack, my first catch for the first round over the trapline consisted of nothing but owls, though fox-tracks had been quite plentiful. Nor had Annakhay and Angashak fared much better. Between them, they brought in a sled-load of eyes, beaks, and feathers.

For two weeks we caught hardly any foxes. Then, when we had the owls under control, trapping improved. But as there were other camps within fifteen miles of us, and everyone trapped near the beach, Angashak and I decided to extend the scope of our activities.

We moved farther inland where conditions were less crowded, setting up a tent on the shores of a lake beside a high cliff, twenty miles in. From this point we ran traps inland as far as Lake Teshekpuk. This lake is one of the largest in

Alaska, being fifty miles long and at least twenty-five miles wide. It is generally avoided by the Eskimos because of the mythical man-eating fish which are supposed to inhabit it.

Our trapline was thirty miles long. The round-trip hike of sixty miles was ample to keep a person on the go during the dark season.

Strong blizzards prevailed, but so long as they were not too savage we accepted them as a matter of course. To buck a blinding gale with face and parka hood a solid mat of ice is the Arctic trapper's almost daily lot.

In the middle of winter, during the trapping season, there is, at best, only four hours of twilight, while on an overcast or stormy day there is hardly any at all; so one might well wonder how a person finds his way around in the course of a blizzard in which it is often impossible to see ten feet ahead. The answer is— he doesn't, at least he doesn't find all the traps. Everything blends into one smeary white blur and one may come within six feet of a trap and not see it.

Even on a clear day, a snow-set, when properly made, is practically invisible. Many trappers set up a snowblock nearby to indicate the trap's position. But in a blizzard all a man can do, if he fails to encounter a trap, is to keep on his way. He is likely to miss every trap unless a fox happens to be standing alive in one and he sees that. I have set traps in December that I did not find again before the weather cleared off in the spring. Usually they were still in good working order and on two occasions held foxes that had been newly caught.

The camp is ordinarily easier to locate, being bigger and as a rule marked by a pole or some other conspicuous object. But sometimes trappers miss that, too, and not infrequently a man is caught in a storm and compelled to spend the night out, which is not comfortable in twenty below when it's "blowing your head off." The wisest thing to do in a case like that is to take it easy and just walk around to keep the blood in circulation, and hope for the best. There are times, however, when a person gets tired of hoping, and once in a while someone freezes to death.

To successfully trap in the Arctic, a person must learn to travel by dead reckoning, to use a nautical term, and the first step is to firmly fix in his mind the position of bluffs, high cutbanks or other prominent landmarks and their location in relation to one another as well as to the general southwest and northeast direction of the drifts, or windrows, which are the Arctic trapper's infallible compass.

Thus Eskimos are not concerned with north, east, south and west. When giving directions they tell the inquirer to cut the drifts at such and such an angle.

Besides that, there is the wind to go by, which is an especially good guide when a couple of points "forward of abeam," or in ahead just far enough so as not to strike a person's face in the lee of his parka hood. In my case, I found that if I "luffed up" into the wind ever so slightly above that certain point, the cold struck me, stabbing my nose with a thousand knives, and I automatically fell off again.

Of course, one must guard against falling off too much. The idea is to hug the gale closely, like a windjammer going by-the-wind. By doing so, one can lay a straight course with amazing accuracy. That was the way I cut a nor'easter hiking out to the beach from our inland camp. The direction was due north.

At various times, to avoid weathering a particularly withering blizzard in a tent shelter, I made the distance to the igloo at night, when at no time in the roaring dark could I see three feet before me. On each occasion I struck the home camp securely on the head.

To cover the trap line required four days if everything went well, but between trips I usually stayed home long enough to rest and thaw out, so that the traps were visited every eight days on an average, provided, of course, I found them. This may be considered too long an interval in other parts, but is inevitable in the Arctic, where long trap lines are necessary, since the white foxes are always on the go and never stay very long in any one locality.

Eight-day intervals between visits to traps is practical also because white foxes, when caught in a trap, lie quietly down and soon freeze to death.

What loss of pelt there may be is largely caused by red foxes when driven out on the open coastal region by hunger. They tear to pieces and often eat their smaller white cousin when they find him fast in a trap. Incidentally, the reds go into a trap as readily as the white ones and in ordinary years account for about ten percent of the total catch. The rest are whites, with perhaps one blue out of every hundred. Crosses, and an occasional black or silver fox are also taken, usually, however, farther inland.

There is good trapping on the pack ice, too, at times. Annakhay, who operated entirely from our home base, did comparatively well out there. That prompted me to try my luck there also, though I did not have very much success.

After running a few traps on the ice for a month, tending them between inland trips, I gave it up. All it netted me was one fox. But this fox, oddly enough, was a blue one—the only blue fox I have known to be caught on the ice. Also, it was a fine skin, and later enriched me to the tune of one hundred and fifty dollars.

A queer occurrence befell one day while we were both trapping out on the ice. That was the time Annakhay and I both got lost on the way home. In the morning we had started off together, but three miles offshore we parted company, Annakhay striking west to visit his traps, while I set out in the opposite direction to look after mine.

The weather clouded up, and by the time I got to the end of my line, visibility had been reduced to the vanishing point. Then, before I knew it, night fell like a sack, and in hope of making camp before it became too late, I proceeded diagonally in across the ice for the beach.

I planned to make a bee-line for camp. I figured it to be about six miles away. But as it was dead calm for a change, and there was much young ice where well-defined drifts had not as yet had time to form, I had nothing at all to go by. Therefore, when I finally hit the beach, I was not surprised to strike a driftwood log with a big root on it that I knew lay on a small sandspit four miles west of the igloos.

But, by groping my way along the shore in the inky darkness, I fortunately made the camp at eight o'clock, arriving there from the west just as Annakhay pulled in from the east. And that was the peculiar part of it, because he had had identically the same experience in the other direction. This so amused his wife she laughed uproariously the rest of the evening.

They are easily amused—the Eskimos. Of a carefree disposition, and easy-going even under conditions of extreme hardship, they never show their sorrow, if they have any. Like the night when Annakhay's old mother died . . . Nobody showed signs of grieving, and I couldn't help feeling that maybe they were glad to be rid of her, so as to lighten the drain on the diminishing grub-pile.

Anyway, "Him long time Innuit," was all Annakhay said, by which he meant she'd been a long time on this earth. I estimated her to be more than eighty years old. We wrapped her in canvas and put her out on the cache until spring.

Although once they merely put their dead in a box and set them out on the tundra, the Eskimos have long been taught to dig a grave and give them a Christian burial.

Early in January, death once more knocked on my door. This time it affected me more closely. I learned that "Gee-pole" Larson, my late partner, was drowned. I had left him at Point Barrow the previous summer and, since the freeze-up, had been anxiously awaiting him to join me.

In company with five or six Eskimos, Larson had gone hunting in a small boat off Point Barrow. They were last seen stalking a wounded walrus among the ice floes when a strong gale came up. What happened to them nobody knows, but mutely eloquent remnants of their splintered boat washed ashore towards Wainwright, were discovered the following summer.

News of this tragic occurrence was brought to us by the first dog team to return from Point Barrow. By this time, everybody along the line was short of food and, tired of eating foxes, had begun making trips to Barrow to trade their furs for supplies. We then frequently had visitors staying overnight or for the duration of a blow, and were thus kept posted on what was going on throughout the region.

A large part of the news passing from camp to camp naturally pertained to trapping. According to reports, the trappers were doing better farther east, on the other side of the Colville Delta. Locally, trapping was not even half as good as the year before and, of the camps in our immediate vicinity, we seemed to be doing most poorly of all.

Angashak and I did not have ten foxes apiece. That made us start to scratch. Hence, when the sun reappeared and the days grew longer, we established an additional camp farther inland, on the other side of Lake Teshekpuk.

The country inland furnished a surprising contrast to the low, monotonous coastal region. It consisted largely of high, rolling hills where dens were plentiful and signs indicated that there had been an abundance of foxes earlier in the winter. Now there were hardly any.

Results fell far short of expectations. Especially as measured against the extra mileage involved, the move was disappointing. Since there were twenty-five non-productive miles across the lake, and we had to trap inland from the other shore, our trapline was more than sixty miles long. Once I made the entire 120-mile round-trip without getting a single fox.

All-in-all, I calculated I walked enough miles that winter to easily go the length or breadth of Alaska. My catch was only twenty-two foxes, which was well earned, especially considering the bitter cold and strong gales we had to contend with. It will then be seen that trapping in the Arctic is no snap, even in prosperous or bountiful years, which 1925 decidedly was not.

Still, many trappers, including Annakhay, got more foxes than I did. Several of the neighboring trappers wound up the season with nearly fifty foxes apiece, while a few caught only from five to ten. But fur-trapping, vital to the Eskimo's economy though it is, is of secondary importance in his scheme of existence. He likes flour and other white man's grub, but meat he must have. That still constitutes his most vital article of diet. No sooner had the trapping season ended, therefore, than everybody started back to Point Barrow to hunt, and I went along with them.

By that time April had been ushered in, the sun was rapidly climbing the sky, leading summer north, and it was nearing the time of perpetual daylight. But new snow lay soft and deep, and it was a long, slow drag over the sea ice to Smith Bay, made more so by the fact the youngest of the two Eskimo girls persisted in wanting to ride on the sled, while poor Annakhay broke his back on the handlebars. His dogs were poor, starved, and quite played out.

At last I could stand it no longer and told Annakhay that I thought it might be a good idea for the girl to get off and walk. But he, looking long and lovingly at her, only shook his head. It was very plain that she didn't fall in with the idea. And as I wasn't the one who was pushing her along, it was none of my business. So I said no more until after we had made camp that night. Then I chided the old people for deferring to her opinion and always letting the girl have her way.

That is when I learned why the old folks were virtual slaves to their youngest daughter's wishes. According to ancient superstitions, which the advance of civilization has failed to wholly eradicate, when an old person dies, his departing spirit comes back to enter the body of the next baby born in the village. Hence, whenever the girl spoke she was in reality expressing through her voice the words of someone else, perhaps the wisdom of some former chief.

As I saw it, she might even be Annakhay's father. If Annakhay was therefore satisfied to break his back pushing her all the way into Point Barrow, that was satisfactory to me, even though it made traveling slow and we were the last to reach there.

When we got to Barrow, everybody else had arrived, some coming from as far east as Demarkation Point. All were devoting themselves to eating and resting, overhauling the skin boats, and sharpening harpoons in readiness to go whaling out on the ice. This activity is followed by the duck, seal, and walrus hunts that crowd with activity the short summer of Point Barrow. After that, they again scatter to the four winds and once more get ready for trapping.

Chapter 7

BUSH MADNESS

November 1939

By S. A. Camp

For several seasons, Bud Smith and I had trapped on a small tributary of the Tanana River. We regularly poled up the river with our winter supplies in the fall. Upon arriving at our cabin one autumn, we found that a prowling bear had smashed in the door, and a roving porcupine had gnawed at the table and benches. Otherwise, everything was intact.

Before leaving camp the previous spring, all surplus supplies had been stored in a cache built upon four high posts securely set in the ground, with tin wrapped around the posts to prevent the possibility of bears or wolverines climbing up and getting at them.

On our return, after storing most of the new supplies in the cache, I said, "Everything's set for a long, prosperous winter, Bud. Tomorrow, we'll go after our meat supply."

"Yep," agreed Bud. "I think I know where I can find a nice, fat moose. After getting some meat, we'll string the traps on the lines and get action with those as soon as possible."

"Sure," I said, "with these cold nights, fur ought to be pretty good, and a snow may come at any time, now."

"I believe," said Bud thoughtfully, "that we didn't get here any too soon, for the river is beginning to freeze in the quiet eddies."

I grinned at him as I replied, "Right, the first guess. Let's hope the migrating caribou will be along here so we can get some of them handy to the shack. It's a big job to shoot moose back in the hills and pack the meat to the cabin."

But the next morning Bud insisted on fishing in the river, saying that he would catch a supply of fish, dry and smoke them, so they would keep indefinitely. This was contrary to his usual custom, but I did not object to anything he proposed, and let him have his own way.

This radical change, however, caused me to do some thinking, but I realized that it would be bad policy to antagonize him in any manner. Bud was occasionally subject to surly spells. He would brood on slight provocation.

Upon returning late in the evening, I said: "I shot a large moose within a short distance of the river, and there is tundra to pack the meat over, so we can avoid the brush. We'll take the boat up there in the morning and bring in the meat."

"I wish that I'd gone hunting, too," Bud rejoined. "I didn't get any fish. Didn't even get a bite."

I regarded him narrowly, but made no reply. After finding out that the fish wouldn't bite, he still had ample time to hunt during the rest of the day.

For several days I strung out traps on our lines, getting them in their proper places, but Bud did not seem interested and made various excuses for not helping to establish the lines.

"Today," he blandly told me, "I went up to the East Fork to see if it would be a good location for some mink traps."

"That's all right," I replied, "but I think we should set the traps on the regular lines first, then we can explore the more remote country."

The caribou soon appeared upon their annual migration. A few hours of watching at one of their regular trails enabled me to add two of their number to our meat supply. Thousands of the caribou passed over their well-worn trails, which had been used for ages.

These caribou were of the barren ground variety, and were much smaller than the mountain caribou found farther south. They wintered near the headwaters of the Tanana River, leaving there in the spring and going hundreds of miles to the northwest.

During the month of December the weather was very cold, and for three weeks the sun did not appear above the horizon. Occasionally the thermometer fell to seventy degrees below zero. The snow was very light and feathery, making the use of snowshoes impractical. The aurora borealis blazed and crackled in the northern sky during this period, adding its weird light to the long hours of darkness.

All this time, Bud easily disposed of the long hours by almost continually sleeping. He had always been addicted to long hours of sleep, but now sleeping was his principal occupation. His melancholy attitude caused me considerable worry. I feared it might assume a more malignant form.

"Bud," I said, "you ought to get outside more. It would add variety in helping you pass the time away."

"Nope, nothing' doing," he replied, "it's too damn cold, and it's much more comfortable here in the house."

He had never before complained of the cold.

"But," I objected, "I have but little trouble in keeping warm, and I'm out on the trap lines every day. I dress warmly. I learned many moons ago to never expose bare flesh to extreme cold."

He was getting more morose every day, and he would glare at me as though he considered me his worst enemy. I was continually watchful, and was worried to such an extent that he was getting on my nerves, but there seemed to be nothing that I could do. I prepared for any emergency by continually carrying a six-gun, whether out on the trap lines or at the cabin.

While Bud was a heavy sleeper at night, I, on the contrary, was a very light sleeper, being instantly awakened by the slightest unusual sound. I was confident that no harm could happen to me during the night.

On one occasion, while following the trap line, I chanced to look back. I received quite a thrill when I least expected it. Bud was sneaking through the brush, stalking me as if I were some wild animal!

When I called to him, he looked around in the brush as though he planned hiding his rifle. He had a wild, maniacal look in his eyes and dilated pupils, but this look soon disappeared during my casual conversation.

"Well, Bud," I said, "have you seen any game, yet? It generally lies low during this extremely cold weather."

Bud's teeth chattered with excitement. "N-no," he replied, "I-I-I haven't been out b-but a little while."

I watched him closely, thinking he might try to shoot me when he thought he was unobserved. I soon gave an excuse for returning to the cabin.

After this nerve-racking experience, I considered the advisability of putting Bud's two rifles out of commission by removing part of the mechanism, but such a course would make him suspicious. He seemingly had unusual cunning. It would do no good to hide the cartridges, for he would know at once that I did it. This might precipitate a climax. If I broke the tips of the firing pins, it would require some time, and Bud always stayed at the house, giving me no chance.

I now realized that Bud was getting worse. He had homicidal ideas. I passed more anxious hours in planning what was to be done before it was too late. If I wanted to keep in circulation, it was high time for me to be on my way elsewhere. Knowing Bud's condition, and having to be continually alert to avoid a climax was making me very nervous. An unexpected sound caused me to have a tingling thrill, which would mean nervous prostration in time. To one who has not gone through a like experience, day after day, for many months, there can be no idea of the nerve-racking conditions. I determined to return home.

I tried to induce Bud to return with me, offering as an excuse that we would trap in a region where foxes were plentiful, but he persisted in saying that he intended to stay where he was until he could go out in the boat.

"But, Bud," I remonstrated, "we're not catching much fur here now, for it seems to be all trapped out."

"Well," persisted Bud, "it would be hard traveling now, and in the spring we can go down in the boat in a half day."

"Yes," I agreed, "that's true enough. We're making but little money here now, and at this rate we won't have enough money to carry us through next summer."

"You can go out now, if you want to," Bud said with finality, "but I'm not going, so that's that."

In the Northland, when two men are wintering together in a cabin, trapping or prospecting, and one leaves before the season is over, it causes suspicion. Many embarrassing questions are asked in regard to the absence of the partner.

When two men are isolated in a cabin during the winter, each should avoid dissentions and arguments in order to live amicably. A party of three should never be considered. Two will combine against the other and open hostilities will invariably result.

I was well versed in the customs of northern Alaska. I realized what it would mean if Bud stayed, especially if he should die before spring, but there seemed to be no way of inducing him to accompany me.

One evening I casually informed Bud that I was intending to hunt bears in the spring, and suggested that he go along, but he promptly and emphatically refused.

I now realized that I was surely "up against it." Should I remain, it did not require much imagination to understand what might happen. If I went out to a settlement before the season was over, and Bud failed to appear in the spring, being subsequently found dead—and his chances were doubtful for living until spring if he was alone—then it would place me in a bad position.

During his waking hours, Bud always watched me suspiciously, while his dilated eyes had a set glare as though he was nursing a morbid grudge. Continued brooding by a diseased imagination could conjure up improbable conditions.

We talked frequently of the proposed trip, for I wanted to allay any suspicion that he might have. It is the improbable that happens most frequently.

Finally, everything was in readiness for the start. I had made a small hand sled from the toughest birch. On this sled I packed bedding, clothing, half of the furs that I had caught, my rifle, and a supply of food sufficient for the trip. Then Bud used my camera and photographed the outfit, with our cabin and the forest for a background, the frozen creek as a foreground.

I had also made a new pair of snowshoes, the ones I had in daily use being somewhat worn. In the Northland it is not advisable to take anything for granted. Carelessness, even in minor details, frequently invites disaster.

When ready for the start, I said, "Now, Bud, if you'll go along and help me move my outfit, I'll pay you well for your time and trouble. You could also get your mail at the post office, and that might be worth your while."

"No, I won't do it," he replied, with a positive shake of his head. "I guess that I can do as I please about it."

As nothing I could do or say would induce him to accompany me, I started just at dawn on a bright morning in early February. Being bitterly cold, it was necessary to use caution to prevent being frostbitten.

The nearest trapper lived forty miles away, on the other side of the mountains. I was unfamiliar with this part of the country, for we had always used the river in coming in and going out. But it was with a feeling of relief that I began mushing toward the settlement.

I occasionally scrutinized my back trail to assure myself that Bud was not following me with sinister intent. I had no desire to be shot in the back. Upon finding a place that offered concealment, I used my field glasses and watched the trail for some time. Finally, I was satisfied that I was not being followed.

The sun rose high at this season in the northern latitudes, but it seemed to have a cold glitter and no perceptible warmth. The air was filled with fine particles of frost that twinkled like myriads of small diamonds.

I had been told that somewhere ahead, in a little side canyon, there was an abandoned cabin, and I hoped to find it before dark. With the extreme cold, a nightly bivouac before a camp fire had no fascination for me, having experienced such conditions many times during an adventurous past.

Late in the afternoon, I disturbed an inquisitive bull moose, the only game found during the day. With the sled dragging along behind me, and the noisy clack-clack of my snowshoes on the still, frosty air, I appeared to be quite a novelty to him.

Shortly before dusk, a full moon arose and shone coldly in a clear sky. As darkness settled down, I anxiously scanned the surrounding country for evidence of a canyon cabin.

Nearly a mile distant, up a small side gulch, was what appeared to be a cabin to my uneasy imagination. A hasty examination with my field glasses verified my surmise. With the light of the moon reflecting on the snow, I had little difficulty in reaching it.

The sight of what had once been a human habitation in this vast wilderness gave me a lonesome feeling.

I found the cabin habitable, although the roof sagged dangerously with the weight of the snow. An old stove in the cabin proved to be in a serviceable condition. When I built a fire in the stove, its warmth soon filled the cabin, but caused the roof to begin leaking in many places.

Before dawn I set out for a hard day of mushing. If I was not delayed somewhere I expected to reach the trapper's cabin late in the evening. Fate smiled upon me, for I arrived there just as the shades of evening were being drawn.

During the remainder of the journey I would be following a stage road, used only in summer. A short cut over several frozen rivers and lakes was used after freezing.

On this road I met two acquaintances. From them I learned the latest news in regard to what the rest of the world was doing. Having been isolated for several months, I had heard nothing of what was happening in a busy world.

One of these friends, Ralph Ludin, asked, "Where are you expecting to stay tonight?"

"With Jake Bendling," I answered. "That is the only place I can stop, unless I travel part of the night."

"I'm afraid that you'll have to guess again," he said with a grin. "Last night we expected to stop with Jake, but he told us to keep hitting the grit. He's as crazy as a centipede on a hot stove and, what is worse, he's absolutely dangerous. On learning that he was so rabid about it, we stopped in the old relief cabin. We've had nothing to eat since noon yesterday. During the night, Jake came out of his house and fired his rifle several times, to intimidate us, I suppose."

I regarded him in surprise. Here was something that I had no counted on. It was a new subject for thought.

"Well," I said, "I have just quit a crazy partner, but I'll stop with Jake tonight if I have to hog-tie him. With this extreme cold, I have not the slightest intention of siwashing tonight and going supperless to bed after this hard day of traveling."

They regarded me closely to see whether I really meant it, then laughed heartily. "Well, good luck to you. When we get home we'll phone to town and tell 'em that you're intending to stop with Jake, and explain what Jake will think about your plans."

"It seems to be my unlucky day," I said. "Out of one mess, just to stumble into another. I've often stayed with Jake."

"Then you've noticed that he was rather queer," Ralph said. "But many people who live alone develop peculiarities. This is a deplorable climax, though, in any man's country."

"It's surely too bad," I replied. "Well, so long. I'll be seeing you."

As I silently mushed along the trail, I thoughtfully considered this new problem. It seemed to me that the world was not built right, but what could I do about it?

Arriving at Jake's house about dark, I found that he was not at home. Probably out on his trap line. Jake's thermometer indicated sixty degrees below zero. In such a frigid temperature, waiting would be rather tiresome; but it surely wouldn't do to go into the house of a crazy man and have him find even an acquaintance there.

But Jake soon returned. He walked slowly, as if in doubt about a near approach. While yet several steps distant, he stopped hesitantly. He glared wild-eyed as though I was some wild animal he feared and wanted to avoid.

"Hello, Jake," I greeted, in my heartiest manner.

He looked wildly at me with dilated eyes, but made no reply, nor any sign of recognition. As I looked at him, he was not an inspiring sight, and a cold chill gradually crept over me.

"Don't you remember me, Jake? I've been here a number of times, and I've known you for years."

He made no reply, nor changed his fixed stare.

I was beginning to have grave doubts as my scalp tingled. Probably my primordial ancestors would have fled from this apparition in superstitious horror.

"Jake, I'm staying with you tonight, and I'll hit the trail again in the morning." This seemed to get a rise. He advanced a few steps, stared fixedly into my face, and mumbled: "Well, w-e-l-l, w-e-l-l," as if worried by conflicting doubts.

"That's fine, Jake," I continued, as if he had consented. "Come on and let's go inside where its warmer. It's too cold to visit out here."

He reluctantly followed me into the house, where he had built a fire in the range, and made preparations for supper. A large heating stove kept the whole house warm.

For some time Jake's sulky mood continued, but finally he was quite companionable. I acted as though overjoyed at again meeting him, thinking it would have a tendency toward overcoming his moroseness. Jake gradually fell in with my assumed mood. I realized that I should be enthusiastic in entertaining if I was to keep him interested.

During his isolation he had woven such a shell about himself that it required considerable effort to crack it, but I wholeheartedly assumed the task. Having lived with one crazy man nearly all winter, I felt that I could get along with another for just one night.

"Jake," I asked him, "did you have good luck with your trapping this winter?"

"Yes," he replied, "I done pretty well. Part of my furs are hanging there." He indicated a number of skins hanging in one corner of his cabin. "All winter I've had out quite a lot of traps."

Going into another room, he returned with an armful of furs, among them a fine silver fox and a very dark wolverine.

Picking up the silver fox skin, I examined it closely. "It is a splendid fox," I commented, "glossy and well colored. You'll get some real money for that skin. That wolverine is the darkest I ever saw. It has a rich, glossy sheen, and the stripes on the back can hardly be noticed. You have an uncommonly fine lot of fur, Jake."

Jake's eyes glowed with pride. "Do you really think so? I didn't know, but I thought they were pretty good. I know little about the quality of furs."

I picked up a fine cross fox. "This is a splendid fox, but when you are skinning foxes you should skin the feet out to the toenails, leaving them on the skin, too. Fine fox skins are generally used as neckpieces, to be worn over the shoulders. They leave the toenails on, and put glass eyes in the head." I then explained the customary methods employed.

On account of his affliction, I had the deepest sympathy for Jake. He apparently had lucid intervals when he was pleased, but I realized that he would cut my throat without compunction when under the morbid influence.

My role was to gratify him as much as possible. I continually evolved ways and means. An extended silence would cause him to revert to the morose state.

During the summer months Jake had used his cabin for a roadhouse, but instead of having permanent inside walls, the rooms were formed of blankets draped on poles. While they offered a certain amount of privacy, security was not a factor.

Being under the influence of the customary drowsiness peculiar to being out in the cold during the day and subsequently coming into a warm house, I retired quite early. Jake followed my example.

Due to long schooling in the wilds, my hearing had become very acute, and the slightest unusual sound would instantly awaken me, with all my faculties alert. Even under my present lethargy I felt that this characteristic would not fail me, so I slept soundly without any misgiving concerning emergencies.

Sometime during the night I suddenly awoke. I could detect a faint rustling from the vicinity of Jake's bed. Then stealthy footsteps approached my own bed. I realized that delay might precipitate disastrous results.

"Is that you, Jake?" I asked. I wanted to let him know that I was not asleep, but was prepared for any emergency.

There was an oppressive silence. Jake did not reply. Here was an emergency that he had not calculated on! His brain did not function with sufficient clearness to formulate a plausible excuse.

Under such circumstances, suggestion is the best means of overcoming the difficulty. By prompting, his mind could be diverted into other channels than the one being followed.

"Were you intending to fix up the fire, Jake?" I asked. "It's a very cold night, ain't it?"

After deliberating for a moment, he mumbled, "Yes, yes."

He went to the stove, opened the stove door. Then he immediately shut it, and went back to bed.

After this disturbance, it was some time before I fell asleep again.

It was toward morning when Jake quietly slipped out of bed again, with the same result as on the previous occasion.

I now had no desire for sleep, and lay awake until Jake arose and built a fire in the range. I greeted him cheerfully and he was soon normal again.

I tried to cheer him up, but never succeeded in causing him to laugh, or even smile. The morbid mood had persisted until it dominated his whole character.

When the time came for parting, I cordially shook hands. "Now, Jake," I said, "you shouldn't just hole up here like a hibernating bear. Get out occasionally and see what your neighbors are doing."

"I never have time," he muttered, " and I can't afford it."

My destination was a small settlement consisting of a post office, a general store and a road house, with several cabins belonging to trappers and prospectors.

I first visited the postmaster, Cleum Browlin, for I wanted to acquaint him with the facts. After cordially shaking hands, he asked, "Where did you stay last night?"

"With Jake Bendling," I replied.

He regarded me closely. "How's Jake getting along now? He hasn't been here this winter, and he gets no mail."

"I'm very sorry about Jake," I replied, "for he's pretty far gone. Dangerous, is the word. And Bud Smith is the same. That's why I left him. He intended to pot me with his rifle. I realized that if I wanted to continue in circulation that I had better take a walk. If he don't last until spring, I'll be in bad, I suppose, but he wouldn't come with me."

Cleum picked up the phone and notified the proper authorities in Fairbanks.

"Cleum," I said, "I've had many close calls in my wandering. I've broken through river ice with my snowshoes on, I've shot charging grizzly bears, I've been knocked out many times, but this is the worst. I never, never want to be mixed up in another case of bush madness."

Chapter 8

THE PEOPLE OF NOME
WERE SCANDALIZED

December 1939

By John B. Wallace

The closing and demolition of the "Stockade" in 1907 created much resentment in Nome, not only among the townspeople, but even among Federal employees who had brought their wives and children north with them.

The Stockade women had been kept almost prisoners in the high-fenced enclosure, being allowed uptown only to do necessary shopping. Now they were to be distributed all throughout the community. Abolition of the Stockade did not carry with it abolition of its inhabitants. It was not that easy. As "Doc" Hill phrased it, "They have taken a boil and scattered it, and now the body politic, instead of having one big boil that can be lanced when necessary, has fifty little boils to be treated."

The married men did not relish the idea of having their families residing next door to prostitutes, but there was little they could do about it. The Federal word was law and there was no appeal except to Washington.

Just why the District Judge decided upon such a drastic step was a moot question. However, the consensus of opinion seemed to be that it was because the Judge and his daughter, who kept house for him, had to pass near the Stockade on their way to and from the courthouse.

Naturally I was not in the Judge's confidence so I must depend upon hearsay and there was certainly plenty of that at the time.

The Judge was said to have been a small town Pennsylvania lawyer whose highest office heretofore had been that of justice of the peace. As a reward for political services, he had drawn the Alaska plum, which, everything considered, was not such an attractive plum after all. It seems that only a strong sense of duty, plus possible financial necessity, could have drawn a man well past the age of adventure to a land which nature provided so sparsely with the comforts of life.

Most of the litigation was over mining claims, and I am of the opinion that little of it was permanently settled at Nome. Just how well versed in the law the Judge was I am not in a position to pass judgment upon, but when it came to knowledge of human nature he could not have ranked very high.

The Judge should have known that a Western frontier town such as Nome could not be governed in the same manner as the small Eastern town where he was justice of the peace. Though the action of the Judge in the Stockade case may have been faulty, his honesty, as far as I have learned, was unquestioned.

When they heard the edict, everyone wondered what would be done with the girls. The newspapers broadly intimated that it was up to the Municipal authorities. People said the Judge had created a problem which seemed unsolvable.

One day, while the abolition of the Stockade was still the main topic of conversation, I wandered out to the Sandspit. I had been interested in the Eskimos and their ways of living and frequently walked out that direction just to watch those simple-minded people go about their daily tasks.

To my surprise, as I approached the farther end of the spit, I heard sounds of hammering and sawing, indicating great activity in house construction.

I had been so wrapped up in the baseball league that I had not been paying great attention to Municipal affairs, but I thought it queer that the newspapers had overlooked what appeared to be a new subdivision of the city of Nome. Here were being built, row on row, lines of neat-looking cottages.

My first thought was that Uncle Sam was going to house the Eskimos, but still I could not understand why nothing had been said about it. With three newspapers, it surely seemed that somebody had slipped a cog in not writing the story.

I hot-footed it back to the *Nome Golddigger* office and informed "Big Mitt" of my discovery. He became as excited as I was and sent me at once to the lumber offices to find out who was purchasing the building materials.

The Editor became even more excited when I returned with the information that the lumber was charged to a man named Larson. Larson was Nome's chief of police and the Mayor's brother-in-law.

Beverley B. Dobbs, the photographer, was immediately commissioned to make a trip to the Sandspit, and the *Golddigger* blossomed forth with an extra which included a front page spread of pictures and copies of the bills of sale for the lumber.

When the paper appeared upon the street, the whole town was buzzing. Here, evidently, were to be the new homes of the "Ladies of the Stockade!" Events caused people to believe that here were homes "thoughtfully provided" by the Municipal Administration, which could be profitably rented to tenants who had little choice in the matter. If the Chief of Police told them that the Sandspit was the only place they could reside, that settled it.

The people of Nome became scandalized. Needless to say, the Sandspit cottages were never occupied by those for whom they were intended.

The Mayor was greatly wroth. He indignantly denied any ulterior motive except to solve a pressing Municipal problem. He swore vengeance upon Big Mitt, and the town waited with great interest the first meeting between the two men.

It did not have to wait long, but the fistic combat that ensued was somewhat of a disappointment to those who had expected "The Battle of the Century." Both the Mayor and Big Mitt were several inches over six feet in height. The Mayor was rawboned and sparely built as was Big Mitt, except for his paunch which presented much the same effect as a good-sized watermelon reposing in the interior of a boa constrictor.

With men of their size and known animosity, it was predicted that blood would flow freely. They met at the Barrel House. I did not see the encounter, but those who did said that they fought like a couple of old women, clawing and gouging. As nearly as I could figure out, the combat ended in a draw, with both promising another meeting which, however, never occurred.

Instead of moving into the little village on The Sandspit, most of the girls took quarters over saloons or rented cabins in the residential district. The Judge's daughter probably rubbed elbows with them much oftener than if they had been permitted to remain in the Stockade.

After this newspaper coup on my part, I thought I had cinched a permanent job on the *Golddigger*, and probably Big Mitt would have kept me on if he had not made previous arrangements which he could not now rescind. When he first talked of hiring me, he had already sent Outside for an experienced newspaper man.

He had told me nothing of this, and I had thought that all I had to do was make good. The reason I kept my job as long as I did was that his new reporter happened to be on the steamer *Victoria*. This veteran of the Bering Sea was caught in an ice field on her first trip north that summer and was carried right into the Arctic Ocean. It was not until the middle of July, as I recall, that she arrived, at last, in Nome.

The first intimation that I was to be supplanted came with my introduction to the new man. Fortunately, the baseball season was not yet over and I was able to transfer my sports column to the *Nome Nugget*, for which paper I worked until I went Outside.

Big Mitt did not have much luck with his new acquisition. The new reporter was an experienced newspaper man who had worked on New York and Chicago papers. He wrote a "swell" story of his experiences on the *Victoria*, but as soon as the paper appeared on the streets he went out to get acquainted. Unfortunately, the only persons for whose companionship he seemed to care were bartenders. He disappeared as though the earth had swallowed him and for three days Steve vainly sought his vanished henchman.

Like a lot of good newspaper men in those days, the new man was a "lush," who went on periodic sprees. These periods of drunkenness had been coming too frequently for the editors Outside. That was the reason he was in Nome. He lasted between two boats, then Big Mitt had to let him go.

I have often wondered what eventually became of Big Mitt. I saw him once in the States several years afterward. He then certainly was down on his luck. I was running a weekly newspaper in a suburb of Seattle. One day my office girl said that a man wanted to see me. It was Big Mitt, looking for a job. He was surely surprised when he saw me. He had not known I was editor of the paper.

I had only a small staff and I could find no place where Big Mitt would fit in the picture. I was compelled to tell him "No."

Big Mitt was one of the last of the newspaper men of the old school. In the *Golddigger* he really got out an interesting paper. Newspapers in those days were not the impersonal organs of today, but really reflected the personality of the proprietor, who was usually the editor.

I received much better treatment from the *Nugget*, but candor compels me to admit that Big Mitt had the better paper. The *Nugget*, notwithstanding it was run by two Irishmen, was colorless beside the *Golddigger*. At least, that is how it seems to me now, looking back through a vista of more than thirty years.

No story of the early days in Nome would be complete without something about the "Pay Streak Express" railroad, on the Seward peninsula. It was built by Major Monroe, who afterward went Outside and founded the beautiful little city of Monrovia, in Southern California. The little, narrow-gauge road ran out to the creeks which it supplied with mining machinery and building materials.

The tracks were laid on the tundra with practically no roadbed. It did not operate in the winter, but the little locomotive was kept busy puffing out to the creeks in the summer. Half the railroad train crew's time was occupied in jacking either the engine or the train of flat cars back on the tracks.

Whenever one of the girls from the Stockade made a strike on the creeks, through grubstaking a miner, she invariably chartered the Paystreak Express to convey her guests to the party that she would throw at one of the roadhouses out from Nome. The singing, whooping party would start out merrily enough, but it was not long before the men would be bending their backs putting the train back on the tracks with the encouragement, vocal of course, of the Ladies.

If the train reached its destination without several such derailments it was a miracle, but no one cared. It was all part of the fun. The girls enjoyed it immensely because it was practically all the wholesome excitement these unfortunate women had encountered since their childhood days.

Even in those days Nome furnished amusement for the sportsmen, although all the hunting and fishing that took place was for a purely utilitarian purpose. Everyone was too busy trying to make money or engaging in that fascinating pursuit of "looking for gold" to hunt or fish just for sport.

Shooting was confined almost entirely to ptarmigan, the quail-like birds that lived on the tundra hills, which in summer were covered with blueberries. The Eskimos found the berries a good source of revenue and brought them in by the bucketsful to sell to the Nome housewives.

There was big game to be hunted in the polar bear, walrus and seal that inhabited the Bering Sea, if one had the time and money to outfit an expedition. I saw two polar bears from the deck of the *Ohio* as they disported themselves on the ice a few miles out of Nome. Dobbs obtained some remarkable motion pictures of walrus and seal hunts.

Both the Snake and Nome rivers were full of fish, Grayling, salmon and Dolly Varden trout were easily caught, if one cared to take the time and trouble. The fish in Alaska have a flavor all their own. I have never tasted fish that I liked better. Perhaps it is the cold water that keeps them firm as rocks. A fish dinner was also about the cheapest meal one could buy at the Nome eating places. This fact made the dish doubly popular with me.

The Bering Sea abounded in tomcod. The Eskimos ate them, but they were too bony for the white men, except in emergencies. However, the dogs did not object to them and we had great sport in the wintertime fishing for them through a hole in the ice.

We did not need bait. Just a red rag tied to the end of a string of hooks. When you felt your line move, you just jerked it through the hole, hooking the fish in the side, head, or wherever the point struck. It was so cold that the cod barely hit the ice before they were frozen stiff. A big sack of them would provide dog feed for several days.

Although I ate enough reindeer steaks, stew and roasts to make me eligible to pull a Santa Claus sleigh, I was in Nome for more than a year before I saw one of these animals. I had to go to Teller, then, to see a real herd.

They were afraid to bring the reindeer into Nome because of the dogs, which were also fond of reindeer steaks. The Eskimos used them for sled work around their igloos and Dobbs got some good pictures of these legendary Christmas deer. Reindeer are good eating, being in flavor a cross between beef and venison. They furnished a great deal of the fresh meat consumed in Nome.

The most vivid impressions that I carried away from Nome were of the long winter nights. Although more than thirty years ago, I can still imagine myself plodding down Front Street, clad in parka, fur cap and mukluks. The sun barely peeked above the horizon for a few minutes at noon, yet it was never really dark, as we count darkness in the South. There was always a semi-violet haze in the atmosphere, something indescribable, but never forgotten. The crisp, crackling snow reflected a light from somewhere, perhaps the North Pole, because we were just below the Arctic Circle.

It was not uncomfortable in Nome in the wintertime. Although the temperature averaged around thirty below for about six months each year, it was a dry cold that would freeze you to death without your feeling it. People in Southern California laugh when I tell them I have been more uncomfortable from the cold down there than I ever was in Nome, but it is the truth.

We were dressed for cold weather up there. The houses were well boarded in. In every store, residence and saloon never-extinguished fires burned day and night. Even when the wind whipped up a blizzard, I did not feel it much except in my lungs, which choked up as if an unseen hand were clutching at my throat.

Walking against that wind was a slow process. It had taken me half an hour to walk just a few blocks, with frequent stops in the lee of a doorway to get my breath. One can imagine the feeling of despair that must overcome a musher on the tundra facing such a blizzard. My brief experience cooking out on the creeks gave me all the blizzard experience I desire.

We had most of the conveniences of the Outside at Nome, including phones and electric lights. There were plenty of books in circulating libraries and magazines, too, in summer. All-in-all, it was not a bad place to live. I have never had better health and I often remarked that I never saw a sickly baby in Nome, and there were a lot of babies there, too.

The air was about as pure and unpolluted as one can get it. I must make an exception, however, to the interior of the saloons when a group of Eskimos came in and stood around in their patient, dumb fashion. They could not buy a drink, but they would just stand and gaze. If you wanted to pass by, you had to literally shove them out of the way. I never saw one of them angry. Like an odiferous bunch of stolid cattle in Nome, they were an entirely different people on their native heath. Some of the girls were really pretty.

I had mentally compared them with the Siwash, who lived in Southwestern Washington where I was reared, but after visiting the Eskimo native villages, I revised my opinion. They are greatly superior to the Siwash and if they had been left to themselves would have been a happy, healthy and contented people.

My voyage Outside was as eventful as my trip to Nome. I had been making fairly good money before I decided that I wanted to see some green trees again, but one could not save money in Nome in those days. If you were broke, you needed never to go hungry or thirsty. It was seldom that one drank alone, always either the whole house or some of your friends were called to the bar with you. But on the other hand, if you had money, you were expected to spend it. Living costs were high and amusements few and costly.

In the summer it was quite easy to get employment, particularly on the creeks, on many of which the gold lay almost on top of the ground and the owners of the claims paid well to get men when they needed them most.

The old *Victoria* was in one day when I suddenly took a notion to go Outside. I got acquainted with some of the boys in the Steward's Department and was promised free passage if I would round up a bunch of workaways at $20 a head.

I thought I had struck a gold mine when I ran into a group of Irishmen who were desirous of seeing the States. They had come direct to Nome from Australia via San Francisco. They had some money, but jumped at the chance to work their way and save a hundred dollars or more apiece.

My success in getting them signed on won me the job of steerage pantry man, which high-sounding title proved to be but another name for "dishwasher." The Irishmen were assigned as waiters in the steerage. All went well until one day, the cook started serving us tainted meat. We stood it for several meals, but finally a mess of rotten mutton stew proved to be the last straw. The Irishmen struck and made me their spokesman.

When the Third or Fourth mate came into the gloryhole the next morning and demanded that we "Rise and Shine" no one moved. Finally, the Second Steward came below and demanded to know the trouble. When I told him, there was strong talk of irons and a report of mutiny to the captain. But, eventually, the stewards pulled in their horns. For one thing, they discovered that I was a newspaper man and, secondly, they were too deeply compromised in the workaway fee matter to stand investigation.

They informed me that if I would persuade the boys to go to work they would see that we got the same food as the passengers. Their decision was hastened by the angry roar from the steerage dining room, where a mob of hungry miners were demanding their breakfast.

The Irishmen went back to work but promised to throw me overboard if the steward did not keep his word. To my great relief he did, and from there on until we reached Seattle we had no complaint as to the quality or quantity of our grub.

I was told afterward, however, that careful investigation was made of the previous occupation of workaways thereafter, and that any person with a journalistic taint was barred.

Chapter 9

MAIN TRAILS AND BYPATHS

December 1942

Three women were being evacuated from Westward Alaska. The boat that was taking them out made a circuitous route which took them to the Aleutian Islands where civilians and soldiers were building roads and airfields. Like most voyagers on the small vessels that visit this area, they wore rough clothes—breeches and woolen shirts and coats. There was nothing glamorous about them.

When the ship stopped at one of these distant outposts, the three women went ashore. They walked up the road toward the settlement where the men were working and stood not far from a promontory looking out toward stormy Bering Sea.

The word soon got around that there were women on the Island. One worker rushed up to a foreman and said in a tone of almost breathless reverence, "There are some women over there!"

The foreman had not seen a woman for eight months. He walked over with the man who had brought him the news and when they approached the promontory he asked, "Where are they?" He did not immediately recognize the forms, roughly clad in breeches, as being feminine.

Soon soldiers and civilians came from every direction. Each seemed to have an excuse to pass near to the three visitors at a respectful distance. They came from the east and they came from the west. They came from the south and turned east or west. Each one seemed to have an excuse to crisscross to get a glimpse of the three members of the opposite sex.

The episode is just an illustration of one of the greatest problems of morale of a military site anywhere—but particularly in Alaska. The hunger for just a sight of sister, mother, wife or sweetheart is liable to get the strongest man down—particularly if he has not previously been away from home.

There never were many women in Alaska, and since the war many of those who were here have been evacuated. A few Army nurses are coming in. Even when a soldier is permitted a day or two in towns he is not likely to see many of the opposite sex. There are men in Alaska from New York, Chicago, Seattle and other heavily populated centers who, before coming here, would not turn their heads to look at a pretty girl on the street but who now would sit down and pour out their hearts for hours if they had an opportunity to just talk to one.

The United Service Organizations are doing a grand job in Alaska in providing entertainment with the help of a few women in the larger cities—where there even are some single women—moving pictures, and talented performers from among the Service men themselves. There is nothing wrong with the morale of the soldiers, sailors or marines in Alaska. It is high. They are itching for the opportunity to get into action against the enemy and go home. Meanwhile they are living in the hope of getting a furlough to go home and see sister, mother, wife or sweetheart—even though they may have to spend ten days traveling just to be home for four.

Chapter 10

MAIN TRAILS AND BYPATHS

February 1943

If there is one thing that will hurt an Alaskan more deeply than anything else it is to have Alaska considered anything but a loyal part of the United States. Yet, many people do think Alaska a foreign country as far as the United States is concerned. They ask for Alaska postage stamps, put five cents postage on letters to Alaska, and sometimes even ask what language is spoken in Alaska.

During the present war, there are signs that official Washington regards Alaska, to some extent, as a "foreign possession"—or at least it does not fully understand Alaska and does not realize what a vast area it covers.

Just because the Japanese have invaded one or two small islands in the Aleutians, the whole of Alaska is regarded as a "combat zone," yet it would be just as logical to consider Georgia a combat zone if the Japanese were occupying a small island off the coast of California. California is just as distant from Georgia as Kiska Island is distant from Southeastern Alaska.

If it were not for the fact that by imposing censorship and restricting travel to and from Alaska, the authorities again were regarding Alaska as a "foreign country," Alaskans would not have much complaint except the general one that they feel such strict censorship—entailing the employment of thousands of persons reading mail—may be a wasteful expenditure of labor and money.

There is no doubt that, in view of the shortage of shipping facilities, travel to and from Alaska should be restricted. It is also probably wise to censor mail going from such well-fortified places as the Aleutians, Kodiak, Anchorage and Sitka, in order that the enemy may not get information as to the number and disposition of troops and artillery, even though the thousands of men going to the States from such places carry the knowledge with them and can talk.

There is a very great question, however, as to the wisdom of censoring mail from the States to Alaska. If Alaska really were such a "hot spot" that the information contained in letters to Alaska could be more readily transmitted to an enemy than information from Detroit sent in a letter to California, then the situation would be different. Now, however, military authorities have their finger upon practically every person in Alaska and nothing has happened that would indicate that information as to what is going on in the States should be withheld from people in Alaska. The military authorities may have good reasons that they cannot divulge, but Alaskans can see no better reason for censoring mail to Alaska than the authorities had for censoring newspapers and magazines going to Alaska—which they did at one time. It seems that they just do not understand Alaska.

Chapter 11

I WAS QUEEN OF THE KLONDIKE

August 1944

By Kate Rockwell Matson as told to May Mann

ueen of the Klondike dance-hall girls; wined, dined and feted by the money-spending lords of the Yukon; sought after by the rough, tough adventurers of the gold dust trail; patterned after the lusty, good-natured, fun-seeking women of boomtown Dawson. I was all that at the turn of the century. Klondike Kate, nineteen-year-old favorite of the hard-living prospectors of a get-rich-quick day.

Numerous legends of the fortunes made overnight in the Frozen North had trickled down to the States and I had answered the lure along with dozens of others. I arrived in Dawson bent, too, on getting gold, but not with pick and shovel, pan and patience. I was singing and dancing at the Savoy, and a skit well received meant pouches of gold dust—the floral tribute of the Yukon—tossed at my feet.

Life was wild, the people hardy, and I loved it. It has been forty-three years since I performed on the dance-hall stages, but looking back, I would not have traded a single moment of the time spent in that exciting era.

As a child, on the banks of the Spokane River, I would boast to my playmates, "I'm going to see the whole world when I grow up." My life eventually proved my childish prophesy to be a true one.

I was the stepdaughter of Judge F.A. Bettis of Spokane, a wealthy political figure. Mother was from the South. I was born in Kansas in 1892, and I have no recollection of my own father, for I was only a small child when Mother married Judge Bettis and we moved to the Northwest.

Our home was one of the largest and finest in the city. I had my own governess, and Mother her own maid. I remember the cook saying to me, "Someday you'll grow up and be a very fine lady like your mother and have a great fine house like this for your own. That is, if you will learn to mind your manners, Kathleen."

My father showered luxury on me. How could anyone imagine that his beloved and indulged stepdaughter, who was being groomed to take her place as a society leader in the city, was destined to become a variety show girl and a Yukon dance-hall queen!

But even as a child I was impulsive and daring, with not a little bit of the gypsy in me. For instance, there was the year Spokane had a big fire and I, a slip of a girl of eight, invited all of the neighbors whose homes had been destroyed to our house. For two weeks every room in the house was filled with beds for our more than one hundred guests.

I'd play "hookey" from school and treat my playmates on Father's charge account. We'd have wonderful picnics on wieners and pickles from the meat shop. Mother would discover my charges and promptly discontinued my credit with the butcher. But that didn't matter. I charged cheese, bread, and fruits. When I was discovered, I simply went over to the bakers and charged cakes.

I loved the outdoors, and was always dancing on the lawns. I would take a lace curtain and drape it around me, then dance under the plum trees in the garden.

I'd take Dad's trotting horses and, against any warning, race them and bring them back in a lather. It wasn't that I was bad, I was just imaginative and full of the excitement of living.

Then Mother decided it was more fashionable to place her daughter in a boarding school. All of the best people in Spokane sent their children to select schools, so I was dispatched to St. Paul's Academy. There I argued that mathematics simply had no place in my scheme of life. I loved music and rhythm. I'd bribe the other girls to do my mathematics.

Even there, under the strict surveillance of disciplinarian nuns, my gay spirits could not be regimented. I was always getting into trouble. During a study hour, I threw aside my books and began dancing the Highland Fling. My classmates were delighted at my daring. The nuns were not. One of them caught me in the middle of an intricate kick. "Very nice," she said. "You can go to Bath Number Three." I knew that meant I was to be locked in the bathroom for the remainder of the day.

There was a clothes hamper of soiled towels in the room. I dumped them down the drain. Remembering that this was the day that the nuns always took their baths, I ran all of the hot water out, so they would have to bathe in cold water.

A short time later, my parents separated and I went to live with Mother.

Our home was sold for $65,000, but Mother had little conception of money. So we began traveling in our usual luxurious manner. We went to South America. On the way I became engaged to the first officer of the ship. Mother was alarmed. She put me in the Convent of the Sacred Heart on our arrival at Valparaiso.

There were many impulsive young Latins who would nod and bow when my chaperon took me walking. And I must admit, I smiled encouragement. Later they would throw notes over the convent garden walls. There was one young attache of the Spanish Legation who was so handsome and so enchanting that it was hard to refuse his proposal. Mother was in England, but when she heard of my crush, I was ordered to return to New York and meet her.

I was put on board the *Willie Roosevelt*, a big five-masted sailing ship. We were ninety-seven days sailing around the Horn before we sighted New York Harbor.

Then it was that Mother disclosed that all our money was gone. We were penniless. She was far too proud to appeal to my stepfather, so she went to work in a shirtwaist factory.

I was only sixteen but I knew I must help in some way. I read an ad in a newspaper. It said: "Chorus girls wanted. No experience necessary."

Dancing was not as difficult then as it is today. I answered the ad and was immediately given a job at eighteen dollars a week. I left on a road tour without telling Mother. In three weeks the company was stranded in Philadelphia. The manager had run off with the company's salaries, and I found myself with less than a quarter to my name.

Desperate, another dancer and I begged a ride on the ferry to Jersey City. There we talked some trainmen into letting us sneak a ride in a freight car. Mother forgave me when I arrived home, only because she was so glad to see me alive.

My next job was at Coney Island, where I was the page-boy who pulled the curtains for the "Living Picture" act.

I was in and out of love with every change of the weather, my mother used to say. I had red-gold hair and violet eyes and long black lashes. I wore pretty clothes. So I began receiving offers to appear in variety show houses.

I received an offer at a good salary with a large advance to "go West." The wanderlust was strong in me. It had always been. So I signed a contract and headed for the Northwest.

I remember my first night in a variety theater. I signed a little book when I checked in. I didn't know what it was for. I went back to the dressing room after my numbers on the stage to await the next show. Suddenly my bell was ringing. I was told to sit in one of the boxes. An old schoolmate joined my table. "Will you have a bottle of wine?" he invited. "Oh, no, thank you," I replied. "I do not drink wine. I only drink lemonade." A bottle of wine cost five dollars and the box waiter all but fainted. My commission would have been $1.25 a bottle.

I went back to my dressing room and began to cry. What was I supposed to do? One of the girls explained the setup. We were not only to sing and dance, but between the acts we were to drink with the customers on a percentage commission. She also showed me how to pour the drinks into the spittoons when the customers were not watching.

I was next booked into the People's Theater in Seattle. Two weeks later I was asked to play at the Savoy in Victoria. That meant "stock." I was the company's soubrette. I had to present two new flashy songs each week, and work in the come-on trade.

Mother was horrified because I was dancing and singing in variety theaters. I told her that as soon as I had saved enough money I would send for her. But it seemed as though I could never save the money. I was always helping someone else. Once I had the money ready for Mother, but there was a young girl in our company who needed hospital care. I took up a collection for her and added Mother's travel money, too. A reporter wrote my benevolent act up in the paper. It was my first press notice. But I had a hard time explaining to Mother.

Billy Jackson and Jack MacDonald of the Savoy watched over me as though I were their own child. I called Jack "Guardy" because he was so strict with me. The girls' rooms were upstairs over the theater, and each night we were checked to see that we were in our rooms on time.

My second press notice was for my number at the Comique, which said that I sang and danced with a French flair. My pictures began appearing in print everywhere. And I became one of the first pinup girls of the Northwest.

The gold-rush was on, and everyone was excited. I kept moving closer and closer to the Klondike. I accepted an engagement to play Bennett, a gold-mad town, where the men outfitted themselves and built scows to freight into the Yukon for gold. It was at the end of the train line—and life was keyed high. Someone recently told me he spent a night in an old hotel in Bennett, and there on the ceiling was my name, "Katie Rockwell," nailed in champagne corks. It was a custom in those days.

I was wild to reach the gold country. The Northwest Mounties stopped women from going down the rapids to Whitehorse, where we could head for Dawson. But I went anyway, dressed in boy's clothes—down through the Whitehorse rapids, down the boiling water.

Then I received word that the Savoy theatrical company of one hundred seventy people was being formed to go to Dawson. I was asked to join the show.

We chartered a steamer and went into Dawson. I shall never forget my first sight of Dawson. Front Street, facing the Yukon, was a solid line of saloons, dance halls, and gambling houses. I wore hiking breeches—a startling departure from the usual dress of Dawson women. In those days women never appeared in anything but skirts. But I was young, and I laughed at raised eyebrows.

I was wearing an engagement ring when I arrived in Dawson. I planned some day to marry Danny Allmen, who was a chap in a minstrel show in New York. He planned to join me in the Northwest. "When we meet we'll part no more," he had written.

He came to the West Coast a few months after I had left for the Yukon. He wrote he would join me in Dawson. But he suddenly became ill in Vancouver, had a cerebral hemorrhage, and died.

For several months I worked hard in partial partnership with Alex Pantages, a Greek immigrant with whom I had fallen in love. We made lots of money, and we saved it. It was not uncommon for me to take in $500 an evening in percentages for drinks and dances. They were one dollar each and the music stopped often. The waiters sold bottles of wine at fifteen dollars and then removed the bottles when they were half full. This kept the men buying more wine. But men rich with gold dust did not care. All they asked was to forget their loneliness for an evening.

Alex Pantages and I laughed, danced, and worked hard during those months at the Old Orpheum. We opened it together and it became the brightest spot north of the International boundary line. In the spring we'd go picking poppies together on the banks of the Klondike. And we'd make plans for the day that we would marry.

I was never a gold digger. The men threw their gold at my feet when my dances pleased them. And I had more than $30,000 in less than a year. I lived over the theater in a beautiful room. It had red and gold wallpaper, and the furniture was of golden oak. The carpet was lush and thick, with a design of great red roses. There were fine Nottingham lace curtains at the windows.

I began my day's work with an hour in a gymnasium to keep in trim. Then I would take my own dog team and go lashing out over the frozen snow. I had my own horse and in the summer I'd drive like wild through that strangely beautiful country.

Spring was the big season in the Yukon. All winter the miners sat in their lonely cabins on the frozen creeks, waiting for the spring thaw, so they could come to town for laughter and song. With gold dust they would drown their hardships and their homesickness and be happy.

Then there was gold in the streets of Dawson, gold in the hills, and gold in the Yukon. And I was named the queen of it all! There were whistles and cheers whenever I appeared on the board streets.

Men dressed in mackinaws and high boots, with their pockets stuffed with buckskin pokes of gold, were ready to fling gold at every pretty face. We wore leg-of-mutton sleeves and gold nugget jewelry and silken petticoats that rustled when we walked.

The clothes for my shows were from Paris. I paid $1,500 for one Worth gown. And all my lingerie was French and handmade. My dresses were covered with rhinestones and seed pearls and spangles and sequins. The dance-hall girls who did not sing or appear in the show wore shirt-waists and long black skirts.

The dance halls were like theaters with canvas covers on the floor and benches and chairs and boxes. After the show the seats were moved back along with the canvas, and dancing began. In the next room was the bar, fifty feet long with mirrors and flashing crystal. And at the tables, faro, blackjack, poker, dice, and roulette were in progress twenty-four hours a day. I have seen men lose $100,000 in one night. They'd come in rich and go out broke to start over again to strike more gold.

Gold dust didn't seem real like silver dollars. The men threw it around freely. Why not? There was always more where it came from. The gold was handed to the cashiers who weighed it out on big brass scales. Gold was scattered about like confetti when we girls were on the stage.

The hard-bitten Alaskan sourdoughs loved old ballads and songs. "She's More To Be Pitied Than Censured" was one of my hit numbers. Another was, "A Man Was the Cause of It All."

"Police Gazettes" were confiscated as obscene literature in Dawson in those days. And I always wore tights on the stage. My most daring number was coming out in a black satin coat and stripping it off to reveal myself in a brief, rhinestone-studded costume with pink tights. It would look very mild today. Then it was considered daring.

I remember one man, a handsome young fellow, who came in one evening and asked to drink wine with me in a box. He said I had little hands just like his sweetheart. He had expected her to arrive that night on the steamer from the States. Instead he received a letter that she had jilted him for another man. He ordered one hundred bottles of wine and drank about eight of them. My percentage was $500 on the drinks. Later he married the Dawson banker's daughter. They named one of their children for me, Kathleen.

Twenty-three million dollars in gold dust poured into Dawson that first year. It was a year of lavish spending and lavish living. One of my girl friends was wooed by an Italian immigrant. He had a rich gold claim and every day he had twenty bottles of champagne delivered to her for her evening bath. She consented to marry him only if he would give her her weight in gold. She weighed 125 pounds, and he weighed out 125 pounds of gold dust. It was $16 an ounce then—$35 now.

I wasn't faring badly. I had a nugget of gold as big as my fist with a huge diamond in the center. I had a dog collar fashioned of diamonds and gold nuggets. And I had belts and bracelets of twenty-dollar gold pieces. It was our custom to wear these bracelets with one coin missing. Some kind gentleman always added the missing coin. I had $250 hats, and my clothes were the talk of the town. I had my own horses and I was in business for myself—in partnership with Alex.

One Christmas Eve I noticed a little Norwegian by the name of Johnny Matson standing watching me. He was like a man hypnotized. Contrary to my usual procedure, I asked him if he wanted to dance. "Oh no, I yust vant to look at yoo," he said, "Yoo are yust beautiful."

Johnny was a shy young fellow. Men and women were laughing and dancing, but Johnny did not participate. His admiration secretly amused me. He stood there in a corner, watching me as I led the grand march to celebrate Christmas. I wore a lighted crown of flaming candles. The wax dripped into my hair, and later I had to cut off my lovely, long red-gold hair.

For some weeks I had been taking care of a little tubercular girl. She was expecting a baby and the man had run off and left her. I kept her in a little cabin near the dance hall. Sure enough, when I slipped out to see her, I found the baby was being born. The girl died in childbirth and I took the baby. I kept him until he was three, then found him a home and foster parents in the States. I sent the money for his college education and he is one of the most successful engineers in the country today. I have never disclosed his identity. He perhaps has never known of me. But I like to think of him as my son.

The Gold Rush was over in a couple of years. Alex and I went back to New York to look around for new business ventures. Then we went back to Seattle. Motion pictures were a novelty then. No one considered them important. But I bought a little five-and-ten-cent theater in Victoria, B.C., for $350. With the movie reels I included a couple of acts of vaudeville. The show made money. I sold it for $1,500 and Alex bought a theater in Seattle and converted it into a vaudeville and movie show house. That was the first of a long string of theaters that was to make millions for him.

I went back to the Yukon. But life there was not the same. Alex had stayed in the States—and now there were new faces. Tex Rickard ran the Monte Carlo Gambling Hall on Front Street. Jack London was in Dawson writing stories, and Sid Grauman, who now owns Hollywood's Chinese Theater, was making his first fortune in the gold-fevered North. I picked up and went down to Texas for the oil boom. I was restless—heartbroken, too. For Alex had married a girl entertainer in his show.

For days I was despondent. Flossie, a girl who had danced with me in Dawson, wrote me a letter. She said, "Don't throw your life away because of one man. Don't make yourself something he will always be glad he was rid of. Make yourself something he will wish he had kept." The day I read her letter I felt better.

I sent for Mother and she opened a profitable real estate business in Seattle. Bend, Oregon, was having a boom and thousands of acres of homestead land were being opened. This appealed to me. I got a homestead relinquishment on the desert, and with $3,500 in my pocket, moved into the little cabin on my homestead, three miles from the nearest store. It was a fourteen-by-twenty-foot shack. I sold my diamonds and my silver from the Yukon days and furnished the cabin with the money I got from the sale. Immediately there was a rush of suitors to my door.

I married Floyd Warner, a handsome chap who stood six feet two. We were married in 1914 and lived on the homestead until he went into the service of World War I.

Floyd was younger than I was, and jealous. He was ready to fight when anyone called me "Klondike Kate." But we loved each other and were truly happy. When he went to war we sold our cattle and our homestead and I went to manage a hospital at Pineville, Oregon.

I knew nothing about nursing, but never lost a patient. Then I went into the restaurant business. I had never cooked more than a kettle of hot cakes, so that was an entirely new adventure for me. I opened and sold four restaurants—selling each one at a profit.

After Mother died, I wanted to travel again. With the Armistice, Floyd and I decided to go our separate ways. I kept a little home in Bend, Oregon, but whenever I had enough money, I was off for a few months' travel. When my money ran low I'd go home and work to earn some more—so I could be off again.

When I was fifty-three, I presumed that I would settle down for the rest of my days like any middle-aged woman. But no. I found life, love, fame, and romance starting all over again.

The Alaska-Yukon Sourdoughs held a reunion in 1931 in Portland. The long banquet tables were glittery with golden banners, and almost a thousand men and women were seated. We were celebrating the thirty-fifth anniversary of the Gold Rush.

"Most of us were broke thirty-five years ago," the toastmaster began. "There are a lot of things we want to remember in our years in the Klondike. And there are a lot of things we want to forget.

"Some of us came here today in our own private railroad cars. Some of us are as broke as though we had never struck gold in Dawson. But all of us remember one person whom we are going to honor tonight.

"She was the girl who danced in the old Savoy in Dawson. The Queen of 'em all. The girl with the flaming hair and twinkling feet. And we threw our gold dust at her feet for just one of her smiles.

"We used to dream about her in our lonely cabins on the frozen creeks. We had her pictures pinned up on our cabin walls. We toasted her at the bars in Dawson's dance halls. Boys, I present the 'Sweetheart of the Sourdoughs'— Klondike Kate!"

Tears were in my eyes when I stood up. Many of these men were Klondike Kings, some were bent-backed broken men. They began singing "Let Me Call You Sweetheart."

Johnny Matson, the Norwegian miner, who used to watch me in the dance hall in Dawson, saw a write-up of that reunion in the Alaska Weekly. Johnny had remained with his gold claim in Matson Creek, operating a string of small placer claims 160 miles from Dawson. He had been out of the Yukon only once in thirty-five years. He read an item about my official designation as "Sweetheart of the Sourdoughs" at the Portland Reunion. So he wrote me a letter.

"I have always been in love with you, Katie, all these years. I never had the courage to tell you before. I have heard that life has not been too good to you. You have had lots of hardship. I would like to take care of you. I would like to have the right to take care of you as my wife."

Johnny came down from Dawson and we met in Canada.

"But Johnny, I'm old now, " I said.

"Yoo look yust the same to me as yoo did years ago, the most beautiful woman a man ever saw," he replied. I could never laugh at his accent after that. So we were married. We went back to Dawson on our honeymoon.

How strange it was to return to the ghost town. The dance hall still stood there facing the Yukon. I wanted to go in and look around, I told Johnny. "I want to bring back the past, just for a few moments. When I walk out of that door, I will be closing it on my old life."

I walked about the hall. The red plush curtains, old and dusty, were still there on the stage. For a moment I could see myself up there in a red-spangled dress, kicking my legs and singing, my eyes dancing, as I watched the men's champagne glasses raised, toasting me in wine, in champagne.

I could see myself tossing my head, laughing as the miners threw pokes of gold dust on the stage. For a second I could hear the music, the piano and the violin and the drums. Then it was all over. And I was just a little old lady standing there. Could I have really been "Klondike Kate"?

Later the dance hall burned down. I am told there was a second gold-rush to stampede the ashes. For gold dust had been thrown around that stage for years. It had sifted down through the lumber, and it proved as rich as any strike for the men who panned it.

Johnny lives on his claim on Matson Creek. My health is not rugged enough for the long winters on the Klondike. Johnny insists that I live in my little home in Bend, Oregon. Every other year I go up there to be with him.

Twice a year he makes the long mush to send me a letter. I worry about him. I beg him to come out and live in Oregon. But gold is in the sourdough's blood. He cannot leave it. He always thinks he'll find another big pocket of gold.

For Christmas he sends me gold nuggets for jewelry. But mind you, he is not rich. He takes out only enough gold to permit us to live modestly. Sometimes he traps furs. I have some martens I treasure because my Johnny sent them to me. During the years I have learned to love Johnny. He is no longer the "funny little yam and yelly man" to me. He is the best man on earth.

I take in boarders to help out and just recently I was in Hollywood where Columbia Studios were making a motion picture entitled Klondike Kate. The title refers to me but no movie could possibly cover all of my life. I've done so much living they couldn't possibly get it all on the screen in an hour's show.

In Hollywood, I found myself, at sixty-three, a white-haired woman, being interviewed by the press—being banqueted. And Bob Burns invited me to appear on his radio show, to introduce "Klondike Kate." It seemed like a dream!

My life was still considered interesting! Even interesting enough for the title of a movie.

If I had to do it all over again, I wouldn't change it—not one little thing. Many times I used to think, what's the use? But if you can make one person completely happy, you have not lived in vain. I know I have made my Johnny completely happy. And in doing so I am happy myself.

Mush on and smile—that's always been my motto. And a lucky one it has been.

Chapter 12

ON THE ICE-PACK'S RIM

November 1944

By Florence C. Dakin as told to Edith Richmond Thomas

I may have had some apprehension when I landed at Barrow on August 6, 1921, to take charge of the little Presbyterian hospital. But I survived eight years of taking pulses and temperatures, and other things not quite so routine—and I was neither frozen to death, mauled by polar bears, carried away on an ice floe, nor forced to eat walrus blubber for sustenance.

There was very little ice in the vicinity of Barrow as we approached, and the Arctic Ocean was free to treat our small boat as it pleased. I longed to reach shore, even though I expected to land on an ice-bound waste. Imagine my surprise to find the country flat and brown, just like the Nome country, with brave little flowers peeping through the grass.

Nor will I ever forget the pleasant surprise in store for me when I had walked across the beach sand to the hospital of which I was to take charge. The building was lighted up in gala array, flags flying, and phonograph playing in honor of my arrival.

The first day I went up into the attic to prepare a place for my supplies. How cold it was! I shook all over, and my teeth chattered as if they would drop out of my head! I confided to Ned, the Eskimo janitor, that I thought I was on the verge of freezing to death. He looked surprised, and assured me that the temperature was just right for him.

One of the first things I did after my arrival was to go on a tour, with an interpreter, to visit the homes of the people who might come under my care. The native igloos were built partially underground and to reach them we had to creep on our hands and knees through the long, dark passages. When we did get inside, standing was impossible. I tried to stand once, but my head almost went through the low ceiling.

Invariably we found the women of the household squatting on the floor tanning or sewing skins. They seemed perfectly oblivious of discomfort. One woman had not walked for fifteen years, and she did not even complain at being buried alive.

One old man, who was paralyzed from the waist down, lived each summer on a bench outside one of the igloos, with only a small tent over him for shelter. In the fall some kind-hearted Eskimo would take him into his igloo to spare him the pangs of freezing to death.

After that first visit to the igloos, I staggered down to the beach for a breath of unadulterated polar air, and a chance to check up on my reactions. Surely I had had enough of a shock for one day! But suddenly a young polar bear cub came bounding into my lap! I hadn't yet recovered from my astonishment when some parka-clad youngsters rushed up and whisked the little white fellow away. Those children didn't realize my near-panic. The cub was their little live playmate.

I soon found I had little time to kill in Barrow. That first year was a busy one. My first recruit to the hospital was a little boy who had tuberculosis; but it was only on his third visit that his terror of the strangeness about him subsided enough that he could be induced to remain for treatment. His first bichloride bath set him howling loud enough to raise the ghosts of his prehistoric ancestors! When he got used to things, however, he rather liked the hospital and his treatments. That first year I attended sixty long-staying patients in the hospital, and at least a thousand temporary cases. Stray ships would sometimes touch at Barrow with a patient or two, and to them the hospital was a God-send. Captain Roald Amundson visited us frequently. He, as well as other noted explorers who have visited that far-north station, declared that the establishment of the Barrow hospital was one of the most beneficial acts any institution had ever performed.

The Eskimos, themselves, are naturally explorers, and think nothing of traveling long distances. I have no doubt that many of them have crossed the North Pole without realizing it. One boy who worked at the hospital had traveled on foot all the way to Demarcation Point—four hundred miles of barren waste—taking the census. Nor was it unusual to have a visitor drop in on his way to or from Siberia in an open skin boat.

The map on the wall in the hospital corridor was a source of great interest to all visiting Eskimos, and it seemed every one of them knew from personal adventure most of the northern points.

Office hours were always mixed with various other activities, and there was no keeping a strict schedule. There was cleaning, taking inventory, handling enough drugs to run a pharmacy, and always the necessity to keep close track of the food supply.

Ordering supplies by mail involved much hard work, for it was hard to foresee exactly how much of everything we should have sent up one summer for the following year. There was no possibility, in those days, of sending a radio S.O.S. and having some forgotten items flown in. My lists included eggs packed in salt, butter in pound bricks packed in barrels of brine, bacon crated in salt, hams in gelatin cases, canned goods, and dried fruits.

All these supplies had to be kept in the laundry or kitchen, where it was warm enough to prevent their freezing. Medicines, too, had to be protected from the cold. During the summer we lit the furnace daily, but through the long winter the fire was never allowed to go out.

Had food supplies from the Outside failed to arrive, we would still not have been in danger of starving at Barrow. In spring and fall, large flocks of ducks and geese fly over Barrow, joining their cries with those of the Arctic terns, whistling swans, phalaropes, snipes, snowy owls, and ptarmigans, until the air is filled with a raucous tumult.

I never tired of seeing the way the ptarmigans decked themselves in white raiment in about the middle of August, so that they blended with the snows of winter. Then each spring they took on the mottled hue that blended with the tundra. The boys who took care of the big reindeer herds used to bring in eggs of the wild fowls, and they were well worth the dime apiece we paid for them.

It may sound paradoxical, but there was a cold-storage at Barrow in which meat for the winter was kept. It was merely a storage room hewn out of solid ice, and entered by a four-foot-square passage. Occasionally the frost on its walls became so thick that it had to be defrosted. About fifty reindeer carcasses always hung in the storage room, and each was as safe as if it were in a private refrigerator. People would go down and cut off their own steaks as they needed them.

No one ever thought of helping himself to someone else's meat. In my estimation, one of the finest traits of the Eskimo is his innate honesty. He simply does not lie nor steal. Our two-hundred tons of coal lay in sacks on the open beach for weeks, but not one sack was touched, in spite of the fact that the poor people needed coal badly.

In the fall the boys would go out hunting for birds, and as they returned across the lagoon with their boats loaded, they would shout, laugh and yell to let everyone know of their success. The birds were stored for winter use, and they supplied the down for innumerable quilts we made.

We always had plenty of fish, and each season brought its own varieties of game. No sooner was duck season over when seal hunting started. Then came the oogaruk, walrus, whale, and caribou seasons. Always in the background lurked that circumpolar navigator, the polar bear.

There were many other pleasures besides hunting. We had picnics, and some of the more energetic went in for surf-bathing and kayak racing. It was not the sort of surf-bathing one enjoys on the warm beaches of California. One time a couple of Eskimo boys stayed in the water a minute too long, and came out with terrific chills. They were rushed to the hospital, but they failed to respond to hot coffee, medicine, or massage. As a last resort, I turned on the phonograph and made them dance.

Those were two patients who had me properly frightened! I thought they would never stop shaking! The last remedy did the trick, however, and ever after that I kept a good supply of lively records.

The Arctic ice was captain of the port of Barrow, and boats could reach us only in the summer. We considered ourselves lucky to get mail twice a year— once in summer by boat, and once by dog team in winter. Sometimes we could see the boats for days before they arrived or before the seas would permit their landing. Then we would nearly go crazy before we could learn what boat it was, and whether it had mail.

Sometimes mail and supplies would be transferred at the last minute to a stray ship en route to Barrow, so we never knew what to expect. At best it might be six months or a year between the time our letters were posted and the time they reached us.

A favorite summer visitor to Barrow was Captain John Backland, of the schooner *C. S. Holmes*. He had been a minister, and he would always oblige us by preaching a sermon in the little Presbyterian Church. He never failed to attract an over-flow audience. He had the faculty of relating his sermons to things the people understood and knew. His "Jonah and the Whale" sermon was a masterpiece, in which he used all nautical terms, and it was so funny that I could scarcely keep from laughing during the entire time of its delivery.

Captain Backland is now dead, and the schooner *C. S. Holmes*, in which he plied the Arctic trade for thirty years, has been requisitioned for war service. His son, John Backland, Jr., who accompanied his illustrious father on many Arctic voyages, is now serving our country as a Lieutenant Commander in the Navy.

A few days after I reached Barrow, one of the eleven white women there brought me an oil stove, saying that I might need it soon. The next morning the ice lay in big slabs all over the ocean; but, as the water was calm, no ice had yet blown up onto the beach.

We could see giant slabs of ice floating by, and sometimes, mounted in the saddles, rode big black walruses. The sight was like waving a red flag before a bull; every last Eskimo would race for his spear. They would pile into their big oomiaks and paddle out in pursuit. It was a gala day in Barrow when a walrus was killed. Jubilant shouting would announce the glad tidings long before the boat reached shore, and the entire populace would rush down to the beach to watch the hunters come in. Each one would do his share of the butchering, and the cut-up carcass would be divided equally among the villagers.

With winter bearing down in earnest, I found I had to have fur boots and a muskrat parka in order to withstand the cold. Summer had been cold, in my estimation. What would winter be like? Suddenly we were frozen in. In a single night, ice had accumulated in huge piles all along the beach. By the first week in October, the ground was white with snow, and the temperature ranged about twelve above zero in the mornings. For some reason I felt the cold more than I did when the mercury fell to twenty or thirty below, later on.

With the approach of winter, the days and nights became indistinguishable. A deep twilight lasted in varying degrees for half the year. The Arctic night at Barrow is actually of seventy days' duration, and ends at noon on January 23. On that day the upper edge of the sun-disc appears above the southern horizon. Then, on the following day, the whole disc is visible.

Each day thereafter finds the sun rising a little earlier, and a little farther to the east, and setting later and a little farther to the west. Sometimes the nights were actually lighter than the days, for the moon and stars shone brilliantly. Moreover, the iridescent colors of the Northern Lights spilled down upon an enchanted world. At such times the land took on an aura of mystery, and we lived in a constant state of thrill.

During the winter we could do little without the aid of artificial light, and the perpetual twilight was trying on the eyes. It was the wind, however, that we dreaded most. It would cut like a knife, and it seemed it would freeze our faces to the bone.

One night I thought I heard the chimneys crashing through the roof, and the roof itself taking flight to parts unknown. We in the hospital sat up all night, too terrified to sleep while the hurricane roared. The entire night was attended by sounds of crashing that were frightful and awful. It was morning before we realized that it was the crashing and jamming of the ice-floes on the nearby reef that we had heard.

The howling of a winter storm was no damper on our Christmas spirits, however. Everyone came to our entertainment at the church. Gifts of raw meat, reindeer skins, deer heads, sinews, soles for boots, paddles, ermine tails, fur gloves, parkas, carved wooden ware, and so forth, were exchanged. The most envied gift was an ermine skull.

Poor Ned, the mail musher, could not get to Barrow in time to deliver his load on Christmas. It was January fifteenth before he arrived, and the mercury still ranged around thirty below. Later he came over to the hospital and had dinner with me. He told me that that trip was the worst he had ever experienced. He lost five of his dogs, and suffered intensely himself.

His poor face was a sight—frozen, swollen, bleeding, and covered with sores. The skin was peeling off, and, although I gave him some ointment to use, I knew it would be a long time before he would look like himself again.

He was scheduled to leave again immediately with the out-going mail; but the storm continued with increasing violence and he had to wait it out. Indeed we were all in danger of being lost the minute we set foot outdoors, for it was impossible to keep a straight course in the sleet, wind, and darkness.

When my cancer patient—who lived in the little village on the Point, about eight miles away—went home from the hospital, I was interested to see how her doting husband prepared her for the trip. They spent all morning getting ready. First she was dressed in all the fur clothing she could stand, then placed on the canvas sled. Over her was spread a heavy eiderdown quilt, the edges all carefully tucked around her. Then over all a little tent was fitted, and inside was a burning lantern to furnish warmth. I was afraid she would suffocate before they reached the Point.

The biggest occasion of the entire year at Barrow comes when the whale hunters have returned to shore. Then they celebrate the festival of Nalukataq. The young women and girls all make new snow shirts and fancy clothes to wear on the occasion. Others busy themselves with cutting up the black-skin of the whale into cubes for their favorite tidbit—muktuk.

Of course everyone went to the Nalukataq. Even the patients from the hospital were carried over, and stayed until evening watching the games. At skin-tossing, the greatest skin-game ever devised, we roared with laughter. The antics of the players, as they bounced boisterously back and forth through the air on the big walrus hide, were something to behold!

The player was proficient only when he could keep standing upright on the skin, and to do so was an almost incredible feat of balance. Some held out for an amazingly long time. Several old grandmothers, probably stirred by the memories of more agile days, took up the challenge with vim and set the Arctic village into an uproar.

Helen, my assistant at the hospital, carried off the honors by keeping her feet and her head for the longest time, and being the first to touch the overhead wire. She, of all those Eskimo contestants, seemed to "know her stuff" best, and I was delighted with the distinction she brought to the hospital.

The skin-tossing kept up intermittently throughout the day, and during the games food and coffee were served to the guests. In the evening the big skin was set aside, and everyone danced hilariously in the big circle, to the rhythms of Eskimo drummers. At midnight the dancing ceased, and everyone repeated the Lord's Prayer in unison—as, indeed, they had done at the beginning of the festivities.

I was amused, sometimes, to hear the reactions to our teachings among the Eskimos. A boy from Wainwright wrote me: "Your question about the airplane will be answered sure. That time I myself got surprise, too, for everybody seemed to marvel at such a big weighty thing so high up in the air like that. It is said that an oldest woman here got so frightened that she had to run for her life. She was an old lady with a very bad tuberculosis too; her age is perhaps ninety. She had to run she got so scared; her heart was beating all the time."

The Eskimo children loved school, and we endeavored to keep them well, and in school as much of the time as possible. I have always felt that my work at Barrow, besides being one of the most pleasant periods of my life, was exceedingly worthwhile. We were extremely proud of the fine records some of our Point Barrow Eskimos were making in the American universities. It is those young people who eventually become the teachers of their race. Our entire work with them was done in the spirit of helping them—teaching them to help themselves.

In 1936, after the depression had long curtailed the funds of the Presbyterian Missionary Board, they were no longer able to maintain the Barrow hospital. At that time the Indian Service took charge, and carried on until the building was destroyed by fire in 1937. It was almost two years later that the present hospital was completed by the Government to continue serving the needs of the Eskimos and other adventurers on the ice-pack's rim.

Chapter 13

WOMAN ON THE DALTON TRAIL

January 1945

By Della Murray Banks

It was in June of that hectic summer of 1898—when the Spanish war and the Klondike gold stampede competed for space in the newspaper headlines—that I went from San Francisco to Seattle to join my husband for our fourth attempt to find a fortune in the North. Two summers, '96 and '97, were spent in Cook Inlet with no success, and a winter at Marble Creek on Prince of Wales Island, working for a grub stake which we didn't get, had been discouraging. But this time Austin had made arrangements to go with a party of nine hopeful gold-seekers from Massachusetts and Connecticut.

None of those men had ever been West, but the leader, Denison Tucker of New Haven, was very enthusiastic about a district a hundred and fifty miles inland from Pyramid Harbor, on the Dalton Trail. Tucker had heard of this district through Homer Pennock, who had been the promoter of our Cook Inlet company.

When Austin met me at the train and gave me his plan, he told me that Tucker had implicit faith in Pennock. I implied that Tucker would get over that.

"I know you don't like Pennock," Austin said impatiently, "But do you have to say so?"

"No, I don't have to say so," I answered with resignation. "I can keep still."

In the hotel lobby we met Tucker, brandishing the morning paper, wildly excited. Disconnected words and broken sentences poured forth. We looked at the paper where a half-column gave a far from creditable life story of Pennock. Austin, who had known Pennock for years and had never heard any of the things of which he was accused, said promptly that he didn't believe a word of it. For that matter, neither did I. Then Tucker turned abruptly to me.

"Mrs. Banks, you would believe what Pennock says, wouldn't you?"

I hesitated, saw the smile twitching Austin's lips, and took the plunge. "I wouldn't believe Homer Pennock on the stand under oath!" Austin laughed at Tucker's dismayed expression, and I hastened to add that, even so, I didn't believe the story in the newspaper. As a matter of fact, Pennock later won a libel suit against the paper.

Then we went up to meet the two ladies, Mrs. Tucker and her sister, Mrs. Hutchins, whose husband was one of our party. They were the most conservative of down-easters. Mrs. Tucker regarded the trip as a lark, wanted to go just for the fun of it, and naturally didn't expect to do any work. She wouldn't think of going if there was any possibility of getting her feet wet! She actually said just that! She couldn't ride a horse—and at best it would be a three-hundred mile trip. She couldn't eat off a tin plate, nor drink from a tin cup; nor could she eat beans or bacon. She lived on cream, milk, and eggs.

I explained that such delicacies would not be found on the Dalton Trail; that it would not be a summer picnic, but a lot of hard work. Later I explained to Austin just why I wouldn't go if those women went. I will willing to do my share, but that didn't include waiting on Mrs. Tucker. I didn't intend to prove the truth of the old saying, "Them as will can; them as won't, don't."

The ladies finally decided to spend the summer in Seattle, where they could keep their feet dry. I smiled when I heard that. They didn't know Seattle!

Besides Tucker and his brother-in-law, Hutchins, the easterners of the group were "Pop" Green, who had once mined in the Black Hills of South Dakota; Kilton, a two-hundred-pound office worker; Stoddard and Smith, also office workers; Thorn, a boy of twenty; Thompson, an artist; and George Townsend, familiarly known as Teddy, a young Yale man. He assured me he had had some experience at roughing it. Ah, yes! He had camped out in the woods a few times! They seemed like a nice bunch of fellows—but as trail mates?

Just before sailing we saw a group of Laplanders in native dress on the docks. They were to drive a Government herd of reindeer in over the trail to the lower Yukon. They were a curious and interesting group, but plainly they resented the amusement their appearance gave Mrs. Tucker, who laughed openly at them.

In telling us about Shorty Creek, our destination, Tucker had said that Pennock had had an old miner with him in New York, and that the miner had been in the district. He told the man's name, and I felt more doubtful than ever. I'd heard of him before.

"There was a little misunderstanding," explained Tucker. "We thought this man Jim said the gold was so thick that it could be picked up by the pan full. But what he really said was 'handful.'"

Forty years old, and as credulous as that! Tucker had much to learn—of gold and of men. Yet we had been as ready to believe anything two years before, when we had gone to Cook Inlet. And we had learned—or had we?

We sailed on July 5, after a lively Fourth. Tucker just couldn't reconcile himself to the fact that the South Highlanders came over from Canada to march in the parade.

"But we whipped them," was his cry. Seattle, however, was celebrating the battle of Santiago that day, and forgetting the Revolution.

We stopped in Vancouver for miners' licenses, and there Tucker came to grief. We had so little time that he thought a taxi up to the office would be best; only a dollar. But when he packed all eleven of us in one taxi, the driver charged him a dollar each. Tucker's thrifty Connecticut soul was outraged.

On the steamer we studied each other. Not one of them had even handled a pick or shovel, yet each was sure he could shovel sand for ten hours a day. Did they think they could do it on the streets of Seattle? No, of course not; but gold-bearing sand would be different. That's true; it is the heaviest kind. But enthusiasm helps even a lame back.

They had grumbled over the steep streets of Seattle, but never doubted for a moment that they could pack fifty pounds over a mountain trail.

We got into Skagway at midnight to find the town quiet under martial law, and Soapy Smith just killed. Soapy had made fleecing the unwary his business, and a profitable one, until his high-handed arrogance and open outlawry had become unbearable. A citizens' committee had been called the night before at the end of the long wharf. Soapy got wind of it, and arming himself, started down to the wharf to break up the meeting.

In the ensuing battle Soapy was killed, and the marshal, Frank Reid, was wounded so severely that he died the next day. There were twenty-four of Soapy's henchmen in jail, and all docks and passes were guarded. The town was buzzing with talk of lynchings.

Skagway lies at the mouth of a narrow canyon, with a wide, shallow flat in front of it, so the docks are all long. There were many cabins, but all small, either of logs or frames covered with tar paper. There were many tents, some well put up, but most of them as slipshod as if the owners were ready to start up the White Pass Trail at a moment's notice.

The projected railroad over the Pass was being built along the main street. It was the only business street, and every other building was a hotel, saloon, dance hall, or gambling house. There was little other business, as Skagway was only a transfer point for hopefuls going on to Dawson, and the lucky or discouraged going back to the States.

We stopped at Dyea, but did not get up to town, as the tide was out and the wharf was cut off from the town at high tide; so if you went ashore at low tide, you might not get back to your steamer.

Pyramid Harbor, like Skagway and Dyea, lay at the end of a long finger at the head of Lynn Canal. There was a fish cannery and a store, and a tent-hotel a mile or so from the dock. The proprietor came across to the boat to see if he had any prospective guests. Austin decided to take me over to the hotel and come back to help unload, as the steamer wanted to go out with the tide.

We got into the rowboat, but soon found that the hotel man had been celebrating the Santiago victory, also. He was an Englishman with a hands-across-the-sea attitude. We were making no progress when Austin took the oars and finally got us to the hotel. It consisted of two tents with a fly between. The larger tent was the dining room in one end, and had bunks in the other.

The proprietor was quite overcome to have a lady present, and routed out the cook at eleven p.m. The cook, a Frenchman, was sober. When ordered to prepare a place for a lady to sleep, he hauled down a big American flag.

"Washa gonna do wiz zat?" inquired the proprietor.

"I want it," was the cook's brief reply.

The boss assured me of my safety there. They might be rough in appearance, but they had hearts of gold. When I was shown to my bunk, I found it draped on one side with the Stars and Stripes. Perhaps the flag was to make me feel safe, but Austin decided to stay there until morning.

The Indians, who belonged to the Chilkat Tribe and were said to be the most troublesome on the coast, had a large settlement there. The cannery had a number of Chinese workers; but white women lived there. I was amazed when a forlorn woman came to me and said, "Do you remember me, Mrs. Banks? I met you in Seattle in '97."

She had been a fellow guest at a Thanksgiving dinner. Now she was planning to go alone to Dawson by way of the Dalton Trail. She told me two other girls were going—one by way of St. Michaels, the other by the White Pass. They planned to meet in Dawson and compare experiences!

Tucker hired two packers, and bought a six-horse pack train to supplement the dozen oxen he had brought from Seattle to pack supplies. Jack Noon, one of the packers, had made the trip to Shorty Creek the spring before. Tom McAvoy, the other, was an experienced packer. It was agreed that I should get fifty dollars a month for cooking on the trip, and if I decided to go home after we reached the Interior, Tucker was to pay my way to the coast and see that I got out safely. Of course I knew I'd have to do the cooking anyway, but without such an arrangement, I refused to go.

Tucker, himself, expected to go out in the fall. He thought he could gather up handfuls of gold in no time, but Jack Noon wasn't optimistic about Shorty Creek. Tucker's education was progressing, however. Before leaving New Haven he had been certain that an ox could carry four hundred pounds and walk at least thirty miles a day, while any man could go as far packing fifty pounds—over any kind of trail and in any weather. Therefore, he knew just how long we would be on the trail.

Jack explained. At best an ox could carry two hundred pounds, and the length of day must depend on where feed and water were found, while wet weather would prevent travel.

That morning I heard voices outside the tent, and thinking Austin was back from the store, I stepped outside almost into the arms of two astonished strangers.

"I—I thought you were my husband," I stammered.

One of the men stared at me, and then exclaimed, "Why, you're the woman who was hurt out in Cook Inlet two years ago!" Yes, I was! Two years ago that week I had burned my hand. "You won't remember me," he added, "but I was captain of the *Sophie Sutherland*. We were anchored in Kachemak Bay the day they had to cut off your fingers."

An old Indian woman came past the tent, walking in the edge of the water with skirts trailing, a kerchief tied over her head, and a long string of fish heads dragging along behind. She looked poverty-stricken, but when she saw my blue-and-white enamel cups, she offered me a dollar and a half each for them. They had cost me only ten cents each, but they were all we had.

Much of the stuff had to be cached at Pyramid, since even the six-horse pack train and the oxen couldn't pack it all. But the Easterners couldn't find anything they could do without, even for a month. Jack explained again. If they did stay at Shorty Creek, they could come out after their precious stuff later.

Tucker missed a gold pan, and was sure the natives had stolen it. I insisted that Alaska Indians were honest, but he knew better—they were all born thieves. When he found the missing gold pan in his own dunnage bag, I suggested he apologize to the natives. But he wouldn't even laugh.

The Indians had a potlatch the last night we were in Pyramid. I wanted very much to see it, but no one would go with me. A potlatch is a sort of tribal festival at which a wealthy chief gives away all his possessions and has a great feast, expecting, in due time, to get twice as much back at other potlatches. I saw some of the Indians in gay blankets and painted masks. We should never have the opportunity to see such a thing again, but not one of the men had the slightest curiosity about it.

We left Pyramid at noon on July 15, when the tide was low, as we had to pass a cliff that couldn't be skirted at high tide. Jack said the rivers were waist-deep on the trail, but that he had a horse for me with legs so long that she only got her feet wet. Jack was Irish, and looked like a pirate—big and burly, with heavy black beard and hair. He always listened to Tucker with a bored air—and explained.

I walked the first afternoon, shedding my skirt after getting away from the settlement. Thus I cleared up a question which Stoddard said had been bothering him—what I could do on the trail in a long skirt. He had asked me on the steamer about it, and I had replied that it wouldn't bother me a bit. When he saw me in knickers, he understood.

We passed a beautiful, two-hundred-foot waterfall, in a stream fifty feet wide and nearly knee deep. Stod and I were ahead of the rest. Stod surveyed the stream and asked me how I would get across.

"Oh, you will carry me," I assured him. He did; but a Westerner wouldn't have asked—he'd have known.

After a couple of miles we turned across the Chilkat Delta. There was knee-high grass, and a number of meandering channels, which brought the query from our greenhorns as to whether we would find any other rivers on the way as deep as that. Jack explained. This wasn't a river, exactly, but a salt-water marsh.

We made camp in the rain at the head of the delta, having gone about seven miles. I got supper in the rain, by the light of a candle. Kneeling on the ground, I mixed biscuits—ninety of them, baked 15 at a time in the sheet-iron stove. Thompson watched, saying that if he had to get supper that night, there wouldn't be any. Well, I had walked as far as he had.

The loading next morning was a picnic for onlookers. One ox bucked off his load and took to the brush; one horse got scared when a stove rattled in his pack and bolted. I had a blanket and rope surcingle on my long-legged horse, Polly, no stirrups nor saddle, not even a bridle—just a rope around her neck. Jack said she didn't need guiding, for she would follow the trail at a walk. True, she would; but she walked at her own pace, and I was alone most of the time. Once a pack train carrying bonded whiskey passed me, and Polly joined them. My emphatic "whoa's" didn't stop her, but the pack train finally outwalked her.

We crossed the Chilkat again the second night, at the Dalton toll station. While we were making camp, a man yelled at Austin: "Banks! What are you doing here? I haven't seen you in years!" Later I asked Austin why the man's voice had sounded so familiar, and he reminded me that it was a man from Denver— that he and his wife had been at our house at a card party in 1895.

Our third camp was on top of a steep hill, and our fourth, on the bank of the Chilkat River again. Jack Dalton had built the trail for packing supplies into Dawson. He had, by instinct, chosen the shortest route, keeping close to the swift, winding rivers, but cutting off much distance by crossing and re-crossing their depths, and taking short-cuts through the hills. Gold seekers were free to use the trail, for a modest fee. The recently built Haines Highway follows closely the Dalton Trail but ends at Champagne.

From the fourth camp we followed the Salmon River, a tributary of the Chilkat. At times we waded the river, itself, to round steep cliffs. We met many men going out, some from the Klondike, and some from Shorty Creek. All had a hard-luck story—especially those from the latter place. Jack called it the "wail from Shorty Creek," and didn't hestitate to say that he didn't think much of our prospects. But why, we asked ourselves, should Pennock and the man named Jim have told Tucker such a story of "handfuls of gold?" They had nothing to gain; and besides, Pennock had sent a party into that district the previous spring.

Jack called his retinue his "kindergarten." All the men went with the oxen except Tom and Teddy. Tom led the bell mare, followed by four ponies. Then Polly strung along with me on her back, and Teddy brought up the rear with Swift, an inordinately slow horse. The oxen were always packed first in the morning, and started up the trail. Then the horses were packed, and soon overtook the oxen. We would go until such time in the afternoon as Tom found feed and water for the stock. Sometimes it would be two o'clock—sometimes five.

Everything needed for supper would be packed on the horses, so that the meal could be underway by the time the oxen arrived. My prevailing memory of that trip was of making biscuits—always ninety, baked fifteen at a time! Smith helped me, bringing wood and water, and doing other odd jobs. The other men looked after watering the stock, watching out for sore backs from chafing packsaddles, finding tent poles and putting up tents, and all the other jobs that go with camping.

It didn't take long to find out who would work and who would shirk. It wasn't the man who didn't know, but the man who wouldn't learn, that made it hard. I often thought of what a woman at Shakan had told me the year before. Knowing I was coming to Marble Creek for the winter, she asked the cook what I was like.

"Well, I'll tell you. Mrs. Banks is the kind of woman who can adjust herself to any situation." I never did like that cook; but I hope I have always lived up to his opinion of me.

Jack eventually made me a saddle of blankets arranged over a packsaddle, and bridle and stirrups of rope. They made riding easier for me, and Polly joined no more strange pack trains.

The Salmon River flows down from a big glacier. The water was so full of sand and silt that we had to strain it through our teeth while drinking it. The stream was swollen from floods, and we had to wait three days for it to go down. Finally we went up a smaller stream. Although the Salmon ran swiftly, most of the smaller streams had little current. Once we had to ford a deep place. The men made a loose raft, stretched a rope across, and ferried our goods over hand-over-hand while the animals swam.

We came again to the Salmon, where it spread over a wide valley and could be forded. There were a dozen or more channels in the valley, and although the trail was plain on land, it was difficult to follow across the water. Often it cut upstream at fords, and was hard to pick up at the farther end.

After leaving the Salmon River, we followed along the side of a bluff, through thick spruce forest for two miles, then up a steep hill. There lay the Klahena River valley, two hundred feet below us. We went down the steep trail to the valley floor, and along gravelly bottom-land to the ford. Except that the water in the Klahena is clearer, it is much like the Salmon. Both have constantly changing channels, and much quicksand.

As we crossed the first channel, which was more than knee deep, Pop Green stumbled, fell, and was swept downstream. Thorn ran out on a sand bar, snatching up a long tree branch as he passed. As the current swung the struggling Pop toward him, he held the branch out from the tip of the bar. Pop managed to clutch the branch, and was pulled ashore. Austin also stumbled, but caught himself by the ox he was leading.

A Dalton pack train passed us, and we followed it through several channels. Then we came to one which their horses had to swim, although it had been crossed with no trouble a few days before. Jack, as usual, hunted a shallower spot.

We camped at the mouth of Boulder Creek, on the Klahena, for two days because of the sore backs of the oxen. From there the trail let through the woods up the valley of the Klahena, which narrows to a canyon headed by glaciers. We had to turn and go over a high hill to get down to Pleasant Camp, the Mounted Police Station and customs house, where we had to pay duty on our goods.

The trail down the hill was still under construction, and in some places there was none. One of the oxen slipped and rolled down with his load, breaking off a horn.

Pleasant Camp was on a flat just above the river. It consisted of a restaurant, "The Old Vienna, Michael Casey, Proprietor;" a Dalton outfit which was working on the trail, and the four tents of the Mounties, which were being replaced by cabins.

The Mounties were three strong and their duties were rather stiff. One of them was to see that no one came out of the Yukon without paying the royalty due the crown on all gold taken out. At the time, some men were trying to slip out without paying the royalty. If they passed that post, they were in American territory and safe from apprehension. I have often wondered if they did.

The Mounties told us that the Seattle girl I had met who was making the trip alone had turned back at the Klahena fords. We didn't meet her, but couldn't understand how we missed her.

The first summit of the Chilkat Pass was four miles away from Pleasant Camp. The first three miles were easy. I was just thinking how glad I was that we didn't have to climb the mountain off to the right, when the trail turned abruptly toward it. The entire side of the mountain was zig-zagged with narrow cattle trails through mud-holes and brush that grew downhill instead of up. I walked, since the sergeant-major of the Mounties had told us that horses had sometimes fallen over backward on the ascent.

I pulled myself up by the brush, and wondered how the cattle and horses could get up at all! There were many beautiful wildflowers I would have liked, if a person hadn't been so busy crawling uphill to enjoy them. And how in the world could there be mud holes on such a steep hill?

On top there was no timber—just lichen-covered boulders with dwarf spruce trees not more than a couple of feet high. This boulder-strewn, slightly rolling terrain stretched on for miles, coming down like an apron from the range of rocky, round-topped hills on the right and sweeping down to the edge of Klahena canyon, which must have been a thousand feet deep. Across the canyon, the high, snow-capped, tooth-like St. Elias Range loomed up. We could see the immense glacial moraines, and in some places, little skeleton valleys, where the glaciers had moved back. Raw, new country this, with hills, small valleys, and empty water courses ready and waiting for vegetation to begin. A world in the making!

Beyond the rolling hills on the right was Mount Staythere, a jagged peak which Jack said got its name because no matter how far you went, it was still with you.

Some of our goods had been taken up the steep hill the day before. When I reached the summit, I went swinging along looking for them when, to my amazement, I ran into two men. They were as astonished as I at seeing a woman up there with no visible outfit nor companions. They hadn't seen the cached goods, and I found that Tom had made the summit on another trail the day before.

The same ox which had fallen previously fell backward on the summit trail, and it took two days to get straightened out. The scenery was gorgeous, but the mosquitoes were so bad they interfered with our pleasure in it. The green wood just smoldered, and would hardly burn. Chopping it was like chopping at a piece of rubber. The larkspurs, violets, asters, yellow and white daisies, wild roses, and other flowers had been beautiful on the hillside, but on top I found, also, small evergreen shrubs not more than three inches high, with a cream-colored bell; and a little vine with a pink bell. There was moss of every variety from cream cup and silver skeleton to every shade of green and umber.

We left Klahena Summit and came down through Rainy Hollow, a low cleft running down to the Klahena canyon; then to Devil's Gulch, a deep gully halfway between the summits, with a steep trail going down and a worse one climbing out. We camped at the bottom of the gulley, and, as there was wood, and Tom reported we'd find none at the next camp, I baked biscuits enough for supper and breakfast, and to carry up to the Chilkat Summit. Two hundred biscuits, and only fifteen to a pan!

Three men came down the trail on their way out. Tucker bought a horse from them, and Teddy found an old acquaintance of college days. His name was Arthur Thompson, and he later capitalized on his trek by writing the book "Gold-Seekers on the Dalton Trail."

Thompson had gone into Shorty Creek with Pennock's first party, under Lieutenant Adair, and he told Teddy of the troubles they had. Adair, as a former Army man, was accustomed to strict discipline; but none of the men with him knew what discipline was. At the start, each man was given a plate, knife, fork, spoon, and cup, and expected to look after his own. Long before they reached Shorty Creek, they were reduced to tin cans and jack knives.

I thought of the time I told Pop to bring the cup and plate back to the stove when, after finishing supper, he had tossed them on the ground twenty feet away.

"Who do they belong to?" Pop asked angrily.

"Well, they happen to belong to me. The outfit doesn't own any," I told him. He brought them back meekly, then.

The Adair company had had other trials. The men were put on rations, which was a new and unpleasant experience for them. They grumbled, although they had to admit that Adair shared equally with them. It wasn't safe to stow a cracker under one's blanket for morning—someone would steal it.

"Thompson says," Teddy told me, with horror-stricken face, "that he was so hungry he could have eaten the bacon rind they used to grease the whipsaw with! And he's a Harvard graduate!"

"But Teddy, I suppose a Harvard graduate can get just as hungry as anyone else. I know a Yale graduate who can."

"I know," Teddy admitted with a rueful grin. "But it does seem so awful!"

Chilkat Summit was about the most desolate spot I've ever seen. Just lichen-covered rocks, without a bit of brush, even! We went down to a small stream where we gathered a few sticks, but one as large as a pencil was a find! The men went some distance and found one small tree that would do for a tent pole.

Austin and I slept under a tarpaulin thrown over piled up bags of flour. Our bed was rocky, and it rained all night. In the morning the fog was so dense that I could hardly see the pony ahead of me. We cooked breakfast by breaking up some boxes. Then the canned goods had to be packed in bags.

We made only six miles that day, camping in a meadow aptly called Mosquito Flat. The cattle and horses had had little feed since leaving Pleasant Camp. Many dead horses lay along the trail over the pass. Two men going out gave us a couple of dried salmon and a ptarmigan, and slept under our fly for the night.

Tucker had learned a good deal since he left New Haven, about what a man can carry. Both he and Thompson were glad to have me put their Kodaks on my backstrap. Tucker carried a small pack, making quite a fuss about it since the other men carried none; but the boys discovered that it was only a light feather pillow.

On August 6, we made Glacier Camp. There was plenty of dry wood, but the water was muddy. We passed a man that day who asked Jack why he had a mule-bit on my horse.

"Because that's the kind I found," answered Jack.

"When you get to Glacier Camp, go seventy-five feet to the left of where the tents were, and you'll find some horse-bits hanging on a tree. Help yourself."

I had started with a blanket and a rope, but I ended up with a good bridle and riding saddle, all picked up along the way.

We saw a herd of reindeer on the mountains above us, and wondered if they were a Laplander's herd we had seen in Seattle.

Thompson, who seemed of a finer nature than the others, appreciated the scenery. But he was utterly lacking in tact. After a hard day he called Pop to come out and see the wonderful view.

"I didn't come here to see the scenery!" Pop exploded. "It's gold I came for."

Another time we were crossing a stream nearly waist deep. Hutchins was halfway over when Thompson called loudly, "Hutch—oh Hutch, wait a minute."

Hutch stopped and turned.

"I want to tell you a story!" said Thompson affably. But it was Hutch who did the talking, and the air was blue. Jack said that what Thompson had to say might be interesting, if his slow monotone didn't put you to sleep so quickly.

The bogs, where beavers had built dams and flooded the valleys, were terrible. Sometimes horses and cattle sank down in them and were lost. The old-timers seemed to feel that no river was deep if you could cross it, and a trail wasn't bad if you could find a trace of it. If travelers didn't like the Dalton trail, there was plenty of virgin territory. The Dalton sign read, "People unwilling to pay toll please keep off the road." However, men on foot without horses or oxen were not charged.

It was insufferably hot above Chilkat Pass and the mosquitoes were a constant annoyance. We sent out mail by Dalton outfits we met, and the Mounties were always passing, asking their usual questions. We might lose ourselves, but the Mounties would always know where we were!

We camped on August 9 on an upland high above the southern branch of the Alsek River. The boys shot a number of ptarmigans, which I cooked after dinner to have for the next day. While the rest were rustling wood and water, putting up tents, and caring for the stock, I asked Tucker to help me pick and dress the birds. Tucker always shirked all camp chores.

After a few minutes he said grumpily that he thought the fellows who shot the birds ought to dress them. I told him I agreed, and moreover, I thought the man who shot them ought to be the only one to eat them. That shut him up. Tucker liked ptarmigan.

Next morning we cut down the canyon to the river on a trail so steep I could hardly stay on the horse. But it was so narrow I couldn't get off, once we started. We could look back up the cleft into the heart of the mountain range, then forward down to the Alsek, with the Dalton Post on the far bank.

The Alsek, a glacial stream like the Klahena and Salmon Rivers, is swift and deep—deeper after a day of hot sun. We camped on a stony flat on a bank, and got our drinking water from a spring a hundred yards away. After supper Kilton came into the tent for a drink. I told him the pail was empty. So Kilton took the empty dipper out of the empty pail, walked three hundred feet to the spring, got his drink, and returned the empty dipper to the empty pail! If I had asked him to get a pail of water, he probably would have done so; but he just didn't think of anyone else.

We used a three-cornered needle to sew the sacks of goods every morning, and we only had one. It was missing one morning, and there was consternation in camp. Then someone remembered that Kilton had used it at night. He didn't know what he had done with it, and he didn't care.

"It was my needle, anyway, so what if I did lose it?" he shrugged. That was his attitude from start to finish.

The days were growing noticeably shorter. We were on the trail from about nine in the morning to three in the afternoon, and were usually in bed by eight o'clock. Five in our tent, eight in the other; the niceties of life were forgotten. Riding over hill and dale, through bog, river, and woods, in sun and wind and rain, feeding twelve perpetually hungry men, my constitution and disposition were beginning to wear. My knees were calloused from kneeling on rough ground, baking biscuits.

On August 11, we camped near the Indian village of Wesketahin. The men came over and asked us not to let the stock wander into the graveyard, where little houses were built over graves. Austin bought me a beautiful pair of beaded knee-length moccasins with fringe down the fronts.

Dead, spawned-out salmon lined the banks of the creeks, and fish in the creeks were so thick the men had to kick them out of the way. For dinner that night I cooked three salmon, the usual biscuits, a pail of thick vegetable soup, and a pail of dried apples. They ate every morsel.

After leaving Wesketahin, we climbed a long hill and kept to the trail until later than usual, having been warned not to camp in a desirable looking meadow because it was full of loco weed. We camped on a hill, in the midst of burned timber, where dust and soot were bad. But by that time we were used to anything.

While I was alone in camp, an Indian brave and two women came by. They sat down on a log a little distance away, stared at me, and laughed heartily. I knew they were making fun of my knickers, and felt resentful until I remembered how Mrs. Tucker had made fun of the Lapps in Seattle, and how they hadn't liked it. My resentment faded into amusement as I thought how indignant she would be should anyone tell her that her manners were like those of the Indians.

We reached Klukshu Camp, ten miles from Shorty Creek, on August 15, and eight of the men went on to the goal. As we rode through the village of Kluk-shu, the small boys yelled, "hello," and in the evening four children came over to our camp and serenaded us with "There'll Be a Hot Time in the Old Town Tonight." Teddy and I fed flapjacks to one Indian until he could eat no more. He explained with a wide grain and expressive wave of his hand over his stom-ach that he could eat no more; but he wanted to take the last flapjack home to his family.

I sold my felt sombrero to a young woman who was attracted to it for the same reason that I had been—it had a narrow, double leather band with two intriguing little leather buckles. She saw it hanging on a limb, and when I agreed to sell it, she spoke to a boy with her. He untied a handkerchief holding more silver than I could keep in my two hands.

A much-disappointed group returned from Shorty Creek and reported that there wasn't even a gravel bank there. Where could Pennock have got the information which led him to send in the Adair party and ourselves? Pennock, himself, had been over the pass the previous spring, and should have learned something. The long weeks on the trail had been just another wild goose chase! Austin and I were getting used to them.

Thorn and Thompson decided to take one horse and go back, giving up the search for gold. Thorn, I daresay, never forgot the trip, nor the number of times his horse bucked him off in the middle of a creek. Tom always said the horse made it in three jumps, but that Thorn only made two.

Thompson had his Kodak views from which to paint, which, after all, was what he had really come for. At Shorty Creek he had slipped and dropped his camera in the water. He told me about it, and asked me if I thought the films were ruined. Of course I thought so; but since he wouldn't know it until he got back to Seattle, I cheered him up by saying they probably weren't hurt. As a matter of fact, he told me later they turned out all right.

The rest of us decided to go on to the Klondike. That suited Austin, and there was nothing else for me to do. So, on August 18, we left Klukshu, trekking through bog and brush, then up a steep hill through small, thick timber. We had a good camp that night, but the wind, which had been blowing steadily for days, threatened to blow us all away. That day we met a white man and woman going out with one pack horse. She looked as tired and discouraged as I felt.

We camped on a flat near Deep River, which was well named. The ford was breast-deep, and on either side one would have had to swim. The men always jumped on the oxen or horses for such crossings. At Deep River, Kilton decided it was too much trouble to mount on the bank, so waited until an ox was in the water, thinking just to step aboard. But the ox was too quick for Kilton; he just got his arms around the pack, and clung there like a fly on the wall. Halfway over he was stopped when the ox ahead stood in the water and gazed calmly at the scenery.

"Go on, Baldy, go on!" yelled Kilton. But Baldy took his time, while Kilton clung and Tom and I sat on the far bank laughing.

We met a number of parties on their way out. If a man could stand the long tramp, it was much cheaper to go out by trail than by boat down the Yukon. Most of those going out were broke and discouraged. Austin, who was behind us with the oxen, asked one party whether they had seen a group of seven horses, two men, and a lady. No, they had met seven horses, two men, and a boy—but no woman, and certainly no lady! I'd been wearing Teddy's cap since selling my sombrero, and, as the wind was chilly, I had his coat on, too. I suppose I didn't look very feminine.

We passed Dezadeash Lake, set in a ring of mountains, and camped well off the trail where the feed was better for the cattle. Even then, the Mounties found us. Our names, please? Where from, where bound, and why so far off the trail? We had to use water from the bogs, and it was unfit to drink, even when made into strong tea.

The next stretch was through a forest fire, which burned ominously on the hillsides, filling the narrow valley with smoke and ashes. Tom scouted ahead to pick up the trail through the burning timber. The horses needed much urging, for the ashes were hot and burning trees fell across the trail. When a blazing tree fell between Polly and the bell mare, it was hard on my nerves, as well as Polly's.

We camped in a grove of young poplar saplings, which Jack assured us wouldn't burn; so we were safe through the night, though fires were thick on all sides and the air was dense with smoke. The cattle, nervous because of the fires, swam the river during the night. Tom and Kilton had to swim after them, and we were very late getting started the next morning.

The trail led us through a mountain pass into the valley of the north fork of the Alsek, where we turned to the right towards the Yukon. Where the trail was not running through bog holes and sand dunes, it was wiped out by ashes from the burned timber, and fire still smoldered in the trees.

There must have been scattered Indian camps through the timber, for one night a small boy, not more than four years old, wandered into camp after supper. He was the only Indian I ever saw who was not hungry. He ate only a little, and then, having satisfied his curiosity, sauntered off unconcernedly. He knew where he was going, even if we were somewhat uncertain ourselves.

The horses of the pack train were very clannish, and showed Polly plainly that they considered her an outsider. Once we passed some horses grazing twenty feet off the trail. Our ponies deliberately went over to bite 'em, just to show that they didn't belong. Just like different people, those horses were different in personalities and temperaments.

On August 27, we came to Hutshi Station, on Hutshi Lake. The lake is twenty miles long, with high bluff banks and wooded islands. The trail led up and up, until we were on a plateau covered with spruce trees. Dalton's station at Hutshi was merely a tent with one forlorn man. There was supposed to be an Indian village nearby, but we found only one cabin, two or three shacks, and nine graves.

The location was beautiful. I can remember thinking what a grand place it would be for a summer resort. A railroad could have been built over the trail. Perhaps the new Haines highway will open that wonderful country to vacationers.

About seven years after that trip, I was doing night work on a Los Angeles newspaper. After a wearying session, an elderly man at the next table stretched his arms wide and said, "I wish I were at Lake Mentasta!"

"Well, Mentasta may be all right," I responded, "but what's the matter with Hutshi?"

He stared at me. "There's nothing the matter with Hutshi—but where did you ever hear of it?"

"I was there—August, '98."

"I was there at the end of July," he said.

He might have been one of the men we met on the trail—one of those who had seen the "boy!"

One night when we made camp, the boys' cake of soap was missing. Who had it last? Each was sure he had given it to another, and finally one man remembered leaving it on a stone. Should he go back and get it? Ten miles or more back, even if he could have located the stone! But he was in earnest!

The ax was always the last thing packed, being slipped under the pack ropes where it could be got at quickly. Once the ax was missing, although Tucker insisted he knew he had packed it. An argument began. The easterners jumped onto Tucker and told him all the things he had done wrong on the trail, interspersing them with "Where did you leave that ax?"

Tucker, reduced to tears, kept breaking in with, "But I did pack the ax!" Then Austin discovered one of the oxen, behind some bushes, still loaded, and on his pack was the missing ax.

"I told you I packed the ax," cried Tucker; but by this time the ax was only a side issue. Hadn't he told them how much an ox could carry and how far one could go? Hadn't he been wrong? Where were those handfuls of gold? Everything Tucker had done was wrong, and the whole fiasco was all his fault.

We heard from someone that the Spanish War was over; but we doubted it, for the same fellow told us that a man named Dewey had blown up all the Spanish Fleet at Santiago, Cuba! The police had no news from the Outside, and to us it seemed of little importance. The question of what to feed the horses and oxen loomed larger than any war.

On August 29 we started following down the narrow valley of the Nordenskiold River. Of everyone we met we inquired how far it was to Rink Rapids, and from each we got a different answer. Sometimes it seemed we must have been going backward.

There's never so lonesome a grave as one beside a trail. We passed one with a square post at head and foot, while a blazed tree carried the name of the dead man and the names of the comrades who buried him. "Frank Goodman, died July 20, 1898." Long afterward I learned that he had belonged to the Thibault cattle outfit, and had died of typhoid fever.

A packer whom Jack knew spent the night with us, and told us that our dinner was the best he had seen since California. He said there'd been a woman with the outfit he had just packed in to the river, and when they made camp at night, she just lay down and didn't do anything. She has my admiration; and I wish I had her nerve!

I had a sinking feeling when Red, the packer, told us that the other outfit had left Pyramid on June 9, and hadn't reached Rink Rapids yet! We had not left Pyramid until July 15. Could I endure forty-six more days on the trail?

On September 5 we decided to leave Tom, Hutchins, Kilton, and Smith to camp on the Nordenskiold to let the oxen rest, while the others of us went on to Rink Rapids with the horses and started building log rafts to float the cattle down to Dawson. There was much repacking and dividing of supplies for the separate parties.

When we saw the Yukon, I understood why old-timers referred to it as "The River." Other streams were called by name, but not the Yukon. It was about four hundred feet wide below the Nordenskiold junction, and swept along in great, smooth curves—as majestic as the Mississippi.

It was hard to believe that the mighty Yukon would be frozen over in six weeks, for our first day along its banks was the hottest we had endured since leaving Pyramid.

With no cattle to care for, and Smith, my helper, left behind, the other boys seemed to leave all the chores to Austin. I explained that they could do their own cooking if it wasn't stopped, and at the next meal time they clustered under my feet like puppies wanting to know what they could do to help.

We passed Five-Finger Rapids, where the Yukon is divided into five channels by four statuesque rocks spaced evenly across. It was picturesque, but I couldn't help being glad we were traveling on land, rather than on the swift, dangerous river.

Halfway between Five-Fingers and Rink Rapids was a sawmill, store, police post, and the end of the Dalton Trail! From July 15 to September 9 we had wound through bog holes, over mountains, through rivers, mosquitoes, forest fires, and rain—"leagues on leagues and miles on miles." Now the trials and tribulations of the Dalton Trail were a thing of the past. But there were others to come.

Jack Dalton kept a hundred horses near Rink Rapids to carry out passengers, but he had no call for them. He offered to furnish saddle horses and food, and allow a certain amount of baggage, and charged one hundred and fifty dollars for the trip. But men who would pay that much would go by boat. But boat fare from Rink Rapids to the head of White Pass was a hundred and ten dollars, with meals an additional two dollars each. It cost as much to get out of the country as to get in!

Our last day on the trail just about finished me. We were going through burned timber, with ashes flying in clouds. I was so near exhaustion that I clung blindly to my saddle, and Jack said he knew I could go no farther. We stopped at a bad place for camping, and Austin carried me off poor old Polly. The cook was a complete wreck! And that was one night the boys got their own dinner.

The next day the boys found a good place for a permanent camp about two miles away. It was on level ground about twenty feet above the river, and offered timber for building rafts. The Dumbolton outfit, which Red had brought in, was camped a half mile below us. I was so curious to see a woman who could go over the Dalton Trail and do nothing that I wasted no time in going down to pay a social call.

She was only twenty-two, and pretty. Maybe that was how she got away with it. A man once described me as the homeliest woman and the best cook that ever went over the Dalton Trail. Ah, me! Well, we can't have everything!

We were short of nearly everything in the way of provisions, and we were always hungry. One sack of beans had been broken, and in gathering them up, they were mixed with sticks and pine needles which eventually settled to the bottom of the sack. It was now our last sack, and almost empty at that. I was picking them over carefully, pouring a few into a plate and blowing off the refuse, when a mosquito lit on my nose. In getting rid of him I knocked over my basin of cleaned beans, and had to get down on the ground, scrape them up, and clean them again.

Austin shot a grouse, and I stewed it with biscuits; but one grouse doesn't divide into seven very large pieces. Mrs. Dumbolton had a live grouse under a box. Her husband had caught it and wanted to cook it, but she felt sorry for it and wanted to let it go.

Teddy and I went to the store at the sawmill, and invested ten dollars in necessities. One can of baking powder was a dollar; three bars of laundry soap, a dollar and a half; seven pounds of rolled oats, five and a quarter; three pounds of sugar, two and a quarter! The storekeeper gave us two small green onions as a treat, and let us read a newspaper dated August 19.

I mentioned to Tucker that we were low on provisions, and he said, "Oh, there's plenty of flour and bacon," He was quite surprised when I pointed to the last half-pound of bacon, and told him it was all there was.

Mrs. Dumbolton mentioned that she was hungry for onions. I told her that the first day I had met her I had wanted some of her fresh bread so badly that if she had turned her back, I would have grabbed a loaf and run. She asked why I hadn't told her, and I explained that I was afraid they might be as short of provisions as we. She laughed, and gave me a loaf of bread. Next time I visited her, I took a dried onion to her.

The men were working in the timber, away from the river breeze, and the insect pests nearly drove them mad. After felling the trees for raft logs, they had to haul them by ropes back to the river bank. The horses, being pack-trained, wouldn't work in harness. Even Polly either couldn't or wouldn't learn. They had to turn them loose; there was no sale for them, and no feed. Hay was five hundred dollars a ton. Would the horses freeze or starve to death?

But much as I longed for the plenty of food, the warmth, and the soft bed of home, I knew that, should I suddenly be transported there, I would feel an aching desire to sit by the Yukon campfire again, with a freezing back and scorching face, smelling the mingled odor of wood smoke and tobacco, while Jack told his yarns. Our camp was a beautiful spot—the mountain across the river was purplish-gray, with splashes of red and yellow of frost-turned leaves against the dark spruce. The gorgeous sunsets gave way to the dancing Northern Lights. The majestic river was a mile wide, with the steamer channels on the farther side, and little islands breaking the green water.

After more than forty-five years I can still hear Austin's tired voice, and see the kindly but serious look in his eyes as he said, "I guess you'd better go back home when Tucker goes." I stood up quickly, the pan I was washing falling to the ground. "It's going to be a mighty tough winter up here," he hastened to add.

His words brought apprehension, for although we had discussed the possibility of my return, and it had been in our agreement with Tucker, still his sudden decision seemed an unexpected and unpleasant reality.

I took rapid stock of the situation: My boots were covered with dust and mud, my knickers torn and dirty, a worn greatcoat buttoned around my too-thin body to keep out the bitter wind and keep in my heart's despair; provisions were pitifully low, the cattle still far behind on the trail; little hope of gold for weeks or months—perhaps never.

Most discouraging of all to us was the complete indifference of Tucker, the supposed leader of the party, to any responsibility. It had never occurred to him that it might be necessary for him to spend a winter in the North, nor had he anticipated doing any work. No—during a pleasant summer's outing he would "pick up handfuls of gold." Now, at the end of the trail which had surpassed in hardship anything he could have imagined, with short rations and a bitter winter ahead, Tucker had lost no time in deciding to take the first boat up the river.

But for me there was the long trail behind—the endless days and desolate nights, the bogs and dust and smoke, the heart-breaking, back-breaking climbs over the passes—and back of that was the terrible winter in the prison-like camp of Marble Creek. Was this, then, to be the end of the glorious vision Austin and I had had?

I looked across at the purple mountains, down at the swift river we had come so far to find. Every instinct rose in me against turning back. But Austin, alone, would be free to go about the Klondike as he pleased; there would be no handicap.

"Yes," I said wearily. "I suppose you are right."

Chapter 14

MAIN TRAILS AND BYPATHS

December 1952

One sign that frontier Alaska is at last "growing up" is the attitude of the people in the cities against the institution of commercialized prostitution, which has flourished in Alaska to a much greater extent, proportionately, than in any other place in the United States.

The "girls" of "the line" were attracted to Alaska concurrent with the earliest reports of gold discoveries. The prosperity of any camp or city could be gauged immediately by the number of prostitutes in the place. As the gold supply declined, so did the number of girls.

In recent years this commercialized vice has again erupted. With prosperity now associated more closely with quick gains in fishing and in military defense construction, hundreds of prostitutes, encouraged by the fact that the people and the officials of most Alaska cities and towns looked with closed eyes upon their activities, set up shop near the business districts. In at least one city, the "hotels" in a row on Main Street are really all brothels. Closely allied with prostitution is the bootlegging carried on by the madams, all of whom serve liquor at "$1 a shot."

In the last few years, however, there has been a constant upheaval, with changes of city managers and police chiefs in Anchorage, Fairbanks and Ketchikan following in rapid succession, because of conflicting opinions about what should be done toward suppressing this disease- and crime-spreading racket—a racket many people thought an evil necessary to a frontier country such as Alaska.

Agitation by law-abiding, Christian people of good morals is causing some action to be taken by the city governments in these cities to close the lines. The madams, most of them older women who have been in one Alaska town or another for twenty to thirty years, are complaining to investigators that "business is not what it used to be."

Opponents of those who want to enforce the laws and close the wide-open "districts" have long been misled by fallacies circulated by the underworld. "If you close the line," they say, "the girls will be operating all over town," and "no man's wife or daughter will be safe on the streets."

Studies by police, the United States Public Health Service, state health authorities and volunteer social hygiene agencies, led by the American Social Hygiene Association, have shown that neither of these arguments is true, and that closing the line always brings about a decrease in the number of attacks on women and a decrease in the incidence of venereal disease. It also makes for a more prosperous community for all inhabitants. Segregation into publicized "districts" increases prostitution, takes money out of legitimate channels and attracts procurers, gamblers, bootleggers and other undesirables.

Many inhabitants of the more prosperous communities have attributed their prosperity to the red-light districts, when the truth is that prostitutes are attracted to their cities by the opportunities for "easy money." The story of many a town in Alaska is that prosperity brought prostitutes, and when prosperity waned the prostitutes left.

The more enlightened attitude which is growing up in Alaska cities is an indication that the cities are growing up into more stable, more cosmopolitan proportions; more families are moving in, and doing something to improve the communities, rather than moving out because of immoral conditions.

Chapter 15

NONE SO BIG

August 1958

By Dolly Connelly

S uch a fish!
The crew of the cannery tender *Quadra* lined the rail and peered into the milling mass of sockeye and pink salmon crowding the trap's pot.

"He'll go ninety!" exclaimed Skipper Chet Small.

"Maybe eight-five," amended Engineer Baldur Johnson. "He's not long enough."

The object of all this attention was a brute of a king salmon, swimming majestically among his crowded smaller relatives and, like them, a victim of another of man's ingenious devices to take fishes from the sea.

It was the summer of 1939, at the Point Colpoys trap on Prince of Wales Island. The *Quadra* and her crew were about to brail the trap and take their load to the Pacific American Fisheries cannery in Petersburg.

Although the big king was definitely big, no one thought that day about world records. To most of the crew members this was just another highlight of another trap brailing. Sometimes hair seals and sea lions are trapped in the pot—sometimes even small whales. A big king salmon was just a big king salmon, another relief in the monotony of shipboard life.

To the *Quadra's* second engineer, young Joe MacKechnie, the big king meant something more, a good fish for his mother's annual canning order. The two trap watchmen, living in their little frame shack on the trap, had been watching for "a good one" for Joe. It was something he always did, every summer. A good, fat, red king salmon, canned in his mother's kitchen, tasted mighty good when the winter snows lay deep in Petersburg streets and fresh fish was just a summer memory.

Although the fish in the salmon traps belonged to "the company," crew members usually helped themselves to a few choice fish each season for their own use—for canning, salting, smoking, pickling, by whatever private recipes they employed.

Cannery superintendents were inclined to be lenient with hard-working crew members who wanted a few fish for their own use. Anyway, the big kings don't fit the mechanical "iron chinks" that cut up the run-of-the-mill sized pinks and sockeyes, and so they have to be hand-butchered for the can.

Tender crews did not, however, advertise their homeward-headed fish when they left the boat. This understandable caution almost cost the world its knowledge of the existence of the Point Colpoys king.

And, perversely, a triumphant display of the fish to a passing tender crew likewise almost kept the Colpoys king story from reaching the public.

Joe had laid his big king on the *Quadra's* deck after a pacifying blow with a marlin spike to the base of the head. While they were washing down the homeward-bound *Quadra*, Joe and Baldur Johnson hailed the passing tender *Rodoma*, another of the PAF fleet. Together they lifted the big king from the deck for the *Romoda's* crew to see and admire, but two things conspired to give both men a wondering shock.

First, the Colpoys king was not dead. Hoisted thus unceremoniously into the air, he came to sudden life and flipped mightily with his great tail. It was then that MacKechnie and Johnson realized they had something beyond the ordinary in this fish.

He was a heavy one—a really heavy one!

A Near Miss

Frantically they hung to the thrashing fish, but he was too much for them. He plunged from their straining and slippery hands to the ship's rail. There he hung, teetering precariously, half aboard and half overboard. Both men flung themselves on the fish and in a wild, head-bashing scramble managed to get the big giant back to the deck.

"I clobbered him good that time!" MacKechnie later said, and confessed that it was at this point that he decided advertising might have its drawbacks.

Not only was it best to keep this fish safely on deck, but a conviction was crystalizing that perhaps this fish should go home after dark.

Thus began chapter two of how the big king almost missed immortality.

Joe carefully stowed the big salmon under a screening cover of bin boards lying conveniently on deck.

Back at the cannery dock in Petersburg, the last sockeye and pink had gone up the fish escalator and the crew had washed down and secured for the night. Twilight was beginning to soften the summer evening shadows when, through pre-arrangement, Joe eased his big salmon over the side into a skiff manned by his younger brother, Don, under the dock. Together the two Petersburg boys rowed quietly up the beach, and together they carried the Point Colpoys king to their back door, where they hung him by his tail.

Life on a cannery tender at the height of fishing season is no eight on and eight off watch routine. It's go and go the clock around while the runs last, and Joe MacKechnie had had little sack time in the past seventy-two hours. Any bunk when you can get into one at this time of year, is a good bunk. A bed at home is something you dream about, and Joe had been at sea long enough to appreciate it. He was asleep a few minutes after he crawled in.

"The next thing I knew it was broad daylight," Joe said, "and mother was telling me Mr. Ringstad was on the phone."

A salmon as big as Joe's couldn't be kept quiet. Admittedly with some trepidation, Joe answered his superintendent's call with a sleepy and stumbling attempt to apologize for bringing the big salmon home. His mother wanted a nice king for canning . . . .

A salmon for mother, that's all right, don't worry, that's all right. It seemed there were a dozen people on the phone. No, he hadn't cut it up yet, he'd just cleaned it.

The News is Out

Dazedly Joe MacKechnie hung up the receiver on a dead line. Doc Rude wanted to skin the salmon. Earl Ohmer, the walking chamber of commerce and head of the Alaska Game Commission, wanted to see it. Scale counts. And Superintendent

Ringstad! Never mind about your mother's fish. Can him, sure, but—with some Scandinavian embellishments—don't, please don't cut him up until they get there!

Outside, a crowd was beginning to gather.

Gutted, and after more than twenty-four hours of draining and heavy loss of weight that always follows death in such big fish, the giant weighed one hundred and five pounds. Biologists, figuring closely from comparative viscera weights, estimated the Point Colpoys king to have weighed 126½ pounds when taken—the largest salmon on record.

The big king was no race horse in lines. He was chunky, like a barrel-chested wrestler, only 53½ inches long but with a girth of 39 inches.

As Donald Rude put it, "He was sure something to see!"

Rude, at that time a boy in Petersburg, is now a practicing physician in Juneau with his father, Dr. Joseph C. Rude.

"There had been quite a few big salmon taken around Petersburg," young Dr. Rude recalled. "When I first saw this one, it didn't look unusually large. The back was to me and it didn't appear thicker than normal, and the fish didn't seem extra long, either.

"But from the side! That was the view that shocked you. From a moderate-sized head, that fish just swelled and swelled into back and belly of tremendous proportions. His girth was thirty-nine inches. There was no doubt this was a salmon among salmon."

After taking precise measurements the senior Dr. Rude carefully applied his scalpel. With head, fins, tail and skin parted from the meat, to be placed as carefully in cold storage, he finally turned to Mrs. Lloyd MacKechnie.

"Now he's yours," he grinned.

Mrs. MacKechnie and her neighbors spent two days canning the giant, putting the firm red flesh into scalded jars, adding a pinch of salt and processing in a kitchen-sized pressure cooker at ten pounds' pressure, ninety minutes to the load. The job filled one hundred and four pint-sized Mason jars.

By the Inch

Cannery Superintendent George Ringstad wired Jonas Brothers, Seattle taxidermists, for a price on mounting the skin.

"Dollar an inch," the reply said.

When Jonas Brothers got their first look at the giant's skin, they must have done some swift, if rueful, arithmetic but the famed taxidermists did not renege.

The Petersburg Chamber of Commerce, the Elks and the Sons of Norway paid the handling and mounting charges.

The Point Colpoys king had become famous. Promoters scrambled in "to get in on the deal," and offers poured in from everywhere, but the biggest salmon ever caught by any gear was destined for more dignity.

A Seattle sporting goods store, Ben Paris', exhibited the mounted brute for the first month and then Superintendent Ringstad became custodian, exhibiting it to crowds in several cities until the following summer when the Point Colpoys king returned to Petersburg, where he is still on display at the City Hall.

Tale of a Fish

His epitaph is a chapter in ichthyology, a life story reconstructed by Biologist Joseph T. Barnaby of the Fish and Wildlife Service.

"This fish," wrote Barnaby, "was the progeny of a pair of kings— *Oncorhynchus tshawytscha*—which spawned in 1933. The egg hatched out during the winter or spring of 1933–34, and the young fish emerged from the spawning nest in April, 1934.

"It stayed in fresh water until the middle of July, 1935, and then migrated to the ocean, a two-year-old migrant. By the spring of 1936 this salmon had attained a size of nineteen inches, larger than average for fish of this period of ocean residence.

"During the summer of 1936, a short period of unfavorable conditions, such as food shortage, was experienced. However, rapid growth soon began again. By the spring of 1938, the fish was forty-one inches long, and by the spring of 1939, had grown to fifty-one inches. Taken in the fish trap a few months later, it was fifty-three and one-half inches long.

"This fish was six years old at the time of capture, and is what is known as a six-two—a fish that migrated seaward in its second year and returned to spawn in its sixth year.

Biologist Barnaby explained that the size of a salmon largely depends upon the length of its stay in salt water. This brute had stayed four summers and a part of a fifth in the ocean, a stay much longer than normal, which accounted for its great size.

There have been other big kings taken through the years that crowded or even exceeded the hundred-pound mark, but none on record comes even close to challenging the Point Colpoys fish.

A Petersburg Indian best described this king among king salmon when he stood before its impressive mounted bulk recently.

"Big!" he grunted.

Chapter 16

THE MYSTERY OF THE BILLIKEN

September 1960

By Dorothy Jean Ray

In 1909 when Florence Pretz of Kansas City was awarded a patent for a "new design for an image" called a "billiken," she could not foresee, even with the wildest woman's intuition, that one day it would be considered an invention of the Alaskan Eskimos.

After its appearance it was so quickly and adroitly adopted by Nome's sharp-witted tradesmen and clever ivory carvers that it became, and has remained, one of the most successful good luck amulets of our time.

It is carried in the pocket, in handbags, around the neck; it sits on desks and tables. It has become earrings, salt and pepper shakers, gavels, pickle fork handles.

The billiken is everywhere in Alaska, but particularly in Nome, the Eskimo ivory-carving capital of the world, where it is made by the thousands. Anyone in Alaska who has any sympathy at all with a billiken knows it is wise to have several on hand because, according to local gossip, it's risky to be without one.

Over the years a number of persons have had their curiosity aroused by this little bullet-headed creature of the pixie ears, grinning mouth, and rotund belly, and I was no exception. A comparative late-comer to the little "club" of members scattered the nation over, I soon got into the swing of asking, "What is this billiken and where did it come from?"

But strange as it may seem, no one, storekeepers, sourdoughs or Eskimo carvers at the very headquarters of billiken manufacture knew its history or origin.

To a question of that nature they usually answered, "Oh, it's just something the Eskimos always made," a very doubtful statement since no prehistoric billikens ever had been found.

A couple of likely sounding explanations turned out, like the rest, to be baseless. One was that it had been a caricature of a well-liked physician of Nome's early days. A friend of the doctor supposedly commissioned a carver to make a "funny" likeness of him in ivory. And, as the story goes, soon the whole town was clamoring at the carver's door for more.

Another tale was that it had been copied after a huge driftwood stump statue on Big Diomede Island. A Nome curio shop even publicized this tale in its advertising, but the Eskimos always vigorously denied that there was any connection between the billiken and the statue.

"Somebody," one man said, "told that store a 'big whopper!'"

Then one summer I returned to Nome for research with the ivory carvers. Here is concentrated the largest number of ivory carvers in Eskimo America when all of the inhabitants of King and Little Diomede Islands arrive in July for longshoring and ivory carving.

All summer long their files and gravers create many objects of artistic beauty. The billiken, which is really very ugly, is viewed by them as a necessary sideline to keep travelers happy with a "typical Alaskan souvenir." Because they prize creativity even in the making of souvenirs, they often make billikens only as a last resort. The billiken with its set and rigid style is about the last word in dullness to them.

One dreary, stormy day in July when it became impossible to discuss serious topics with "Big Mike" Kazingnuk because he had to keep jumping up to plug the holes in the roof, I asked him where he thought the billiken had come from.

"Why, don't you know?" he asked astonished. "Happy Jack made the first one!"

It was as simple as that. Prior to that summer I had not met Kazingnuk, a man not only equipped with a remarkable memory, but whose sister had married Happy Jack, probably one of the most famous ivory carvers of all time.

Truth at Last

Almost fifty years had elapsed since the carving of the first ivory billiken, too long ago for most memories or knowledge of it. But Kazingnuk had resided with Happy Jack for several years, learning to carve and listening to stories of days before Nome existed.

"I think it was about 1909," Kazingnuk said, "when a storekeeper who the Eskimos called 'Kopturok,' which means 'Big Head,' asked him to do it. Someone had brought one of these statues up from the States. That storekeeper showed Happy Jack that figure which looked like a Chinese God sitting on a slab of something, and right away Happy Jack made one exactly like it. He made some more and they sold fast."

I knew, at last, that this was the real story of how the billiken got its start in Alaska. I had heard vague rumors of plaster-of-paris billikens which young ladies placed on their dressers for luck before World War I. But where had it come from in the first place?

Good luck never rains but it pours, and through the sheerest accident I discovered who "invented" the original billiken. On a visit to Seattle's Ye Olde Curiosity Shop, a magnificent conglomeration of priceless ethnological objects and just plain tourist gewgaws, who should peer out at me from behind a mass of baskets, boat hooks, and mustache cups, but billiken. Not a little ivory figurine, but a big, gray, cast-iron bank.

An almost illegible number on the back turned out to be patent D-39,603 which appears to have covered all of the uses to which the billiken was put in its short and ephemeral non-ivory lifetime. In 1909 the billiken was manufactured as a bank and statuette followed by dolls the next year. The American Doll and Toy Company made more than 200,000 of the latter which were the rage for six months, then disappeared. At the same time the Times Publishing Company (Seattle) sold small billiken figurines as a publicity stunt for the Alaska-Yukon-Pacific Exposition.

In 1910 St. Louis University's athletic teams began to be known as the "Billikens." When the billiken's popularity was still at high heat, a staunch fan of the university's athletic department, Charley McNamara, made a sketch of one, displaying it in a soda fountain where the athletes and their admirers often gathered.

In the mysterious ways of naming, the football team found itself known as "Bender's Billikens," after John Bender, the coach at that time. The name was enthusiastically endorsed by the local sports writers and the subsequent publicity gave the team its permanent nickname.

Two magazines have used the name. "Billikin's Philatelic Magazine" was published in 1910 in Columbus, Ohio, and "Billiken; revista illustrada" appeared in 1920 in Caracas, Venezuela. The former was published "every now and then" by Mr. William I. Kin, which explains the title and the spelling.

The latter magazine combined fiction, poetry, and contemporary news of the theater, sports, and travel in the Spanish language. The billiken figure is used in many ways throughout the magazine, but in a manner more reminiscent of a kewpie doll than the original billiken.

The billiken and the kewpie doll are similar in that both are based on the principle of good cheer obtained through an exaggerated external gaiety. Rose O'Neil dreamed up her kewpie doll the same year as Miss Pretz her billiken, but in contrast to Miss Pretz who wrote not a word about her invention, Miss O'Neil penned volumes. A closer resemblance to the billiken is seen in Miss O'Neil's "Buddha-Ho-Ho," a later "invention," a seated, rotund, boisterous-appearing figure with both hands resting on fat garmented knees.

Miss Pretz had a real flair for reinterpretation. Not only is her billiken a highly romanticized caricature of a Buddha, but the slogan on the base of the plaster-of-paris statuettes reading, "The God of Things as They Ought to Be," is a paraphrase of Kipling's famous words from "L'Envoi": "Shall draw the Thing as he sees It for the God of Things as They Are!"

By late 1910 the billiken's adventures swiftly ended in the continental United States but already had begun its spectacular career in Alaska.

The most interesting fact about today's billikens is the remarkable similarity to the original Pretz design. Kazingnuk told me, "Happy Jack carved it exactly the way the little statue was made, toes, belly, fingers, and head." And up to this day, the carvers have continued to copy faithfully Happy Jack's copy.

The most popular and prolific form is a pocket piece, one to three inches high. But in the past there have been those so tiny that a carver used a magnifying glass to make them, and those as large as a walrus tusk or sperm whale tooth permitted.

The carvers at times have attempted to portray the billiken in action—bowing in a subservient position, fishing through the ice, or dancing—but it never has been successful. With these changes the billiken assumed human characteristics which even from the first it was never meant to have. After all, was it not "the god of things as they ought to be?" Miss Pretz's inspiration, travesty though it is of a Buddha, remains in the spiritual, not the human realm.

One variation of brief popularity which is still occasionally made nowadays is the "milliken," a billiken with breasts, supposedly suggested to the carvers by soldiers stationed in Nome.

Recently, factory-carved billikens of the United States and Japan have almost out-billikened the billiken. Instead of reflecting a subdued and self-contained optimism, their willowy gaiety pours on the good humor a little too thickly. An exception is a Japanese-made pair of ceramic salt and pepper shakers in the form of seated billikens. "Billiken" is engraved below one who sports the traditional grin, but below the other, with downturned mouth is proclaimed "Billikant."

A number of unique attributes have become attached to the ivory billiken. For example, in Nome it is said that there are three kinds of billiken luck: Good, better, and best. Billikens bought and used by the same person have good luck, those given to a person have better luck, but those that are "borrowed" surreptitiously bring the best luck of all. But, woe to any future luck if you are caught!

Make a Wish

The billiken can also be manipulated to make a wish come true. The preferred method is to rub its fat stomach, but an alternative one is to tickle its toes.

The name of the billiken has become so firmly established in Alaska as good luck without peer that numerous ventures either have used the name of billiken somewhere in advertising or have adopted the figurine as its mascot.

Although the billiken has traveled far and wide in its first fifty years, the crowning achievement of its career may be its inclusion by a Soviet Arts and Crafts Board at Uelen, Siberia, in a newly revived program of Eskimo ivory carving there.

V. V. Antropova illustrates three of them in an article about contemporary Siberian ice carving. All are dead ringers for Alaskan billikens. This is not at all surprising. The Bering Strait between the two continents has served as a great

Eskimo highway as long as anyone can remember. Siberian and American Eskimos traded goods and visited each other frequently before travel barriers were erected. Kazingnuk, himself, had carved ivory there.

But, no matter where the billiken is made, in Russia, Japan, or Alaska, it is still the original billiken—wide grin, pointed head, immobile arms. By some quirk of fate it has become known as one of the Eskimo's own, old objects. A secure place in the history of Alaskan Eskimo ivory carving is already reserved for it in spite of its being invented by a Missouri girl.

But, that's luck, the kind that could only happen to a billiken.

Chapter 17

ALASKA TERROR

August 1965

By Art Kennedy as told to Herbert E. McLean

A lot of people asked us what we were doing out there on the ice. Well, I'll tell you, we weren't out there having a party—not in fifteen degree weather.

Actually we were taking lake water depth measurements for scientific studies of the Portage Glacier area. I'm a visitor information specialist with the U.S. Forest Service. The three other fellows were students from Alaska Methodist University in Anchorage, and Ruth—Dr. Ruth Schmidt—is a professor of geology at Anchorage Community College.

I had just read the sounding dial. Five hundred and thirty-four feet of water, three feet of ice. Then I heard a sound that was sort of like an iceberg turning over—a low, deep-throated rumble. Then across the lake, from the direction of the glacier, came the shattering growl of ice breaking.

Next thing I knew the ice under our feet was heaving and shaking like some huge hand had grabbed it.

I looked down into the hole we'd drilled in the ice. The water had dropped right out of sight!

Suddenly huge cracks opened in the ice in all directions. It sounded like someone ripping open a huge, rusty zipper—and we were right in the middle.

"It'll stop! It'll stop," I yelled, trying to convince myself. But it didn't. It was splitting open all around us.

Then I looked for Ruth and Mike Mitchell. They were gone.

Now, from the mountains overhead, the sickening spew of crushed rock and snow avalanched around us, thundering in our ears like the devil himself.

The snow flew, and through my speckled glasses I saw Steve and Howard looking at each other in stark, bone-deep disbelief. They were just standing there, speechless.

Again and again the mountains shuddered, the ice heaved and fell and cracked as we struggled to stay on our feet.

The ice quieted down for a minute, but up canyon we could hear the treachery of rock avalanches as they ripped downward.

"This has got to stop, it's got to!" I kept muttering.

I wheeled around to look over our own private disaster and there, through the flurry, came Mike and Ruth, who'd been out across the lake.

"For Pete's sake let's get out of here!" someone yelled.

I looked around and thought better of the idea.

"We'd better stay where we are; we'll never make it out," I countered.

The snow was coming down fast now, and it was getting dark.

We had to do something, so we loaded the sounding equipment onto a sled behind the Arctic Cat.

Things quieted down a bit, so we got into the Cat and started feeling our way forward. Visibility was down to 10 feet as we tried to follow our tracks back to shore.

As we inched along, the snow lifted just enough to lay out an appalling sight immediately ahead. Jagged, razor-sharp lake ice lay shattered, upended, sprawled grotesquely in our path. In between, frigid swirling water.

We were trapped.

Somehow—I don't know how they ever did it—Steve and Howard moved out over that ice, roped together, seeking some way out. It was darker now, and a chill breeze stung our faces.

The boys found an ice bridge that looked like it might take us to shore.

Suddenly I heard rushing water.

"Get back, it's turning over," Steve yelled in the face of a huge chunk of floating ice.

Now we heard water all around and I saw the unbelievable—the entire lake was heaving and falling. Water around shore was spilling up and out like coffee from a cup.

We could hardly see now. I figured we had less than an hour of daylight to get off the ice. The cold was beginning to bite; the clothes we had on were no challenge for a night like this. Groping through the semi-darkness on the cat and on foot, we probed for an escape route to shore but found none. That surging water was a sickening sound as the canyon heaved and crumbled.

We were clustered together closely now, secretly relieved when a little snow flurry would hide the reality for a minute, then shocked when we could see what was happening.

Then we found an ice floe that had overridden itself. It seemed to lead to shore.

Using our snowshoes now, we picked our way through the jagged, upended ice.

I looked at my watch. 7:20 p.m. Almost two hours since the quake.

Then my feet gave way and I plunged downward into the water. I was too scared to think of death, but somehow I caught hold of something and braced myself before I was completely drenched. The ice water pricked and numbed my legs.

The others were slipping and falling too as we made our way over that frozen treachery. But we didn't say much. We just kept on going.

I don't know how we ever did it, but one by one, we negotiated the frozen maze and suddenly felt the blessed solidness of sloping ground. We'd made it ashore.

We hadn't been thinking about anything else, just to get off that floating death trap. But now we began to wonder what was next.

It wasn't long before we found out: We were just as trapped here as we were on the ice. We were literally surrounded by 5000-foot peaks. The only way out was over the ice—God forbid that—or through either of two railroad tunnels.

Having seen these mountains open up and shatter, we knew it was pure madness to consider the tunnels. But the idea fascinated us.

Somehow in the darkness we found the rail line and stumbled down it—heading toward Anchorage.

The ground still trembled and rolled as the blackness of the tunnel loomed ahead. We stopped, faced each other in the dark and in our madness decided to enter. Ruth took out a tiny pen flashlight and we went in.

Suddenly the earth pitched and groaned as rock cascaded down in front of us. We wheeled around and groped our way back to the entrance.

Our bodies cold with fear, we trudged up the tracks, tripping and picking our way through the maze of earth-cracks that spread in darkness before us. I'd remembered an abandoned cabin somewhere up this way. Maybe I could find it.

A half-hour later our hearts jumped. There, as we rounded a bend, was the cabin with a light in the window.

We were almost running now. Inside, we could see through the window, were a man, his wife, and their daughter, eating supper. Hoekzema was his name, Max Hoekzema, patrolman for Alaska Railroad, living there and watching for rocks in the tunnel area. Colleen, his wife gave us some chow. We tuned the short wave radio to Anchorage, then settled down to the slow torture of speculating about our families. We rigged a coffee cup "seismograph" and watched it arc 15 degrees either way from the end of a string. Somehow we got some sleep between tremors as that ten by fifteen foot cabin swayed through the night. The last thing we saw before we turned in was a strange, bright orange glow through the snow mist. We didn't know it was Whittier, going up in flames.

Next morning the reality of our ordeal caught up with us. Slogging down toward the lake, we saw the result of the quake's fury. The ice lay around the shore like so much crinkled glass. Overhead, nasty black earth-gashes streaked the mountainsides where avalanches had thundered. Proud Portage Glacier, whose sheer ice face I'd pointed out to visitors on many occasions, lay fractured and broken, flattened into a gentle slope. Out over the lake I saw the desperate, circling track marks of our Arctic Cat from the night before. I traced our escape route through a treacherous mountain of rubble ice, the only route off that floating hell.

A rescue 'copter picked us up and took us back down to the lodge by the highway, a highway completely deserted and crossed with gaping crevasses. The rails alongside lay contorted and twisted like strands of spaghetti.

There had to be a sweet ending, and so there was.

We ambled down to the Portage Café, which had sunk three feet into the ground.

"You boys want some ice cream?" asked the lady there. From the shambles inside, she salvaged three gallon containers of black walnut, chocolate, and strawberry.

We stood there amid the wreckage, eating our ice cream in the fifteen degree morning. It tasted great.

Chapter 18

HUSLIA'S HOLE HUNTERS

June 1966

By Mike Cline

The crisp snow crunched as Fred Bifelt and I walked out of the village and moved up the Koyukuk River on ten inch thick ice. As we moved briskly in the zero degree temperature, Fred pointed to first one track and then another—"Fox," "otter," "moose," "squirrel," "wolverine," he said as we passed their trails imprinted in the snow.

After traveling about four miles, we cut into the woods in pursuit of fresh moose tracks. Fred moved up in front and said, "We'll go slow now," and indeed we did. Because of the brush it was exceedingly difficult to move quietly. After we had traveled about a quarter of a mile, Fred suddenly moved off to the left, cleared his throat and said, matter of factly, "There's a bear hole here."

We had discovered, to our delight, the object of much hunting. Each fall after it has grown cold and the black bears have denned up, the men of Huslia begin their search for the highly prized succulent flesh of the black bear (fat and in its prime). Some go in sno-gos, some take dog teams, and some walk, but all have in mind one quarry—a bear den—and in it a sleeping bear.

The fact that bear dens are hard to find I would willingly attest to, for this was my third trip out and I hadn't seen so much as a likely looking hump. In this brushy country, the bears gorge themselves in the fall on berries, then look for a secluded hole in the ground in which to spend the winter. These holes are usually under a partly overturned tree or in a hole dug in a bank. As preparation before Mr. Bear enters his den, he gathers grass and moss to line the den and then he constructs a door of this same material to plug the entrance. This finished, he gathers the grass, enters the den, closes the "door" and curls up for a long winter's nap—or at least so he thinks.

As I hurried over, Fred busied himself cutting a long slender willow wand to stick into the den to find out if there was really a bear in there. He gingerly put the stick in the hole and dropped it. It moved slowly, up, and then down. "Well, I guess there's one in there," he commented. "You can hear him snore. Listen."

I cautiously put my head down by the entrance, surely expecting an enraged bear to come charging out bent on our destruction. However, all I could hear was the muffled sound of heavy breathing.

While Fred cut two large poles with which to block the entrance to the hole, I surveyed the area. It was a typical dome-shaped mound about six feet in circumference with the entrance leading down to the den so that the den was about two feet beneath the surface of the earth and about four feet back from the entrance. We plugged the entrance with two stout poles and roped them in place. Then Fred began to chop a hole in the roof of the den to see what position the bear was in and where we would shoot him. The frozen earth was hard but finally Fred had opened a small hole about six inches across. We looked in . . . again I thought we would see gleaming white teeth eager to sink into human flesh, but nothing happened.

It was so dark in the hole it was hard to discern which was bear and which was hole. Fred threw a little snow in on what proved to be the bear's head and he shoved his rifle forward and fired. We heard a gurgling sound yet the animal was still breathing. I carefully eased my .270 closer to the bear's head and pulled the trigger. All was silent in the den. The bear was dead. Fred muttered, "Now the fun ends and the work begins."

Removing the bear from the den was no small chore for we wanted to leave the den as nearly intact as we found it for reference in future years. (Men here have observed the same dens for fifty years and they seem to pass from father to son.) After much struggling we fixed a rope around the bear's neck and with much prying, pulling and tugging, the dead bear emerged . . . a medium-sized female with two bullet holes in her head.

As we were skinning and cutting up the meat I asked Fred if there was going to be a bear party soon. He said, "I think so, maybe next Sunday."

Sure enough the next Sunday afternoon a bear party was held. The party is held to celebrate the catching of bear, to share the meat with those unfortunates who did not have any luck, and perhaps more importantly, to provide an excuse for all the men and boys to get together. The location for our party was about two miles out of the village so most of the men and boys went by dog teams or sno-gos. It might be added that only men and boys attend bear parties for it is bad luck for bear hunters if women eat bear meat at a party such as this. At other times, however, it is perfectly permissible for them to eat bear meat.

When we arrived at the site, a huge bonfire was roaring while all the men and boys were busy gathering wood for the fire and with which to make tables. A number of large pots were filled with water and placed on the ends of sticks over the fire to boil. While this was happening, Jimmy Huntington, the chief of Huslia, arrived with the bear meat. He and Stephen Attla immediately set to work cutting it into chunks and putting it in the now boiling water. After this was done, several men cut short sticks, impaled bear paws on them and began to singe and scrape the hair off the paws. The paws were then placed in the pot for about two hours. When done, the outer skin of the paws could be peeled off and the cooked flesh eaten.

When the meat was finally done it was rescued from the pots by dumping out the water and putting the steaming pieces of parboiled meat on chunks of wood split especially for this occasion.

The older people, Chief Henry, Grampa George, Attla, Tony Sam, Sr., Richard Derendoff and Edwin Simon were served first. They had their choice of the assortment; after that it was every man for himself. Each person brought his own cup for tea, his own utensils including hunting knife, spoon, plate, and salt, and anything else he wanted to eat with the meat.

Upon receiving a piece of meat I stared at it with mixed feelings. I had never eaten bear meat and the smell was not what I would call appetizing, but, there must have been at least ten kids watching me (the teacher!) closely. I sliced off a small piece, salted it, and popped it into my mouth. It was delicious! I whacked off some more and began stuffing it in my mouth. As Jimmy walked over, I said, "This meat is really good!" He answered, "Yes, we like it, but a little bit goes a long way." He explained that bear meat has a lot of fat and this fat "does things" to a man's stomach, especially if he hasn't eaten rich meat for quite a while. I had to forcefully restrain myself because the meat was good.

As I looked around, everyone was busily eating, but because of the cold (it was about zero) we had all moved in closer to the fire. Then the bear feast tales began with Jimmy as the main storyteller. These stories of bear maulings, old time Indian tales, and woodsmen, fascinate young and old alike even though some of them have been told numerous times. One of the stories still stands out fresh in my mind. It was one that revolved, not around a woodsman, but a woods woman. These "woods women" people live by themselves in the woods and are ascribed to have magical or supernatural powers.

It seems that a man's daughter at the junction of the Kateel and Koyukuk Rivers (south of Huslia) had been ill for some time. The medicine man, knowing this, tried to cure her illness, but during the treatment she went to the river for water and disappeared. Her disappearance instigated a search for her, but her father found nothing and concluded she had drowned.

Sometime later, tracks were seen by her father further up the Kateel River on a sand bar. The father searched again, but again found no trace of his daughter.

The village of Koyukuk, located on the Yukon (fifty miles down the Koyukuk River) began missing dried fish. However, after that winter nothing more was missing at Koyukuk, but three hundred miles down the Yukon, at a village called Holy Cross, dried fish and fish eggs stored in little birch cups began disappearing from the smoke houses where the people stored their meat. One day a seventeen-year-old boy was out in the woods when he saw a woodswoman returning from a smoke house with stolen dried fish. Now, these people believed that a person who saw a woodswoman and reveals this to others will die. The knowledge worried the boy so much he could not eat or sleep for a number of days. He began to lose weight and became increasingly morose. Finally, his sister, who was about his age, realized something was bothering him. She took him from the village, cooked him some fish and said, "You will die if you don't eat, so eat and tell me what is bothering you." After much coaxing he finally told her what he had seen.

The story was circulated in the village, but the older people would not have anything to do with it. Then five young men (about the age of twenty) decided to try to capture the woodswoman. They dug holes in the ground and climbed in and covered themselves with grass. The seventeen-year-old boy that had seen her was to be the lookout and he would signal them by whistling when she came. When she finally did come he tried to whistle, but he was too scared for any sound to come out. Another young man thought he heard something and peeked out of the grass. When he saw the woodswoman he yelled and reached out and grabbed her leg. The young men came scrambling out of their hiding places to assist him. They were able to catch her, but it took all of them to hold her. When the six men had her tied up they then had to decide what to do with her. They could not kill her for superstition would not allow it. All agreed to carry her back to camp and build her a small cabin. They then piled logs on top of it to prevent her from escaping. At first she refused to eat or drink. Finally the seventeen-year-old boy fed her and she began to eat. They eventually cut her ropes off and she became more friendly. She knew none of their language nor did they know hers. One day they let her out of the cabin and she walked down to the Yukon River holding a small girl by the hand. She had the small girl wash her body very carefully and when she came back she was a "new person." She stayed with the people of Holy Cross and gradually learned their language. It was from the people of Holy Cross that this story traveled to Huslia.

As the flames gradually diminished and the coals glowed more dimly we realized it was getting dark. Time to get home and feed the dogs. The remaining meat was split up and everyone headed for home, full and contented, yet eagerly awaiting next year's bear party sponsored by Huslia's Hole Hunters.

Chapter 19

THERE WERE WOLVES...ALL AROUND ME

October 1967

By Paul Kinksteater as told to Anne Purdy

It was around one in the afternoon on a day in mid-December, 1965, when it happened.

I go over my trapline often to prevent needless suffering of the wild animals I trap for a living, and to see if any traps are empty and sprung. More fur means more bacon and beans for me and my family.

My wife and three children have a wilderness paradise on Healy Lake where the Athabascan Indians once had a village around fifty miles northwest of Dot Lake, which in turn is around 160 miles out of Fairbanks on the Alaska Highway. Only around fifty people call Dot Lake home. Usually twice a month in winter I take my dog team for some twenty miles to a rough road where I keep my truck parked and then drive on into Dot Lake.

Although we have no close neighbors we enjoy our wild bush life and we sure hope this lovely spot can stay untouched by the march of civilization.

But back to our story . . .

I had harnessed eleven of my dogs on this particular day to go over the trapline. The dogs were in good shape. They needed exercise and they strained and tugged to be off. Tails up, those malemutes just sailed down that hard packed trail, the sled slipping smoothly and the pooches yipping happily.

When I had gone as far as possible with the dogs, I stopped and tied them to a spruce tree. There was no good trail ahead, but plenty of windfalls. This, of course, is dangerous for a dog team. It can mean a broken leg or tangled mess of fighting dogs.

Mounted on snowshoes, I took off on a side trail with a pack on my back. I made sure I had my gun. I always carry a rifle in the wilds. It's a good law to follow because you never know who or what you are going to meet on the trail at this time of year. Sometimes an ornery old grizzly doesn't get fat enough to hibernate. He's on the loose, hungry as all get out and not at all particular as to what kind of grub he finds.

I walked about a quarter of a mile from where I left the dogs tied and arrived in the middle of a pot hole lake. In the Northland one unconsciously is always on the lookout for game. Hence, when I stopped, I unthinkingly scanned the horizon.

I stared unbelievingly, but couldn't accept what I saw. There, just ahead, running off the hill at breakneck speed were twenty or more gray and black timber wolves. The huge animals were between the dogs and me. No doubt they had heard the dogs yipping.

I immediately got ready for the oncoming horde. Off came my pack and the first wave of wolves swept up to within one hundred yards of me.

Automatically, I started shooting, but the pack kept on coming. They split on both sides of me and charged to where the dogs were tied.

Usually I carry plenty of ammunition, but on this trip I only had ten shells. I shot three wolves, and as they went down I realized I only had seven shells left, but within a matter of minutes I shot five more wolves within thirty or forty feet of my position.

Completely ignoring me, the pack jumped over one wolf that lay on the lake and headed for the dogs. Reloading as I ran back to my team, I found only two bullets in my pocket.

Terribly frightened, my dogs cowed in complete silence. Dogs instinctively fear wolves.

Again and again, the wolves circled the bushes surrounding the terror-stricken dogs. Pouring off the hill in waves were additional packs of wolves, charging in to join the others in the attack. I am sure there were a hundred or more wolves in the combined pack.

When I reached the dogs, the wolves weren't visible, but they were there in the bushes howling and crying. They moved off a little as I came into view and the fact that I'd killed several of their brothers apparently dampened their enthusiasm a little.

As I left the lake, a wounded wolf had dragged himself a short distance. I easily followed his bloody trail and found him dead. Wolves were crying uphill, downhill, everywhere, creating a bedlam.

A steady stream of wolves were running down the hill following the tracks of the leaders out on the lake then splitting and scattering in the brush around the dogs.

I had shot eight wolves by now, and my footsteps didn't lag as I returned to my frightened dogs. I loaded three of the huge animals on the sled, all that my dogs could carry. Each weighed well over one hundred pounds.

Never in all my dog mushing days have I seen dogs travel with such speed and harmony as we flew down that homeward trail. Wolves were howling and crying right and left, everywhere around us, but we were secure in the knowledge we were headed for the safety of home.

The next morning I returned to the battleground and brought in the remaining wolves I had shot plus two more of the pack which had been caught in snares I had set in that area. My total take from the big pack was ten wolves.

When I returned, I noticed the ground around the dead wolves was all tramped down by the pack, but no wolves could be seen or heard. The carcasses hadn't been damaged by the pack. If wolves are hungry they will eat their own kind, but these wolves weren't hungry. Those I shot had deep layers of fat over their entire bodies.

It should be noted that the wolves made no attempt to attack me. There was apparently not a man-hungry one among them. In winter the wolves are nearly always fat and in their prime because the heavy snow traps the moose and wolves can more easily finish them off.

Although they didn't succeed, those wolves had been definitely out to get the dogs. They know most dogs are powerless against them. A wolf has no sense of sportsmanship and neither gives nor expects any quarter.

Why did that giant pack want to get at my dogs? I don't rightly know. They certainly weren't hungry. Perhaps it was just pain cussedness or orneriness. Or maybe their attack can be attributed to a wild hatred built up through the ages to wreak vengeance on their civilized and domesticated brothers. I just don't know.

Chapter 20

ENCASED IN ICE, I NEARLY DROWNED

February 1974

By Frank W. Johnson as told to Ola M. Hughes

During the fall of 1971 a man nearly 50 years my junior approached me to go trapping with him. I had known him and had had a few business dealings with him in years past, when I needed help fishing, seal hunting or with some other work. I'll call him the "Kid" in this account.

He suggested we go to Dry Bay, which is about 50 miles south of our home at Yakutat. It was an area that we both knew well, and it hadn't been trapped for 20 years.

I was reluctant. The Kid pointed out that he had a family to care for, and that hunting was bound to be good. He needed meat and money and offered to do all the trapping and hunting. He wanted me to cook and do camp work, so that he wouldn't be alone 80 miles from home. The Kid thought he could make $3,000. I decided if my half was even $500 clear I would be satisfied. And since I had spent most of my 79 years out of doors, one more winter didn't seem overly important. I finally consented to go, against my better judgment.

I hired bush pilot Dick Nichols to fly us out and made arrangements for him to check on us every two weeks, weather permitting. I bought $300 worth of food and small supplies and we took off for the Dry Bay camp on November 4.

We found the cabin on the Alsek River, where we planned to headquarter, in bad shape. It needed a lot of work to make it comfortable for winter. First, we had to find an oil drum and make a stove. While I worked on the cabin, the Kid set out each morning to hunt for camp meat. He reported lots of moose and fur in the area, but he didn't bring in any meat.

I urged him to build a couple of line camps and get traps set out first. It usually takes about four hours to build a line camp, which is built something on the order of a pup tent with a sturdy ridge pole and green boughs of hemlock leaning against it for sides. When the overlapping boughs are covered with snow, the shelter is warm and green boughs on the floor hold a sleeping bag off the cold ground. These shelters are built one day's run apart. As far as I know, the Kid never built a line camp, and when the plane came back after two weeks, he still didn't have any meat to send out.

A week or 10 days later, we had deep snow and we knew the plane couldn't land there again all winter. The deep snow was a little earlier than expected, but it didn't bother me, for I am no stranger to snow. We get about 129 inches of precipitation a year in my home town of Yakutat, Alaska, where I have lived for 30 years. Yakutat had more than 400 inches of snow that winter. It also gets pretty cold in Greenland, and on some of the barren, windswept Aleutian islands where I have spent other years.

The only inconvenience the snow could cause, I felt, was the problem of getting a plane in so we could go back to Yakutat for a few days at Christmas.

The Alsek River follows a single channel for about three miles below the cabin where we lived, then it spreads out into Dry Bay. Three miles farther, the bay drains into the Gulf of Alaska. The ocean beach was only six miles from our cabin, then, and we could walk down and wait for the plane there if we wanted. Or with a boat, we could float most of the way at high tide. So the Kid found some plywood and built a small boat.

One morning 40 days after our arrival, the Kid decided we should walk to Yakutat. Cabin fever, I guessed, caused him to make such a plan. I pointed out that we had only to walk six miles to the beach to be picked up by Dick Nichols for our Christmas trip out. We had plenty of food, so that wasn't his problem.

The trapline had produced only one squirrel, one marten and one weasel; our camp meat tallied two ducks.

There was nothing to be gained by staying. We were barely speaking by this time, so we put a few things in the boat and started down river. It was a much worse trip than I had anticipated. The ice on the river was very rough and we had to drag the boat over and around it. We got about halfway the first day, but we were on the ocean beach the second night.

High tide was coming up to the snow line, and in the bit of daylight left, instead of digging into the snow or building a snow house, I built a sea wall that would protect us for the night. We both had good sleeping bags and good tarps to lay under them and over them.

I slept well. It wouldn't have worried me to have stayed there a month. We had brought food and could have returned to camp any day at high water for more without missing the plane because it could only land at low tide.

After breakfast we found we were only 100 feet from a cabin I had left there many years before, but a sand drift had blocked the door and window. We had a tide book and knew that the tides would come higher each day for the next several days, so we had to move.

I started to dig into the cabin, using a camp ax, a gallon can, and a short board. But when I started, I got sick. I had a chill which had nothing to do with being cold. I felt similar to the way I once felt on a hot day on a Florida vacation. I had to lie down, and in a few hours I awoke feeling perfectly well.

When I awoke, after being sick, and found him gone, there was a heavy storm on, with a high offshore wind. I knew I was safe for another night, for the wind kept the tide below the sea wall I had built. I had another good night's rest as the storm raged.

I awoke once and realized that I needed air, but I had taken a stick to bed to poke for air in the event of a heavy snowfall, so I poked and got air, as I have often done in the past.

When daylight came, I found that I was on my left side and frozen in solid. I couldn't even turn over.

The storm had picked up spray from the bay and carried it across the spit a thousand feet to drop and freeze it on me. Try as I might, there was no way I could move to exert pressure on my icy cast from the inside out. I could only lie there, helpless. I knew that the tides were increasing, and I could hear the water coming, far out in the bay. It was eerie to lie there, wondering if it would wash me loose or drown me.

I had married late in life and have no children of my own. My beloved Indian wife had children when we were married. Ours had been an especially good marriage. I knew my stepchildren would bury my bones beside my wife's grave. I had no special reason to live or die, but man doesn't usually stop running the race of life of his own accord. If the high tide set me free, I would survive. If it froze ice deeper on me, there was nothing I could do.

I was alone and could only wait. I got more sleep but the heavy breakers on the night tide came over me and pounded me about half an hour. The backwash of every breaker came into the breather hole and filled my sleeping bag with ice water; the zipper was open and it drained away.

Then I was cold. The ocean is warmer than the land, and it melted enough around my feet so I could kick, and I spent the next 36 hours sleeping a little while and kicking the rest of the time.

The third night the tide was bigger and waves pounded me for more than three hours, but I was still able to trap enough air in the bag to breathe between breakers.

That tide melted me almost free. But I had studied the tide book and I knew that the fourth night's tide would be so high that I couldn't get any air. About noon I managed to tear the bag and plastic tarp and get the lower half of my body out, but I still couldn't break entirely free. My wet bag froze in the below-zero temperature, and I couldn't get back in it.

I knew then that I couldn't last more than an hour and a half hour or so.

Then, far away, I heard planes. One was that of Dick Nichols, and the marshal was with him. The other was a Coast Guard plane.

They circled and landed, and soon strong men broke me free.

Within hours I was in Providence Hospital, in Anchorage. Altogether I spent nine months in the hospital and in a rest home, and came out with the loss of only five toes.

Chapter 21

RESCUE FROM DEVIL'S CANYON

October 1974

By James D. Greiner

In most places below its confluence with the shallow and swift Chulitna, five miles above the approach to Don Sheldon's backyard airstrip at Talkeetna, the Susitna River, or "Big Sue," as it is known to Alaskans, is at least one-half mile in width.

There is, however, a place 65 miles above Talkeetna where this generous breadth shrinks to a measly 50 to 75 yards between vertical rock palisades. Here, during spring, the Susitna's 6,750,000-gallon-per-minute flow attempts to surmount itself in a roaring dervish of hissing gray spume at a place called Devil's Canyon.

Sheldon had been almost content with the transport of itinerant fishermen, miners, and homesteaders during the weeks that followed his rescue of a woman from the Talkeetna River, but this contentment was overshadowed by a vague restlessness. It was 1958, Sheldon was 36 and was more convinced than ever that his specialty flying would become the profitable venture that he had hoped for.

The arrival of the northbound train from Anchorage, an event of regular though transient interest, took on new dimensions that same afternoon. Sheldon noticed that a crowd had gathered on the planking near the station almost before the engine jarred to a stop and braked against the slight grade. Resting on a special flatcar like some huge landbound ark was a bright yellow boat, its bow decked over, and sporting two formidable looking engines in its capacious stern section. The detachment of U.S. Army scouts that presided spelled property of Uncle Sam.

As the 50-foot boat was being offloaded, Sheldon joined the group of curious spectators, and found that little if any information was being offered by the Army as to why the boat was there, or what it would be used for. Speculation was the order of the day, and Sheldon had already heard several rumors, when he spotted a vaguely familiar face among the GIs struggling with the boat. The officer was a lieutenant with the Search and Rescue section at Fort Richardson in Anchorage, and a casual acquaintance. He was busy checking a sheaf of dog-eared papers.

"Hi, hi! How've ya been?" grinned the pilot.

"Good, Don. How's yourself?"

"Great. Hey, what's the deal here? You guys goin' fishing?"

The officer glanced once more at his paperwork and allowed that the boat was to be used in an attempt to chart navigable watershed in the Susitna drainage.

Sheldon was incredulous. "Hey, you don't mean you're going to attempt to run this thing up the Susitna and through the canyon?"

The lieutenant, who had never seen Devil's Canyon, missed the surprise in Sheldon's voice. His reply was curt and precise.

"That's exactly what we plan to do, and as soon as we can get under way, the better."

There wasn't time for Sheldon to appraise the real chances of such a mission on such short notice, and even if there had been, he was sure that the officer was not particularly interested in his homespun opinions. He did, however, have a very vivid picture of the Devil's Canyon, and had serious doubts about the possibility of the mission's success.

"Lookee, I've got a heck of a lot of fishing traffic up that way in the next few days, and I'll check on your progress from time to time."

With the boat successfully launched, the small detachment of scouts that comprised the crew cast off, and with the powerful engines churning the current-roiled river, disappeared from view around the first upstream bend. Sheldon had flown over the five-mile stretch of boiling water in Devil's Canyon many times. It was, in fact, a very familiar landmark to the pilot, one that he used often. From the air, the sheer rock walls of the canyon rising to 600 feet produced an awesome corridor, above which the air was characteristically turbulent, and at the bottom of which existed almost continual shadow. Of the current, Sheldon says, "The current here is so swift and heavy that even the salmon get beat to death trying to swim upriver."

The day after the scouts started up the Susitna, Sheldon flew over the river to make a casual check on the progress of the boat, but did not see it. Since he was not really searching for it, he did not fly over the entire section in which he judged the party to be.

On the second day, he was curious, a trait which to date has accounted for not only his promptness in times of trouble, but to his own personal safety as well. This time, with two elderly fishermen aboard, and en route to Otter Lake north of Takleetna, he deliberately flew up the Susitna to the tail of the Devil's Canyon rapids. As he reached the flume below the fast water, he banked sharply to the left, and rolled the portly Aeronca Sedan up on its ample side. Something had caught his attention at the periphery of his vision, and when he identified it on the second swing, his skin crawled.

"I was shocked to see pieces of yellow wreckage floating down the river. It was boiling."

He continued the 10 miles to Otter Lake, offloaded his passengers, and quickly retraced his path to the rapids below Devil's Canyon.

"I had a feeling this was a fresh wreck, and they'd really gotten clobbered. I saw barrels of gasoline bobbing around here and there. The wreckage was strewn downriver to a point almost 25 miles below the canyon, and it consisted mostly of bright yellow chunks of the boat's hull and other debris, but no people."

Sheldon then flew upriver, above the canyon itself, down to a point just above the rim, and after making several passes in the seething air, spotted a huddled group of men on a narrow ledge of wet rock in the shadows at the base of the north wall. Even from his vantage point, he could tell that they were in bad shape and in desperate need of assistance.

"They were in a terrible condition, cut up, and barely managing to cling to the shelf of rock. Their clothing was literally torn off, and a few of them still had life jackets on. These were also in shreds. They had apparently floated down about 60 percent of the canyon, a distance of about three miles."

Because he knew the place so well, Sheldon could rapidly appraise his chances of retrieving these men, and they looked poor. The canyon walls at their top were but a scant 200 yards apart, and the river was a closed succession of hissing combers broaching over house-sized boulders in the river bottom.

His chances were not only poor, but probably nonexistent, for the Aeronca, though heavier than the Super Cub, weighed only a scant 1,400 pounds empty and would be tossed like a tiny rock, even if he somehow managed to land it on the surface of the river below, a feat which at this moment looked impossible.

To drop onto the surface of the rapids here would be suicide, for the floats needed a flat surface upon which to dissipate the inertia and forward momentum of the airplane. Sheldon needed little or no imagination whatsoever to visualize the results of running headlong at 65 miles an hour into any one of the tumbling white crests of water that surely towered up to six feet above the surface of the river.

"There was no place to land below them, it was just more of the same terrible rough water. I did a 180-degree turn, and about a quarter mile above the guys, I spotted a slick, high-velocity stretch of river that looked like it might be big enough. I made a couple of passes to try it on for size, and then set myself up for an up-canyon approach to the place. It looked mighty small."

As Sheldon dropped the Aeronca below the tops of the canyon's walls, he found himself flying in a narrow alleyway of wet spruce and vertical rock. The wings rocked with the turbulence produced by the unstable air of the canyon and he carefully adjusted his glide path. The floats were causing his airplane to respond to the controls in a delayed manner, which is normal, due to a lowered center of gravity, and in a routine landing produces no problems. Here, control of the airplane was everything, and Sheldon hitched forward as far as his seat would allow, to gain every last inch of forward visibility.

Even before the floats touched down, spray and mist from the river surface were streaking the plexiglass windshield of the Aeronca, and Sheldon had the compulsion to firewall the throttle plunger and climb away from the terrifying spectacle of the gray water, but he resisted it. Then he was down.

Sheldon was landing against a current in the magnitude of 30 miles per hour, and the plane decelerated at an alarming rate. When an airplane is moving through the air at an airspeed of 90 to 100 miles per hour, the control surfaces—ailerons, rudder and elevator—work at optimum efficiency. This is due to the rush of air over the wings and tail surfaces, produced not only by the forward motion of the plane through the air, but by the slipstream blast of the rotating propeller.

An airplane, out of its design element and on the ground or water, is much more difficult to control, primarily due to the loss of this forward velocity, when all that is left is the rush of air produced by the propeller. In addition, an airplane on floats is infinitely less maneuverable than one on wheels or even skis, and as a result, the Aeronca became an unresponsive deathtrap as it almost immediately began to accelerate downriver with the current.

"The nose wanted to swing in about every imaginable direction, but somehow I managed to keep it pointed upriver with the throttle. I was floating backward at about 25 miles an hour, the windows were fogged, and I couldn't see where I was going."

Sheldon was certain of one thing, that behind him was the beginning of the heavy stretch of boiling rapids he had seen from the air only moments before. He was at that moment like a man blindfolded, rolling backward toward a cliff in a car without brakes that he could not steer. Sheldon will never forget those moments that elapsed so rapidly that they precluded panic.

"As the plane backed into the first of the combers, I felt it lurch heavily fore and aft. It was like a damned roller coaster, the water was rolling up higher than my wing tips, beating at the struts, and I could barely see because of the spray and water on the windows. All of a sudden the engine began to sputter and choke, and I knew it was getting wet down pretty good. If it had quit, I'd have been a goner, but it didn't."

Suddenly, he saw the huddled group of Army scouts on the small rock ledge, through the Aeronca's side window. Like white images on a frozen screen, they stared with open mouths as the airplane backed past them. And now the most critical and delicate aspect of the entire rescue began.

"After spotting the men, I had to stop the airplane's backward motion, which I did with full throttle, but I knew my problems had only begun. I had to get the airplane close enough to the ledge for the guys to jump out onto the float and get aboard without damaging a wing on the rocks. If they missed, in their condition, they'd drown for sure.

"I jockeyed around and finally got the wing angled just enough to get one of them on the left float, and still keep myself from turning downstream."

Once aboard, the grateful GI managed to balance-walk long enough to get into the cabin while Sheldon was already making his next move.

"Because of the heavy current and extremely rough water, it was impossible for me to taxi upriver, let alone take off in that direction, so all I could do was continue to float backward as I had been doing. It was a mile and a half downstream to the end of the rapids, and that first trip was one of the longest rides on a river that I've ever taken. It was a shocker."

Once below the rapids, Sheldon was able to turn the plane and make a downriver takeoff. He would make three more of these landings for there were seven men on the ledge, and he could only remove two at a time due to the need to keep the plane as light as possible for maximum maneuverability.

With the unbelievable taken care of, Sheldon now accomplished the impossible. He returned to the rapids three more times without damage to the airplane, himself, or the rest of the stranded scouts, and then turned his attentions to the eighth man. Sheldon had ferried the seven to the tiny settlement of Curry on the Susitna, a way station for the Alaska Railroad, and then returned to the canyon.

"I flew upriver, looked and then looked some more. I still saw a lot of debris, but no eighth man. I was just about ready to go back for another load of gas when I finally spotted him. The guy had dragged himself out of the river, and he was about 18 miles below the canyon. He had floated all that way hanging onto a piece of debris, and when I got to him, he was a shock case and could barely crawl aboard. The water was about 55 degrees and he was all skinned up and bruised, but had no broken bones."

The rescue at Devil's Canyon had been a marvel of efficiency. It was the first of a multitude of tasks that Sheldon would accomplish with the passage of time. Many would be of milder cast, while some would exceed the events that had transpired that day at Devil's Canyon. Today, Don Sheldon is well aware of the part that luck played in the four landings and subsequent takeoffs, for not even he could gauge the depth of the water as it plunged over the jagged rocks in the floor of the Susitna, yet somehow his floats missed them all four times.

Don received a special citation in a formal ceremony from the U. S. Army, Alaska, and today, when asked which aspect of the entire Devil's Canyon episode he remembers best, he smiles thinly.

"I guess it would have to be the expressions on those guys' mugs as they crawled aboard my old floatplane."

Chapter 22

MY SUNSET MOOSE

October 1975

By Charles G. Mayse

F ine," I whispered, "fine!" warning myself against drawing a coarse bead. Sloppy sighting had almost cost me a moose in the recent past, and I was in no mood to repeat that miserable performance.

I had stumbled upon an unexpected boon—if what I was aiming at was really a moose. I had hunted all through this area three hours previously with no results. But just at sunset, entertaining neither hope nor real expectation, I had returned to Goose Puddle, which a long, hot, rainless summer had transformed into a cindery meadow. Immediately I had spotted this suspicious dark mass, which the eye-searing sunglow allowed me to see only vaguely behind what could have been a pair of weathered spruce snags, or even two dead birches among the thick willow shinnery.

And so I hesitated, peering uncertainly down the gun barrel, crossbolt safety on the "fire" position. The question of the moment was whether I was really aiming at a moose, or only another one of the 10 million brush clumps populating the area.

"But no," I reasoned, "there could never be two evenly spaced snags, no two identical dead birches anywhere in the whole wide world."

Then I bethought myself of a ruse which must have been invented by Caveman Number One, which was merely to drop into the prairie hay. The results were satisfactory, for the dark mass took two curious steps out of the direct sun glare into the thin shade of a willow clump and became a lordly bull moose.

Drawing practice beads over the past several days had revealed an appalling unsteadiness of my left arm. If it shook now, I was unaware. Nor do I remember gathering in the trigger slack, nor gradually releasing breath, as I like to do at the critical moment of firing. Neither was I conscious of the authoritative explosion, nor of the sudden recoil, which in the Winchester Model 88, caliber .308, is not excessive.

But across that grassy meadow the ancient drama and excitement and compulsion of the chase was reenacted. A sudden loud "Whop!" and a simultaneous grunt were followed by a distinctive and dismaying thud as that big, black animal, his impressive antlers sagging, struck earth with a half-ton impact.

This wasn't exactly the way I had planned the culmination of my fall hunt. For the previous three days I had been assiduously afield from when I could vaguely distinguish the gun sights in the early dawn until they were no longer visible in the blue eventide, hoping earnestly that I could make suitable moose contact within easy carrying distance of the cabin.

The results had been zero.

I had found recent tracks, bent-grass beds, a few nugget piles and antler-raddled willows where an imaginary enemy had been fought and vanquished. Other bushes were frayed and broken where antlers had been rubbed free of velvet. Nothing more.

Despairing of success, I had canoed to a more distant hunting ground across the river. And there at sunset my quarry and I had met.

I have long entertained a nightmare of some dead moose returning unexpectedly to life and bringing into play vicious antlers and tremendous hoofs. So immediately after the kill I make certain that the game is thoroughly, safely dead. I delivered the *coup de grace* with a shot point-blank into that great Roman-nosed head.

As I propped the reloaded gun against a willow and shucked the pack, I recalled that I have long had the habit of removing the pack before making a shot; a backpack tends to make me shoot high. Perhaps there would have been time for its removal, but a turn and two quick steps would have put my moose safely beyond bullet reach.

The 200-grain Western Silvertip bullet had penetrated a between-ribs interval and plowed through the left lung area. I found it, thoroughly fragmented, in the lungs and on the ribs of the right side.

Indian hunters have told me that even in -40 degree temperatures entrails left overnight in a moose contaminate the meat. With reluctance I forced myself to proceed with the butchering.

For cutlery I had a Marble's Ideal hunting knife. Although a trail companion for 25 years, its performance had been less than satisfactory, for it is too hard-tempered to respond to anything but a coarse file or stone. Long whetting had put an edge on it as keen as it was capable of taking, and I had thought to bring along a mill file and Carborundum stone.

I have a wry but tolerant familiarity with the literature, complete with neat artwork, which outdoor editors foist upon gullible readers on the eve of open season, on the subject of butchering game. It has never worked to my advantage; in this case mostly because I had too much animal for my fortitude: I simply couldn't turn the big carcass over.

I had a 10-foot length of line and tied it to the moose's right hind foot. Then I cut, sharpened and drove a willow stake, took as strong a pull as I could and tied the leg up out of the way. The arrangement was not entirely satisfactory and tripped me up several times before darkness forced me to desist. This was not until after the bowels, liver, kidneys and lights had been removed and the body cavity propped open to cool.

Then I began skinning. The hide itself weighed around 120 pounds. In order to get it back to camp I decided to cut it in half lengthwise along the spinal column. Even then it made as heavy a pack as I could manage, but some of the older Indian women at the village, cheerfully undismayed at the required soaking, the hard, tedious scraping and careful smoking over a rotten wood smudge, would use it to make 20 pairs of velvety moccasins. It was too valuable to be casually wasted.

Before deciding to call it quits, a slight miscalculation, due to poor visibility, brought knife point and my ring finger into brief but painful contact. The result was an angry gash into which slime and bile, dirt, hair and I don't know what else entered. I had no antiseptic with me, and the light was too poor to examine the cut critically.

No illuminating device was included in my stampede pack—not so much as a battered candle stub. A robust blaze would have allowed me to proceed cheerfully and comfortably with the task at hand. But the shoulder-high redtop grass and sedges were thick and dangerously dry. Even a hat-sized watch fire would have been a hazard. During my Alaska years I have helped stomp out three or four forest and tundra fires into the ground and I hope never to see another one—let alone start it.

The big red-gold hunter's moon of two days before had gone into another phase; it did not rise until midnight. By that time the cloud cover was dense enough that its light did not penetrate.

A brief rain pattered, and I crouched under a plastic sheet fetched along, hopefully, to spread under the meat. What with the stress and excitement my heart thudded alarmingly in my ears; the sound, magnified by my ratty old hat and the plastic, was like a distant freight train rumbling between wild rock-hung canyon walls.

Between fitful dreams I tried to remember some of the widely separated and not always comfortable places I had overnighted; airport terminals, fleabag hotels, YMCAs, city parks, open fields, deep forests, overturned canoes, Indian and Eskimo cabin floors, fish camps, snowy sled trails, river bars, under bridges. Never before had I spent a night beside a fresh moose kill, the delicate and delicious aroma of which might entice a prowling and hungry bear.

"At least it's not 40 below," I consoled myself, although in the morning I found the moose hide frozen stiff along the back. This meant that it was meat-keeping weather. One of my great worries is of making a kill which results in spoiled and wasted meat due to mild temperatures.

I had flopped down onto a soft spot on the hard ground, and gradually the cooling night stole my body heat. Shivering in my clothes, sweaty from the day's labor, I got up and ran in place, arms swinging, to activate sluggish circulation.

What if every star in the constellation fell, or if the ice age suddenly reversed itself? I had taken my winter's meat, and a few hours, a night, a week even, of minor discomfort was a piddling price to pay. All I had to do now, after the butchering, was to get it safely to camp.

I had neglected to bring any drinking water. Belatedly I recalled that I had forgotten even to take the last available drink before leaving the river, and by now I had sweated myself uncomfortably dry. But there was nothing to be done over thirst and pain and I consoled myself with the idea that I could drink to my heart's content sometime early tomorrow—and so I did; enjoying it to the last cool drop.

The long night finally waned. I had left my battered Ingersoll in camp, so there was no knowing what o'clock it might be, as if it mattered in the least. But trees on the distant riverbank began standing out in relief, and I realized it was light enough to resume butchering.

When I was done I straightened the kinks in my back and legs, loaded the packsack with meat, and lit a shuck for camp.

With the meat hung where the breeze had free access, I warmed water on the barrel stove to treat my injured finger. The gasoline box medicine cabinet failed to supply any hydrogen peroxide. Luckily there was a partial bottle of Lysol. Alternate freezing and thawing had thickened it, and I was careful to pour only a few drops into the water, and to have the solution barely at a comfortable temperature, so as not to risk further complications with a fresh burn.

After I had soaked the finger for a while I put my glasses on and gave it close scrutiny. It was a cut and no mere scratch. With medical attention 100-plus miles away and no line of communication, it was a matter of grave concern. Blood poisoning is not to be taken lightly. But I was lucky; the wound healed slowly but healthily, though it remains tender.

With a combined supper and breakfast inside me and thirst finally assuaged, first with cool river water and then boiled coffee, I slept for an hour, rather than day-long as my tired old carcass demanded. But I recalled that several hundred pounds of prime moose meat awaited timely disposition, and the reluctant number twelves went firmly to the floor. "You've got to do it, Boy," I told myself and shrugged into the Trapper Nelson packboard and resumed the outward trail.

I no longer recall the number of trips necessary to fetch the meat into camp. But my run-over waffle stompers scuffed through the fallen leaves, brown and red and gold from the frost, up the little hill, through clutching wild rose briars, across the swale, over the slough, through slashing wolf-willows, down the riverbank and onto the sand bar, where I was able to bring the canoe and make the final water-borne journey of a quarter-mile. But it was enough to put me in sympathetic mind of an overburdened pack mule, such as I had seen often in mining-camp country of California.

Habitually I approached the kill area fully alert and with rifle chamber loaded, half expecting to see a ravenous dark form tearing at the moose carcass. Or to find the carcass under a clawed-up mound of earth, sod, grass and brush from a claim-jumping bear. Then the decision must be arrived at, and quickly, by the original owner—me—whether, with my slender ammunition stock reduced to eight cartridges, my claim was worth defending at the jeopardy of my life.

I had been jubilant over the kill. There had been no second thoughts, no finger-on-the-trigger hesitancy, no regret. When that great hairy body, my winter's meat, struck the earth with a thud, I rejoiced. To pass the long night as I lay beside my prey my songs had made the welkin ring.

But gradually revulsion at causing the death of so noble an animal intruded. I had tumbled from its ecological niche a major something. I began to wish, perhaps not too devoutly, that my shot had gone astray; that I had failed to make contact with that fine bull; that my hunting had not meant the death of that proud animal. I regretted that he was not still alive and parading his massive antler proudly, if not belligerently, through the deep Alaska midlands; that he was not still lord of the lakes and moors and winding streams where he had been born.

But the second day after the kill, on the lazy evening breeze I caught a new sound—wolf song. First upstream on the river's left limit. Then downstream a mile or two. The friendly pastoral environment had changed to one of menace and hostility.

The last load brought from the kill was the antlers. They were not in the Boone and Crockett class, with only 16 points per side. However it pleased me to have them as a frail memorial to another successful moose hunt. And with the hunter poised on the brink of his 70th birthday, probably one of his last.

In their green state, the antlers weighed about 70 pounds. Due to their 62-inch spread, from tip to tip, I had to rawhide them lengthwise down the narrow snowshoe trapping trail I had slashed through the shin-tangle many years before.

One trip more would have fetched the last few usable pounds from Goose Puddle—front and hind lower legs and what was left of the neck. All tough but tasty pieces with proper cooking. Then just as my feet crossed the cabin's worn threshold outward bound, the dreaded wolf song resumed. The pack had swum the river and had found the kill site, and they were sounding their wild, ululating ahs of satisfaction.

This translated into the fact that every scrap of meat, every dollop of marrow, every random piece of bone, every drop of blood had been picked up slick and clean. All that would remain to mark the spot would be the half-digested wood fibers of the moose's stomach contents and its stinking excreta.

Gradually my low mood dissipated. I became philosophical and almost light-hearted once more. How long could even that fine, physically perfect, mature bull (I estimated his age at five years) have withstood the onslaught of eight or nine determined wolves? The slow, torturing death they were capable of inflicting was not pleasant to contemplate.

Then I rejoiced that it had been my single, two-bit bullet that had caused his swift demise. The sunset of that beautiful, bluebird September day had been the sunset of his life, which ended as quickly, painlessly, and humanely as possible.

Chapter 23

HOW I KILLED THE WORLD'S LARGEST BROWN BEAR

January 1978

By Roy R. Lindsley

This is to certify that the new world's record brown bear entered by the Los Angeles County Museum was awarded first prize in the 1953 North American big game competition. Witness the seal of the Boone and Crockett Club this 25th day of March 1954. Signed, Karl T. Fredrinds, President.

The above certificate and a medal award are on display in front of the brown bear habitat group at the museum. The record bear, standing 8 feet, 8 inches tall, dominates the bruin family of four, which also includes a female and two yearling cubs.

I killed that bear on Kodiak Island 25 years ago, and the record still stands.

At the time I worked for the U. S. Fish & Wildlife Service as fishery management supervisor of the Kodiak area. Russell Hoffman, manager of the Kodiak National Wildlife Refuge for the USF&WS, and I were invited to guide a Los Angeles County Museum expedition to kill a male brown bear to complete a habitat group.

Others on the expedition were Melville Lincoln, senior habitat curator, Herman Beck, taxidermist, and Robert Sewell, artist.

We flew to Karluk Lake, which is prime bear country, 60 miles south of the town of Kodiak. Next day we cruised around the lake in an outboard-powered boat, watching the mountainsides for suitable male brownies. We saw several bears but none of the size or quality we wanted. That evening Russell was called back to Kodiak to attend to urgent business. Before he left I borrowed his

.30-'06 rifle to replace the .405 I had borrowed from a friend for the hunt. I did not own a gun at the time and hadn't since my early years in Alaska when, as a commercial fisherman, trapper and bounty hunter, a good rifle had been a necessity.

Late in the afternoon on the second day of hunting we located a large male brownie in favorable position to stalk. Herman and I commenced climbing toward King Kong, as I later named him, while Mel and Rob watched from the lakeshore. It was 6:15 p.m., May 23, 1952, and barely two hours of shooting light remained. We fought through several alder, willow and elderberry thickets and finally broke out onto a dry grass swale that led uphill in the direction we wanted to go. There we stopped to rest.

Wiping leaves, twigs, mosquitos and no-see-ums from my sweaty brow, I examined the hillside above us through binoculars, looking for the brownie we had spotted from the lakeshore half an hour earlier. I could not see him.

We continued, soon reaching the top of the swale and were about to cross a narrow alder shelf when suddenly we heard piglike grunts and tremendous crashing in the brush just ahead. I caught a glimpse of a huge brown bear rump disappearing into the alders. I threw a shell into the chamber and stood ready. Nothing happened. Mr. Bruin had slipped away.

"Let's climb to that open spot," I suggested. From there we would be able to see down into the alder jungle. After a few steps I saw the bear's tracks in a shallow patch of snow. When Herman saw them a look of astonishment crossed his face. "Man, they're big," he exclaimed.

We climbed to the open spot and sat facing the alder shelf 100 feet below. We watched for 10 minutes but saw nothing. It is strange how an animal that large can disappear so fast so completely.

I was disappointed for I thought we had jumped the bear we were after and had lost him. We were near the proper elevation and about a quarter of a mile downwind from where we had last seen him. I stood and looked upwind. Surprise! There was a brownie, 75 yards away, walking along the mountainside directly toward us. With binoculars all I could see was a bobbing head and a pair of muscular shoulders. I handed the glasses to Herman. After a brief inspection, he whispered, "I can't tell whether it's a good one or not, but, boy, it's sure getting close."

We'd have to do something soon or that bear would be upon us. I didn't want to shoot if it was not a suitable male specimen. It might have been a female for all I knew. I waved my arms and shouted, "Hi, you, hey there!" thinking it would rear up or at least turn broadside and give us a better look. It did neither. That bear kept coming straight toward us, and now was only 25 yards away.

We'd have to get the hell out of there soon, or stand our ground and take our chances. I made a fast decision, sat down abruptly and faced the oncoming beast. I raised my knees to rest my arms on, pointed my borrowed .30-'06 in the direction of the shaking bushes and waited. Seconds later the bear's head and forelegs pushed through the brush into the open spot where we were sitting. It stopped and glared at us. I centered the front sighting bead between its eyes. *Don't ruin the skull,* flashed through my mind, and I lowered the sight to just below the jawbone.

I could hear Herman breathing heavily behind me. He whispered hoarsely, "Shoot, shoot." I squeezed the trigger. Wham!

The bear fell instantly, rolled, crashed downhill through the brush and landed on the shelf below. It lay there for several minutes, then slowly struggled to a sitting position with its head lying low. I poured three more shots into its spine just behind the shoulders. With the last shot it sprawled and lay still.

We sat watching it for a full five minutes, both of us trembling from excitement.

Before venturing to the bear I stepped off the distance to where it had first fallen. It was 32 feet, later confirmed with a steel tape. Too close for comfort.

We approached cautiously, but the bear didn't move. Herman announced, "It's a male." There was a small rubbed spot back of his head, but otherwise he was fully furred out, deep brown and big. Very big. My first thought was, "He's a giant—just like King Kong. Wouldn't it be something if he were a record?"

King Kong had been fighting. One canine tooth was broken and his face was badly scratched. Maybe that's why he paid no attention when I shouted at him. Probably he was intent on following another boar, perhaps even the one we had jumped, to continue a fight, for breeding season was near.

We each took hold of a leg and after much tugging turned him on his back, a feat akin to rolling a tractor over. Unaccountably, neither of us had a hunting knife. Herman attempted to clean the bear with his penknife but succeeded only in scratching the hide. He hung his hat on one of its legs to help ward off scavengers during the night. Then, with twilight near, we hurried to the lake and our waiting companions.

Mel and Bob looked expectantly up as we approached. "We got a good-sized male," I said, "but I'm not sure it's the one we were after."

"It must be," Mel cut in, "we watched it walk directly over to where you fellows were; we thought it might bump into you."

"It almost did," Herman replied.

It was long after dark when we reached our cabin. Fortunately our outboard motor functioned flawlessly and somehow in the darkness we managed to miss the chunks of spring breakup ice still floating in the lake.

The following morning we climbed back up the mountainside and found the bear untouched. Herman set to work taking measurements he would need to accurately reconstruct the bear at the museum. Afterward we cleaned, skinned and dissected the carcass, saving hide, skull and selected bones.

Bob also found a bullet in the body cavity and handed it to me. The 180-grain soft-nosed slug had mushroomed considerably but remained intact. He also pointed out the path of my first shot. That bullet had ticked the jawbone, breaking it loose from the skull, then ranged back through the neck and emerged from the spine between the shoulders. It was a deadly first shot. It's amazing how the bear was able to regain consciousness and lift himself to a sitting position. It emphasizes what Alaskan bear guides say, "Make a good first shot. When the bear goes down, keep it down."

To ensure collecting authentic weight of the specimen we had with us a 100-pound capacity scale on which we weighed every ounce of meat and bone. We added 30 pounds for blood and lost body fluid, giving a total of 1,033 pounds. The green hide was too heavy for the scale, and we had to weigh it later at camp. The hide weighed 157 pounds, giving the animal a total weight of 1,190 pounds—not bad for a spring bear without an ounce of fat on it. In the fall, after feasting on salmon, berries and lush vegetation, that same bear would have weighed several hundred pounds more.

When we finally finished the messy task it was late evening. Mel picked up the guns, tools and bones and hurried toward the lake, struggling with his unwieldy load. Bob cut a Y-shaped pole and tied the pelt neatly to it. We took hold of the makeshift come-along and began to pull. The going was easy down through the open swale, but when we got into the thickets that danged hide hung on everything in sight. It finally came off, so we pulled it strung-out, skin side down. It slipped along easily that way. After reaching camp that night, we salted the hide, ate a hurried supper and fell into bed.

Next morning we took out the salt, smoothed the pelt on the ground and measured it at 11 feet, 2¼ inches wide and 9 feet, 8½ inches long. It squared (average of length and width) 10 feet, 5⅜ inches. Some rug. If stretched unsalted it would have been considerably longer.

Next we were ready to take the most important measurement—that of the skull. With bears, the skull is measured for the greatest width and length, with the lower jaws removed, and the total, in inches, is used to determine the bear's rank for the record book, the biggest skull being considered the largest bear.

At the time this system was devised growth patterns of bear skulls was not well known, but those who devised it made a lucky guess. In recent year's Alaska's bear scientists have learned that male brown bear skulls continue to grow as the bear gets older, so, generally speaking, the system is reasonably accurate, although it is true that some small bears have large skulls and some large bears have small skulls.

Herman measured the skull with steel calipers: The greatest length was 18 inches and the greatest width was 13 inches, for a score of 31 inches. I knew then what I had earlier suspected—the bear was either a new world record or mighty close to it.

A year later, after shrinkage, the skull was shipped to the Boone and Crockett Club in New York where it was officially measured for a score of 30 12/16. It exceeded by three-sixteenths of an inch the previous world record brown bear, which was killed prior to 1908 by Captain Wagner at Bear River on the Alaska Peninsula. The skull of that bear is in the University of California Museum.

To this day King Kong is number one in the trophy record book, the world's largest brown bear. He's truly the king of carnivores, for the Alaskan brown bear is the largest of the world's land carnivores. For the past 24 years he's been on display at the Los Angeles County Museum, where thousands of people pause to stare at him daily.

What a fluke. It was the first bear I had ever killed—with a borrowed rifle, no less—and I tried to scare him away.

"Hi you, hey there!"

Chapter 24

A TRAPPER LEAVES THE COUNTRY

June 1981

By Scott Fisher

The trapping was over for another winter. Now, in the month before the salmon started running, it was time to leave the trapline and the home cabin and the world across the river, and return to the village. It would be the last time.

We stood on the bank and watched upriver as his long, handmade, wooden boat poked its bow around the tip of the island and entered the main channel. We relaxed and smiled. He had always come back, of course, every spring for the past 19 years, but the worry was always there in the village just the same. When a man lives by himself most of the year, anything can happen: Ice can break, axes can slip, legs can twist, guns can misfire—and the land is dotted with the graves of those who discovered that depending only upon themselves and their dogs was sometimes just not enough.

Every year we would watch and listen upriver and wait and wonder—and then the chug of the outboard would drift in on the wind. The boat would appear, swinging downriver into the channel, then turning toward the village, sliding through the high-water passage between the sand bars in front of the town. Village dogs would howl greetings to his dogs tied in the boat, and kids would gather to help him as he landed.

The blue and white boat was loaded with gear and guided by him at the stern. He wore a floppy black hat. He angled toward the village, and no dogs howled. He swung and landed under the bank in front of his cabin in the village, and no dogs strained to be untied and let loose on dry land. We knew the truth we hadn't wanted to face—that the time had really come. He stepped from the boat and shook hands; none of us looked in the boat, none of us said a word about it. We pretended it was just like it always had been and always would be, but it really wasn't and we all knew it.

The relationship between a man and his dogs is as close and as deep as the man's relationship with the land. It is a closed relationship—he is theirs and they are his, and when the relationship is broken, it is done with a swift finality that allows for no suffering or risk of mistreatment by others. A man can leave the country, but his dogs cannot, and so they are shot. That spring there were no dogs in his boat as he landed and stepped ashore. He was leaving.

As the winter comes in to claim the land, there is one less dog team running down the narrow trails through the spruce trees. There is one less person out there, leading the kind of life that once many lived and now we only read about. He was the one who, when you heard about him, made you say, "I didn't know people could live like that!" He was the one who made you wonder why you couldn't.

For nearly two decades, he had lived without electricity, without a watch or a calendar on the wall, without a radio or a television or a telephone, without a gasoline engine of any kind (save the small outboard for his boat), without a city or a shopping center, without a daily—or even a weekly or monthly—newspaper or mail service. His only concessions to the latter half of the 20th century had been the boat's outboard motor and a subscription to a weekly national news magazine. These piled up in the village post office and were read sequentially when he came into town. Watergate, presidential elections, international crises—all had come and gone before he found out about them. And yet he had everything he needed or wanted.

He had the land to tell him the time of year and the sundials he had built to tell him the time of day. He had his dogs and his snowshoes to travel in the winter, and the boats and canoes he had made to travel in the summer. He had his old crosscut saw to cut wood and his ax and knife to build houses, furniture for the houses, and dishes for the tables in the houses. He had his guns to get meat and the river to give him fish. He used only what he needed and bothered no one.

As the years had passed the times had changed, affecting even someone living as he did. Once cabins and caches and camps could be left stocked and open, but now no more: They had to be locked, or the supply you were counting on might not be there. Once the country was open and free, but now it was divided, regulated, argued about. Lakes where once only he had canoed and hunted were filled with city airplane hunters in the fall; there was talk of oil exploration in the area; a bridge even spanned the Yukon—("If I don't see it, I don't have to think about it," he once said).

And he grew older. The life he lived in this land demanded care and attention and safety and fitness. It is a life filled not only with flowers and sunsets, but with hard work and the shadow of death. If the story of Alaska is the story of people who lived as he did, it is also the story of people who have died trying to live that way. One spring, across the river at his home cabin, he untied his dogs for a walk; one bumped into him and he lost his balance and fell, twisting his knee. That winter he had trouble walking on snowshoes. The next year he said it would probably be his last season: He depended too much on snowshoes to risk his safety much longer.

On the last day he stood by the door of his cabin and raised his blue tin cup. "Well," he said, "this is my last drink of Yukon River water." He remembered his sourdough, and he gave it to the old man saying, "I've had that 15 years and I'd hate to see it go to waste." With the sourdough passed on, it was time to leave: The mail plane would be coming.

He threw his baggage into the old wheelbarrow and began the walk to the village airstrip. We stayed behind, letting him walk alone. And we noticed there was no backward glance at the cabin now sold, the high caches now empty, the silent doghouses, the outhouse we had all watched him build one hot July day while the rest of us hid indoors from the heat and the mosquitos.

He walked along the trail beside the river, past the village cemetery filled with its white crosses. He had carved many of those crosses for friends during the long winters on his trapline—elaborate black-lettered crosses with carved hills and boats and snowshoes and wolverines and high-flying springtime black ducks. In earlier days, refugees from the gold rush and leftover stampeders—wanderers in search of a dream and in love with the land—had settled in the village. Some had stayed and become trappers and had finally come to rest under one of the crosses in the cemetery. Others, after staying a time, had finally gone back Outside to search for new dreams. His departure, as he walked by the cemetery, was one more in a long line that the village had seen.

In his shirt pocket he carried an old, expired passport, from his time with the Army in the '50s. He had found it last night in the last old trunk, after he had announced his plans to travel by bus. Someone had reminded him he would need identification to cross the border. For 20 years the only identification he had needed was his hunting and trapping license. Then he remembered the old passport.

As he came to the airstrip, he found the rest of us gathered there. We sat and talked and joked and told stories. Stories piled up over the years, and he was a person who, because of his isolation most of the year, enjoyed the visiting and the talking and the stories when he came to town. He would come across from his trapline for a Christmas visit, dog team flying down the river, down the fresh trail a friend from the village had broken and staked several days earlier. And in the spring, after breakup and before the salmon came, he'd come again before moving upriver to his fish cabin to catch and cut and dry the food for his dogs for the winter. (One summer a television crew, trying to duplicate life in '98, rafted right past him, thereby completely missing the real life they were only imitating.)

When the fish racks were full, he would return to the village and prepare to go back to his trapline across the river, because that was his real home, the land and the creeks and the sloughs, stretching far into the foothills of the distant mountains. It was his because he had made it so, and he knew the land well enough that he could tell a visitor that springtime day the ants had first appeared in his yard. This was the cycle he had lived, alone with his dogs and the land, throughout the 60s and 70s. And who is to say that was not a good way to spend those particular years?

And then the airplane's high-pitched whine sounded over the village. Now it was finally and really going to happen, and the jokes stopped.

"Well, good-bye," he said, first to his friend standing back by the tail of the plane, away from the cluster of people. This was the friend he had known the longest, the friend who had first brought him to the village, the friend he was closest to in the secrets of hunting and trapping and life in the woods, the friend who broke and marked the trail for him every Christmas, the friend to whose son he had given all of the trapline and the trapping cabins and the home cabin. With that first good-bye we all stepped forward to shake hands and say good-bye and wish him well. We were all men back there that morning and tradition has it that men do not show emotion and so—as memories began flooding in of yapping dogs and stories by the light of the coal oil lamp and silent crosses in the cemetery and brightly beaded dancing boots and strangely fermenting home brew and the old-time blue and white boat putt-putting back upriver to the trapline—he cut it off and said good-bye and got into the plane and shut the door.

The spell was broken. The crowd drifted away, leaving only the old man and me. We stood and waited and watched, because you don't leave until the plane has finally and safely gotten off the ground. The propeller started up and the plane taxied away and, gathering speed, rose into the air. It disappeared over the dark green trees and the wide river with its sloughs and creeks and islands, over the moose and the black bears and the young ducks and geese and the beaver and the marten and the lynx, over the village and the home cabin and over the trapline cabins and over the trails, and into the clear blue summertime sky.

On the Fourth of July, 1979, a small group of people gathered at the bus depot in Fairbanks, waiting for the bus to leave. Among the visiting grandmothers and tourists and wandering young folks was a man in a plaid work shirt, work jeans held up by suspenders, and a pair of battered moccasins. A snuff can bulged from one pocket; an expired passport stuck out of another. On his head was a floppy black hat.

In the fall of '79, the friend and his son took the blue and white wooden boat across the river to the home cabin. They wanted to check what supplies they would need to run this trapline. The cabin and the caches were completely stocked with everything they would need for the winter, from fish for their dogs to a brand-new set of dishes.

The trapper bought a farm and settled in the Lower 48. He is too far south to see the northern lights.

Now that he has left, your life, like ours, like Alaska's, is a little bit diminished. You knew him, though you may not have realized it. He was the one who lived on the edge of your dreams.

Chapter 25

AVALANCHE

March 1982

By Tim Moerlein

The avalanche itself was about 200 or 300 feet wide and 300 to 400 feet long. Heather and I were carried about 200 feet. The slide does not sound too vast, but when Heather was buried, the avalanche looked huge. Every time I walk on a football field, I imagine myself trying to find someone buried below and the same feeling comes back.

Barney, Janet, Heather, and I, longtime friends who were skiing together on a local high school team, had been on a 12-mile cross-country ski tour over Indian Pass, south of Anchorage. Only the temperature—an abnormally warm 35 degrees—distinguished this day from any other cloudy, winter day in Chugach State Park.

We were undaunted by the ominous-looking sky, and the warm weather was a pleasant change. The fact that a young man and his dog had perished in an avalanche two days before on this same path, only mildly concerned us. We had ropes, crampons, avalanche cords and, we hoped, enough sense to turn back should the traveling look dangerous. Thus equipped, we had started out.

We had to climb a steep slope to reach the summit. The route was not difficult, but a large cornice, like some gargoyle, hung above us where the almost constant wind had deposited layer upon layer of snow. Barney led, picking a route that hugged the rock of the mountain, away from the cornice. Our only real cause for concern was the warm weather, which oftentimes is a factor between a hunk of ice or snow holding on until spring or choosing the next moment to come crashing down. With the brightly colored, lightweight, nylon avalanche cords tied around our waists trailing off down the hill, Heather and Janet followed. I trudged up behind carrying an armload of our skis for the descent down the other side. We continued one step at a time until all that remained was the final conquest of the cornice.

When heights are involved I am a self-professed sissy, so we decided to rope together with the heavy climbing rope. I had the longest reach and went ahead, chopping hand and foot holds as I went. Standing on the broad, snow-free area of the summit, I was then able to belay the others as they climbed up.

Within minutes we were eating candy bars, mushy sandwiches, and all those aluminum-packed goodies hikers pride themselves on having invented. Our spirits picked up as we congratulated one another on how well prepared we had come. What remained of the tour was a seven-mile downhill run with little to worry about and lots to look forward to.

We packed the ropes and avalanche cords. With skis back on and whooping it up, we plunged off the top and headed down for the tree line. The first run was rather unexciting.

We followed a path parallel to the mountain and skied down to an area where the slope dropped off steeply. One last traverse was necessary before we could head over the front and down toward the spruce- and alder-covered terrain of Indian Creek.

Where the snow had been loose and powdery as the four of us climbed the mountain on the other side of the pass, here it was hard and wind-packed. Although we were heading down the mountain, a gully of 200 yards or so had to be crossed before we could get to more protected grounds. I arrived first at the gully's edge, so I started across. The valley floor was far below, but with plenty of ridges and bushes between me and the valley, my only concern was trying to get my ski edges firmly in the snow. Janet came across, then Barney, and then Heather, who was having a time just trying to stay on her feet. Our skis were fiberglass, hers wooden with rock-worn edges. With each step her skis came out from under her and she was sliding farther down the hill. By the time I decided to ski out to help her, Heather had slid 20 or 30 feet from our path. I side-slipped down to help her.

Who knows what actually triggered the slide: Whether it was the warm temperature, my sideslipping, our added weight on the snow cover, vibration, or a combination of these. Whatever the cause, the result is still videotaped in my mind. Everything around us settled with a noise similar to a huge mattress being thrown off a building, then came a split second of silence followed by the dull roar of pounding snow. The whole side of the mountain seemed to be coming, and I was in its midst, moving very fast and feeling very small. Where seconds before 15 inches of snow had lain, there was now a torrent of waist-deep snow pulling at my skis and poles and contorting my body. The avalanche lasted only seconds, but many thoughts went through my mind in that time, and a few stayed. I could not see Heather and hoped the slide had missed her; I could not believe I had actually gotten myself into an avalanche; I could not believe the power of it; I knew it was too warm to go ski touring, and I should have stayed home; I thought the slide was a bit exciting. Then it stopped. It did not slow down, it just stopped dead.

The snow had seemed so light plummeting down, but it was now wedged: Packed tight. Everything seemed quieter than before the slide had started. One of my skis was already off, but my legs and the other ski were buried. I am not sure why I was able to keep most of my body above the snow. I had tried to use my arms and legs as if treading water, but I knew it was mostly luck that had kept me from being totally buried.

It took a few minutes of digging to free myself, and then I was up on my feet looking up to where the snow had broken off the mountain. A distinct, jagged line was left there, and the rubble of fallen snow could easily have covered a football field. Alders were twisted and bent; three-foot chunks of snow were strewn everywhere. Heather was gone. Not a ski, hat or pole protruded above the snow. Waves of panic and hopelessness pushed through me.

Barney and Janet had seen the entire event, but had not gotten caught because they were on the ridge off to the south side. They realized what was wrong immediately, and ran down to meet me. All of us were familiar with avalanches. I was stunned—a moment ago the four of us had been talking and laughing, and now one was gone, buried somewhere in the field of snow at our feet. We flipped over chunks of snow looking for any sign of Heather. We screamed for her, cursed the snow, and pleaded for her to show up, but to no avail.

I had read an article about avalanches less than a week before, but all I could remember was that calling was fruitless because anyone buried would not likely hear the call, and that if they were calling, their voice could be drowned out. We had spent perhaps 10 minutes in frantic searching, and with each passing minute our hopes died and our anxiety grew. Barney, Janet, and I had spread out over the face of the avalanche. We had no idea where to look. Slowly we moved together, searching as we came, to plan our next actions. We decided to keep quiet and listen, search for a few more minutes, and then send Janet down for help. The three of us were at the point of sobbing, and where once adrenaline had flowed, we were now just numb. Barney headed back to where I had been trapped, and where my skis had been set as markers. Janet and I searched below. Another five minutes passed as we walked back and forth, looking for any sign and listening intently. Barney screamed for us, and we reacted instantly, running and stumbling to his side.

"Listen, she's right below me."

Janet didn't hear anything, and I didn't hear anything, but this was the first glimmer of hope we had had. The three of us dropped to our knees and began digging. We had only our hands, and the deeper we dug, the more the snow fell in on itself. The circular dish we were digging became wider, but we found nothing. Then we dug deeper. We were three feet down when Heather's long brown hair appeared mixed in with the snow. She lay face down and spread-eagled. We cleared the snow from around her head and face. We had difficulty determining if she was injured because she was so numb, and much snow remained tightly packed over her. She was dazed, shocked, and crying, so Janet tried to comfort her and keep the snow from falling in on her face while Barney and I dug the snow from on top of her. Almost an hour passed before we finally freed her and wrapped her in all of our down clothing. The immensity of the sequences of events slowly sank into us as we sat on the snow looking at each other without a word.

Heather was badly shaken, but after sitting in a cocoon of down for some time, she was able to regain her feet. Both her ski poles had been swept away. We shared the remaining three pairs so Heather always had a pair. Four hours later than we had anticipated originally, we reached our destination. It was well past dark and our parents had already notified the Civil Air Patrol. We simply explained that the weather and snow had been bad and left it at that. We had learned an invaluable lesson, and had word of the event gotten out, it would have meant an end to our tours. Any reprimands our parents could have imposed on us would have done nothing more in impressing the severity of the matter on us.

Heather only recalls bits and pieces of the avalanche itself. She had felt pressure on her head when Barney had walked across her, and she had screamed. The area covered by the slide was so large that such a recovery still seems amazing to me. All of us continue to enjoy touring, but we have a great deal more respect for the area in which we are traveling.

Chapter 26

ACCEPTANCE

April 1982

By Mike Davis

When I returned to the village that evening, the brilliant arctic sunset had disappeared and night had fallen on the small Eskimo community. I quickly unharnessed the dog team, fed them, and hurried to the steam bath, or maka as it is called on the Mulchatna River. Earlier, while Issac and I had been working in the woods, we had challenged each other to a duel in the steam—to see who was tougher.

As I passed between the scattered cabins, it warmed me to see the red blaze pouring from the short stack of the maka. The small log building's dimensions were only about 12 by 5 feet. The ceiling was about four feet high, but on many occasions the maka would accommodate 13 or 14 bodies.

I bent down and pushed open the small door to the dressing room. My face met a wet cloud of moisture.

"Any room?" I asked.

"Lots of room!" someone replied.

There was always "lots of room" no matter how many people were already there. I carefully maneuvered my large white body into a very crowded dressing room. Barely visible through the steamy air were the men's smaller, tan, muscular bodies. A small kerosene lantern next to an old porthole provided the only illumination for the dressing room and the steamy room. The cloudy room was cluttered with parkas, long johns, boots, and various other winter gear. I managed to find a seat and began to undress.

Inside the steam room, I heard Issac's voice.

"Issac, how is the steam?"

"Hot one!"

Hurriedly, I finished undressing, piled my clothes in a corner, and crawled toward the door. Cries of pain and shouts of victory came from inside the steam room and the men engaged in their nightly battle. The door burst open and out poured men and steam. Now there was room for me. I crawled across the frozen floor and into the steam room.

Issac was sitting next to the door. I took a seat next to him on the bench. In front of us was a 55-gallon drum covered with rocks. It was glowing a deep red.

"Nu-tan maka (Just right)," I said, trying to remember when I had seen such a blaze. Already my muscles felt scorched from hot blasts of air. Quickly, I wet my hair and covered my head with my wash cloth to protect it from the heat.

Issac reached over next to the drum stove and grabbed the dipper, a tin can attached to a wooden handle. He filled it with boiling water from one of the two Blazo cans that were in front of the opening to the drum. An old man said, "Doy, Issac," indicating that it was hot enough without more water being poured onto the rocks. Issac refused the old man's request and began to slowly pour the water onto the stove.

The old man, Ivan, and I melted into the bench.

"Akca (It hurts)!" The old man grimaced.

Slowly, with each splash of water, the heat grew more intense. After Issac had emptied the dipper, we sat fighting back the pain, trying to hold on, to stay just a little longer. I thought, "I have to show myself to these people, to prove myself—to show that I am tough."

I watched Issac. He too was doubled over in pain. I waited, wondering if he would reach again for the dipper.

Then I heard the metallic clink of the tin can. He was going to pour more water. With this threat, the old man said, "Winga tauqa! (I quit). Winga tauqa!" Moving fast, he broke open the door and was gone.

The cool air rushed in. I welcomed it and longed to go out, too. It was now Ivan, Issac, and me. The event took on some seriousness. With the old man gone, Issac readied himself.

"Chalie qa (More)?" Issac asked.

"As much as you want." I said boldly.

"Ya, there's been a big draft in here," Ivan added.

Issac was annoyed at this arrogance. "Now, let's see just how tough a white man's skin can be!" he challenged. He quickly heated the place with an entire dipper.

With this new blast all three of us sank off the benches and onto a blazing floor.

"A-na-up-a (Too much)!" Ivan groaned.

"A-na-u-duk (It is too much)!" I cried, wondering what crazy masochism had brought me to this excruciating sport. All of us were turning backwards, lying on different sides, desperately trying anything to gain some relief from this torch.

Slowly, gradually the inferno subsided; all of us were in a state of exhaustion. Any more water was unthinkable. Insane. We all looked and I felt like the orange metal before us. I was sure my body had been scalded by this torture.

Then I saw Issac's hand reach for the dipper. I couldn't believe it. It had to be a bluff! But, I couldn't give up now, not after all this.

Ivan said, "Issac, you're crazy!" He then said to me, "You cooked me." He quickly rose and crawled out.

The men outside knew this was a final test; they waited. Issac fingered the handle of the dipper. Then, he poured the steamy liquid back into the Blazo can. "I'm tired," he said heavily. "You're getting pretty tough." Tiredly, he carried his body toward the door.

With the duel over, I immediately followed Issac. As we filed out, a group of men came in. I threw myself on a nearby bench. Steam billowed from me in the sub-zero cold.

"You're getting pretty tough. Tougher than me tonight," Ivan conceded.

Ivan was an important leader in the village; I felt a surge of pride, as if I had passed a rite of acceptance.

"Too bad I am so tired tonight, or else you would have really got it." Issac snorted.

The language changed to Inupiak. Familiar phrases were woven into many I did not understand. My concentration drifted away from this pristine world. My eyes fixed on the kerosene lantern: I thought briefly of the warm beaches of San Diego . . .

The arctic night soon jarred me back. I became chilled. Scalding temperatures forgotten, I scrambled back to the fire to warm up.

Chapter 27

OF TRAPS AND TREASURES—KLUTUK

September 1984

By Fred Hatfield

I got to know some of the old-timers in Dillingham that year of 1936, after my tough winter at Togiak. Among them was Butch Smith, who was quite a man. He had lost his teeth to scurvy on the Yukon. He was gray-haired, but strong. His eyes looked like two pieces of blue glacier ice. His cabin in Dillingham was a gathering place for old-timers.

"Fred, do you plan to trap this winter?" he wanted to know.

"I'll be going somewhere, Butch."

"I know of a place you'll like. There's no one in there. Come to my cabin and I'll show you what I can."

He spread a map on the table.

"These are the Tikchik lakes—five big lakes all tied together with rivers. I spent a fall there with Harry Stevens, the old man who used to trap that country. I was prospecting. His cabins were here," he pointed, "and here. They should still be in good shape."

"Where should I start, Butch?"

"Why not the first lake? There's a cabin right at the foot of it. Matt Flensburg can set you down there and you'll be home. It's good fur country, with plenty of game."

I told Butch that was what I'd do.

"Do me a favor, Fred. Jake Savolly, an old-timer, and an old friend, has a cabin on the Nuyukuk River. He comes down the river every spring. This year he didn't show up. It will be a 15 mile hike for you. Jake never goes beyond there. His cabin is at the foot of a bad set of falls.

"There's something else you should know, Fred," he said. "Last year the bodies of three government surveyors were pulled from the Nushagak River at the village of Ekwok. All of them had been shot. The opinion seems to be that it was done by Klutuk, an old Eskimo who lives at the mouth of Klutuk Creek, way up the Nushagak River.

"He didn't come down the river in the spring, like everyone else did. Kid Wilkins, Sam Donaldson and I agreed to go upriver and bring Klutuk to town for questioning. I guess I knew Klutuk better than any white man, and I thought I could bring him in with no trouble. It took us ten days to get to Klutuk's place. He seemed willing enough to come downriver with us.

"We made camp the first night and we left Sam there to watch Klutuk while Kid and I went to find some meat for camp. When we got back Klutuk was gone, and Sam was lying by the campfire with our double-bitted ax driven into his head. I knew Sam a good many years and he wasn't a careless man, but he was careless that night. He let Klutuk get behind him.

"I'm telling you this for one reason: The Big King Salmon River isn't far from Klutuk's place. The headwaters drain from the northeast plateau of the Tikchiks. It's good caribou country and I'm pretty sure Klutuk has his camp in there. That's at least forty miles from where you'll be, so I don't think you have to worry about him, but it might be a good idea to keep your eyes open."

I worked for Tubby Griffin all summer, and in early August Matt Flensburg flew me in his float plane to the foot of the first Tikchik Lake, not more than five minutes' walk from the cabin that had belonged to Harry Stevens. We unloaded, and this time I had everything I would need: I didn't want another Togiak winter.

Matt was to pick me up April first, while there would still be plenty of ice on the lake for his ski plane.

Harry had taken quite a bit of care when he built his cabin. It has a nice big window on each side, and it was roomy. I got settled, and in a few days decided to do as Butch Smith had asked—check on Jake Savolly.

I left early one morning. Fifteen miles wasn't far, but the trail followed the river and there were several places where grizzly bears had hauled salmon from the water, so I kept an eye open and didn't travel too fast. Bears are touchy when they are feeding.

In about five hours I reached Jake's cabin. It was on a high bank overlooking the river. The falls Butch told me about were there, and it was easy to see why Jake couldn't take his boat any farther up the river.

Somehow the cabin didn't look as though it had been used for some time. The door was fastened with a latch, and I went inside. The place was barren. The only things in it were a stove and a chair. The stovepipe was in place, and a stack of wood was against the wall. Every trapper saves empty coffee cans, for they have a dozen uses. There were none in this cabin.

I was a little tired. I always carried my tea can; it had been a three-pound lard pail. It had a bail and a tight cover and I kept a small cloth bag of tea in it. Hot tea is fine for tired bones. I lit a fire in the stove and went to the river for water. Jake's boat had been pulled from the water far enough so the winter ice couldn't reach it, and turned upside down.

I was puzzled now. Jake hadn't used his cabin or his boat for a long time. I got my water and went back to the cabin, put the water on the stove and sat down. I dozed off a little, and dozens of squeakings and nibbles on my hands and wrists roused me. My pants were a moving blanket of shrews. I jumped up and stamped and brushed them off, and they disappeared into various corners and crevices.

I had planned to spent the night at Jake's cabin, but not now. I fixed my tea and drank it and went outside. Jake hadn't attempted to go down the river in the spring, something he had done every year. Someone had cleaned out his cabin, and it hadn't been Jake. I walked around to the back of the cabin.

Jake had been there a long time.

He had been dragged there, for his arms were stretched out above his head. There wasn't much left; mostly bones and a few shreds of cloth, and the shrews had polished the bones. I looked him over carefully. One of his ribs had been cut by a bullet, about four inches from the spine. I stood there for a while, and went back and sat in the open door of his cabin to figure things out.

Jake had been shot in early winter. Klutuk used a dog team. Sound carries a long way on the water, and Klutuk had heard Jake's outboard before freeze-up; figured about where the cabin was. After the first good snow he had slipped in close. He had tied his dogs as soon as he smelled smoke or heard the sound of an axe. He may have walked two miles or so to get to Jake. Jake had been easy to kill. After killing him Klutuk had brought his dog team and sled to the cabin and loaded Jake's supplies. The outboard was gone. It must have taken two or more trips for Klutuk to move everything.

I had time to make it back to my cabin before dark, so I started off.

I tried to keep Klutuk out of my mind and pay attention to the trail. Jake had been man number five for Klutuk. He had without question heard and seen the plane set me down at the foot of the lake. I didn't intend to be man number six. If you know the habits of any animal, he's easy to trap. A man isn't any different. I had to figure out the habits of Klutuk. I had to know when he made his moves and why. I intended to trap him.

When the weather got cold enough for it to keep, I shot a moose for my winter's meat. And then the snow came. Lots of it.

I made up a pack and set out. Butch had told me that he thought Klutuk's camp would be at the head of the King Salmon drainage. That put him about 45 miles northeast of my camp. I didn't travel fast. I listened for the bark of a dog, any sound or sign that would tell me about the man I was after. The days were still fairly long and even at my slow pace I made close to twenty miles that day. I made a cold camp that night, but I was used to that.

Next morning I set out again, and after perhaps five miles I found more than I had hoped for: a dog team trail followed the side of a partly open stream. I followed it and came to Klutuk's first mink set. I pulled his trap, snapped it shut, and placed it carefully on the bank. I found about twelve more traps, and pulled them all.

I headed home then. I made circles and cut back on my trail. Klutuk wouldn't follow that trail very long. He'd never know where I might be waiting for him. I had him penned in. He wouldn't dare stray very far from his camp. I made another cold camp that night and got home the next day. After two days of rest, I set out a good mink line. I wasn't worried any. I had Klutuk tied up for the winter.

The hum of Matt's airplane was a welcome sound on April 1. I had my fur ready. Everything else I left for Klutuk. I knew he'd be at my cabin the day after he heard and saw Matt's plane come in to pick me up. He would spend the summer there and wait for me to come back in the fall. He'd have me then.

The trappers hadn't arrived at Dillingham yet. There was still ice on the rivers. It seemed that some of the boats almost followed the ice down the rivers. The trappers had put in a long winter.

Butch Smith was late getting down the river. He took his time. I saw him one day standing in front of the trading post. I went to him and we sat on the long wooden bench against the wall.

"What kind of a winter, Fred?"

"I went down to Jake's place, Butch. Klutuk had been there. Jake had been shot and dragged behind his cabin."

Butch didn't say anything for a while.

"Klutuk knows you were there, Fred. What are you going to do?"

"You told me Harry had a cabin at Rat Lake. That's where I'm going. When Klutuk sees the plane drop down there this fall, he'll know where I am. He knows the country better than I do. When I leave there next spring, I'm going to set a trap for him. Right now he's waiting for me at the head of the Nuyukuk. He's sure I'll be coming back there this fall. He'll know he's lost a year when he sees where the plane drops me off.

"He has lots of patience. He'll be at Rat Lake after I leave there next spring, and he'll wait for me there. But next spring I'll have him.

"Butch, they used to use a lot of strychnine around here. They almost cleaned out the arctic fox between here and Nome with it. Can you get a cup of strychnine for me?"

"I'll have it for you before you leave in the fall. I hope you know what you're doing, Fred."

"I'll see you after fishing season, Butch."

I didn't know anything about commercial salmon fishing from a sailboat, but I went fishing with Henry Field that summer, and he knew his business. We did well and the credit was Henry's.

Rat Creek, where I planned to trap that winter, drains the lake and joins the Tikchik River. I found a canoe I could use—I wanted to look over the river country and the canoe would be handy.

I saw old Butch and he had the strychnine I had asked for. "The amount of strychnine you can pile on a quarter will kill a 150-pound wolf. I hope you have all the luck there is," he said.

Matt put me down on Rat Lake in mid-August. I watched as he gunned his engine and rose from the water. I knew Klutuk would be watching, too. He'd be puzzled for a while, but he would soon put the pieces together and make plans for me.

I didn't do too much trapping that winter. A small creek flowed out of Rat Lake and I picked up some mink there. I was tired of not being able to spread out and trap the country the way I should. I had grown cautious. I had a Swede saw with me this time: It was only two feet long, nothing more than a steel bow fitted with a thin blade. It could cut through a log with no more sound than a whisper. I wanted to be able to hear the smallest sound. Klutuk was a dangerous antagonist—five dead men told me that.

One evening at dusk I heard a distant rifle shot. Klutuk had probably taken a caribou. I was glad to see spring arrive. I had told Matt to pick me up the first of March. I wanted Klutuk to have plenty of good weather for dog-team travel after I left. I wanted him at the Rat Lake cabin.

I made my set for him a week before the time for me to leave. I had a small glass jar with a screw top. I followed the instructions from Butch and measured my strychnine and sugar carefully at the ratio of two tablespoons of sugar, and all the strychnine I could pile on a quarter. I filled the jar with this mix to where it started to neck down for the cover.

It was an obsession with me now. I once read that man hunting is the king of sports. I didn't find it that way. I hung my tea can and the small Swede saw from the rafter in the overhang in the front of the cabin. I added a few #4 beaver traps, and it looked just the way it should. Klutuk wouldn't pass those things up. When he opened the tea can and saw the jar of sugar and the small cloth bag of tea, those things would go with him.

When Matt came I was glad to get out of there. When Klutuk saw us lift off, I knew he would head for my cabin and the supplies that were there. This time, he would think, he would have me. He would wait and take me when I came back in the fall.

We landed at Dillingham and I couldn't wait for fishing season to end and get back to Rat Lake. I had to know. I left town early that fall. Matt circled the lake and landed. He taxied the plane up to the shore not more than 100 feet from the cabin door.

"Matt, wait here a minute," I asked. I wasn't sure what I would do if my bait was still there. I walked to the cabin and looked up at the rafter where I had hung it. The tea can, the saw, and the traps were gone. I opened the cabin door, and if Klutuk had taken anything with him, it hadn't been much. I knew I had him.

"Matt, let's get this stuff unloaded."

We put everything in a pile in front of the cabin and covered it with a tarp. Matt left, and I watched the plane become small in the distance. I took my rifle and crossed the small creek where it left the lake. There was a colony of beaver down the creek a ways, and something told me that Klutuk had gone after beaver. I followed the creek down, stayed back from the bank a ways, and walked easy and soft on the moss. Even now, Klutuk commanded a lot of respect, and I stayed in the timber on my way down.

After two miles I found what I was looking for. Across the creek I could see strips of torn tent canvas. I crossed over to it and knew it had been his camp. A dog sled was there, turned on its side. He had cut a branch from a spruce tree, leaving a stub for a hanger. My saw and traps hung from the stub.

A .30–30 rifle was on the ground, and dozens of shells for it were scattered around. There were plenty of .22 shells there, and I knew he had taken that rifle with him. The bears had been there and his campsite was a debris of scattered equipment. I picked up his rifle. The front sight had been replaced with one carved from ivory, and it was a beautiful job. I tapped the sight out of its slot with the handle of my hunting knife. It wasn't the only souvenir I wanted, and it wasn't for me.

I found Klutuk not more than a hundred yards down the creek from his camp. He had been a small man, not much more than five feet tall. I walked back to his camp and saw my tea pail lying to one side. The jar of sugar with the strychnine was there, and the lid had been screwed back on. I could see that a little of it had been used. I tossed it to one side and walked back to my cabin.

After all these years I'm not sure how I felt. Relief, of course, and a measure of feeling that I had won. Perhaps there may have been a tinge of remorse, but if there was it wouldn't have been very much. Klutuk had killed five good men. He had been morally insane and was better off where he was. My two years of feeling hunted were over.

Back at my cabin I took a few things to eat from under the tarp. There was plenty of daylight left. Somehow I was tired. I sat in the open cabin door for a long time, looking out over the lake. When dusk came I saw a cow moose, her calf following her, wander along on the other side of the lake. I finally went inside, fixed something to eat, and lighted the lamp. I sat at the table reading a book, trying to get my mind onto something else. When darkness came, it brought with it a feeling of finality. It was over.

A *tap tap tap* on the window across the cabin caused a sudden stillness in my heart. I was 28 years old, and didn't have a nerve in my body, but I couldn't stop the small shiver that tried to crawl up my spine.

Klutuk? I had seen Klutuk that day and he hadn't looked as though he'd be tapping on my window. And yet . . . I grabbed a flashlight and went to the window. Nothing. I went back to my book, but it was hard to focus on it. *Tap tap tap* came on the other window. I turned my head, deliberately slowly, not too anxious to see what was there. A mink sat on the window ledge. He tapped the windowpane again and disappeared into the darkness.

I slept well that night, considering the day and evening before. The morning was bright from the sun peaking over the mountaintops. I started a fire in the stove and stepped outside. A loud hiss above my head made me move quickly, and I looked up. A mink sat above the door. Two long porcupine quills were deeply imbedded in its head, answering the question about its strange behavior the previous night.

I killed it with a stick.

I went down to Rat Creek and covered Klutuk's bones.

This was my third winter in the Tikchiks, and it was the first time I was able to trap the way I wanted. I paddled the canoe down Rat Creek and found Harry Stevens' old cabin where the creek entered the Tikchik River. It was in good shape and I used it. I was able to trap both ways from the cabin, up the river and down. I had a beautiful catch of fur that winter.

When Matt came to pick me up in the spring, I was ready. I needed to see some new faces.

One day in late May I found Butch sitting at the counter in the restaurant. I slid onto a stool beside him and he turned and looked at me with a question in his eyes. I reached into my pocket and took out a small piece of rolled up paper. From it I took the ivory sight and placed it in Butch's hand.

"That's the sight from his rifle, Butch. He carried a .30–30. He won't need that anymore."

The legend of Klutuk lived for a long time. People wondered where he had gone. They wondered whether he was still alive. The story stayed around as long as the old-timers lasted. Butch Smith died in the Pioneers' Home at Sitka.

Butch wasn't a man to talk very much. I know that the story of Klutuk stayed with him.

I never told anyone, until now.

Chapter 28

RELUCTANT HERO

December 1984

By Julie Collins

T rapper stood watching as I struggled in the freezing black water. He made no
move to help, to throw me a stick or rope, but at least he was there, worried,
wanting to help, but afraid. After all, he is a dog.

It had been just before seven o'clock—not quite dawn—when my sister
and I slid the canoe into the silent black water slipping past our isolated trapping
cabin on that particular morning in mid-October. Trapper, our 85-pound malamute, jumped into the canoe. He preferred riding to dashing along the riverbank
as the current sent the canoe whipping downriver. My broad paddle drove
through the great clots of snowy slush which had been drifting down the river
ever since the beginning of freeze-up two weeks earlier. Even the thaw of these
last three days had not affected the river as it sank into the lethargic state that
precedes the closing in of the shelf ice on the current.

This was no time to be taking a journey of any distance, for the swamps
were still soggy despite several inches of snowfall, and the lake ice was still soft,
especially since this last thaw.

But travel I must, for the sake of our dog team. Our brother was taking
care of the dogs at our home 18 miles away, but now he was leaving and I had
to take over. Eighteen miles in hip boots is no easy chore, even with arms strong
from sawing wood and paddling a canoe. Walking is another matter. Nobody in
his right mind goes hiking across the marshes at freeze-up.

The first two miles by canoe went quickly. Where the trail cut away from
the river I left my sister and set out with Trapper and a light pack containing
lunch, a sleeping bag, and a plastic bag of birch bark tinder.

The first five miles crossed low hills. Trapper and I had a fine time. Then
we followed a tiny creek across the low country with its taiga and marsh, spindly

black spruce and tamarack. Once I cut across a broad bend and lost the creek. In the flat country it's easy to head off wrong, and the solid overcast hid the sun and cut off all sense of direction.

After two miles of hiking I climbed a tall tamarack to get my bearings and found my way back to the creek a quarter-mile from where I had left it. I was tired from wading hip-deep drainages, tired of walking in those heavy boots, and tired of the monotonous gray of the sky, the trees, and the snow.

Trapper was weary, too, and when I stopped for lunch he seemed grateful for the rest. I saved the last bite of meat and crackers for him. Despite his training as a sled dog, he was a good companion dog, and for hiking and packing he was magnificent.

I elbowed him away as he ventured to lean against me, for he was wet. He had fallen through some ice in the creek. After struggling vainly to climb out, he had bawled until I crept up, staying on firm ice, and pulled him out by the scruff. There was no doubt about it—for all his show and bravado, Trapper was a coward. He was beautiful, and he knew it; he was powerful, and he knew it; but he only thought he was brave. When the chips were down, he'd start blubbering.

This was not the only time he fell in. About six miles from home we had to cross the open creek. The water was 10 feet deep, and the slender pole we called a bridge sagged as I inched across it.

Trapper was no acrobat, but he did well until he was halfway across. Then, fearful, he hesitated, lost his balance, and panicked. A scurry toward the bank resulted in a splendid splash, and for the second time that day I helped him out.

Six miles to go, and they should be easy, for there were no more marshy areas, only a string of frozen lakes. Walking along the ice would be a pleasant change from the muskeg where my feet sank ankle-deep into wet moss at every step.

At least it would have been pleasant if the ice had been strong. What concerned me most was the half-inch of water covered with a skim of ice on top of the main ice. This made me suspect melting, rotting ice, and the skim of ice above it crackled with every step and effectively drowned out the lower pitch of the main ice cracking.

The first of the six lakes was solid white ice; even the marshy border was frozen. The second lake showed patches of weaker black ice, but I was able to skirt most of them. The third lake was better, the fourth worse. I made a mental note to find a good, sturdy pole as soon as I came ashore to carry with me across the remaining two lakes, so I could get out if I fell in over my head. But I was tired, I'd been on the trail for nine hours, and I forgot.

The ice was bad on the fifth lake. I walked near the edge, but not too close, for it was weaker near the shore. The skim of ice crackled, the water beneath it splashed forebodingly, and I could imagine the thicker underlying ice bending with my weight. I speeded up my pace, some awareness deep inside me turning me toward shore.

There was no warning. One moment I was hurrying lightly over the ice; the next I was in six feet of water which rushed around me, driving rods of cold through my thick wool sweater and undershirt and pouring into my tall boots as great air bubbles burst upward.

The cold took my breath away, but there was no real fear—not yet. It didn't occur to me that I might not be able to get out. All I wondered was whether I'd have to light a fire and dry off, or could I make the last two miles.

With my forearm on the ice edge, I reached out with my other hand and heaved myself up and forward. I came part way out, kicking furiously, angry at the hip boots that weighed down my legs. One more pull and . . .

The ice gave way under me, slowly sinking, and the gut-freezing water swelled over me again. The edge of the ice simply wouldn't support my weight.

I had no choice but to try again, with all the strength I could muster. Heaving and kicking, I rapidly used up my energy. Again I was on the brink, half in and half out, my strength gone. I stopped, panting, on the ice edge. Slowly the ice sagged, gave way, and thrust me back brutally into the abyss. This time the cold was overwhelming. Panic rose. As my lungs cried out for air I started gasping.

I tried again. And again, each time more aware of the consequences of failure. I was a good 30 feet from the swampy shore. If I could keep going I might be able to break my way ashore.

As I rested a moment from the struggle, I saw Trapper near the shore watching me. I started to call him to me, memories of childhood stories of hero dogs running through my mind, but then I realized he might fall in, too, and might shove me under as he tried to climb out.

"Stay! Stay!" I roared as he started forward. "Lie down! Stay!" The malamute sat down obediently but it was obvious he knew I was in trouble.

My own fear was rising to unknown heights. The cold was paralyzing my limbs, and I could hardly pull myself up onto the ice, yet in order to break my way to shore I had to lean repeatedly and heavily on my boots.

My hip boots were full of water now and heavy as I kicked and pulled. Every ounce of energy, every scrap of concentration went into supreme effort to heave out once more. And again I sagged back as the ice broke away. I had used up all my reserve energy to struggle 10 feet; how could I manage the next 20?

Head down, legs limp, elbows gouging the ice edge, I started to say my prayers. Suddenly I was aware of something above me, something alive and breathing. Trapper had crept up to me unnoticed and now hovered over me.

I could see his forepaws sinking in and yelled for him to get away. I tried to push him back, but the ice collapsed and his front feet fell into the icy water. His hind feet backed up instantly on firm ice, and he wheeled around to run away from that threatening black hole.

As he snapped around, my hand whipped out and miraculously curled around the base of his white tail. He tried to run, but my grip on his tail stopped him. At the same time I let out a dreadful roar, such as a husky heard only when a loaded sled hits deep overflow: **"Hike, Trapper, hike!"**

That stern command, coupled with his own fear, bestowed wondrous strength to his already powerful legs. As if he were in harness, Trapper lowered his head, dug his claws into the soft ice, and pulled.

The single tremendous thrust heaved me halfway out of the water, farther than I had been able to get on my own. Realizing I was holding him back, close to that deathly hole, Trapper turned halfway around and began sobbing.

There was no time for pep talk. I eased my grip on his tail momentarily. Thinking he was free, he started off again. Again I clamped down on his tail, again I roared, "Hike!" and again a huge pull brought me almost free of the water. I let go of his tail. He could help me no more, and his weight was a hindrance. He was off like a shot, leaving me to scud along on my belly until the ice became more solid. Then I crawled ashore.

After pouring about two gallons of water from each boot, I set off at a brisk pace. It was six o'clock and almost dark, but within a mile I was moderately warm from the rapid march—particularly from the rough part going around the last lake—and after one more mile I was home. With Trapper.

Good old Trapper. He dearly loves to be a hero—as long as it doesn't threaten his own health. It's kind of nice to know that I pulled Trapper out and he pulled me out. He had saved my life. Of course, he didn't do it on purpose; after all, he is a coward.

A heroic coward.

Chapter 29

CHERNOFSKI SHEEP RANCH

April 1985

By Cora Holmes

When I married Milton Holmes in 1980 and brought my two sons to live on the Chernofski Sheep Ranch on the remote Aleutian Island of Unalaska, it was a whole new way of life for us—and for Milt, too, for he had already reared two sons. Instead of the small farm in Idaho that we had known, Chuck, 16, and Randy, 12, suddenly had 152,000 acres to explore.

We chose our own horses from the ten saddle horses on the ranch. We didn't know what it meant to have a close personal relationship with a horse. Both boys chose mounts that Milt had got in a horse trade. Randy picked a big, rawboned sorrel named George, and Chuck took a placid-looking animal called Gray. Milt chose mine, a huge gelding that he had broken himself from the wild bunch on the west end of the island. Since the early days of the ranch, there have been wild horses on the west end, about 100 now, all descended from one Morgan stallion and a small band of mares.

I have fallen from and been bucked off that horse countless times. I've cursed and cajoled him. I've dragged him through bog holes, and I've got him stuck in the mud.

When we first started going on long rides, the boys argued about who would stay back with Mom in case she had to get off her horse, because I could never get back on by myself.

Milt has lived here permanently since 1960, and he has owned the ranch since 1964, and he must have wondered at the advisability of marrying such a greenhorn. He first came to Chernofski in 1949 to manage the sheep ranch for The Alaska Livestock and Trading Company. At that time the ranch was owned by the Bishop family, who also owned the Oregon Worsted Woolen Mills in Portland, Oregon. The ranch itself, operating since the 1920s, was

Classic Covers

1935-2002

January 1935

April 1935

December 1936

February 1937

August 1938

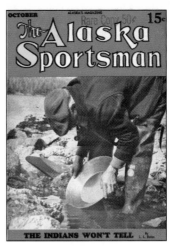

October 1938

April 1939

July 1939

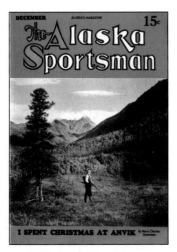

December 1940

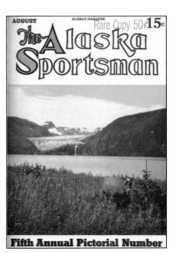

August 1941

April 1942

June 1943

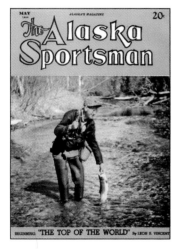

May 1944

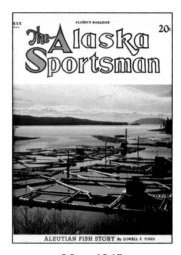

May 1945

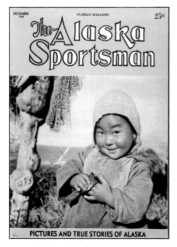

December 1946

December 1948

May 1949

September 1949

December 1949

October 1950

December 1950

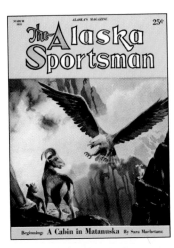

March 1951

July 1951

May 1952

October 1952

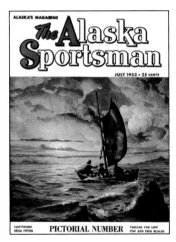

July 1953

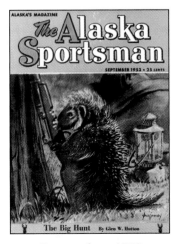

September 1953

December 1953

May 1954

February 1955

March 1955

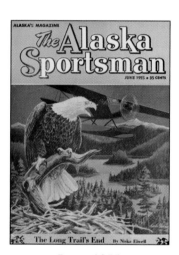

June 1955

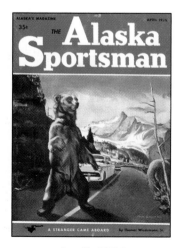

April 1956

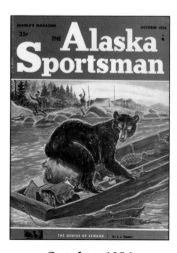

October 1956

December 1956

November 1957

December 1957

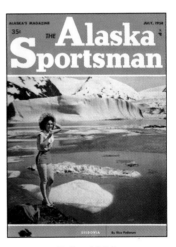

July 1958

November 1958

June 1959

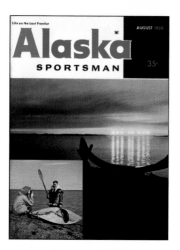

August 1959

August 1960

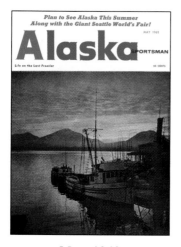

May 1962

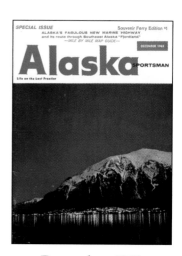

December 1962

June 1964

January 1965

February 1966

February 1967

January 1968

June 1968

October 1968

February 1969

July 1969

September 1969

October 1969

May 1970

October 1970

December 1970

January 1971

April 1971

March 1973

March 1974

March 1975

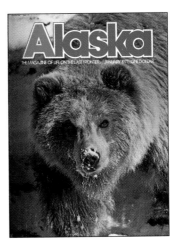

January 1977

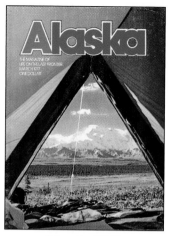

March 1977

September 1978

April 1979

August 1980

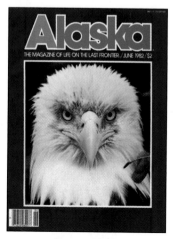

June 1982

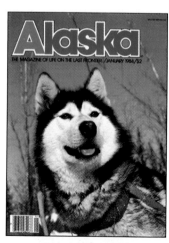

January 1984

November 1984

July 1985

November 1987

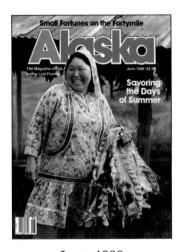

June 1988

September 1988

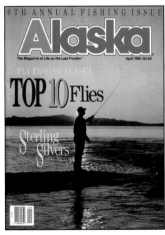

April 1990

June 1990

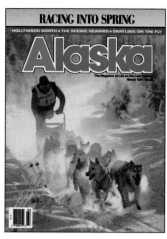

March 1991

May 1991

July 1991

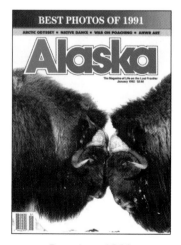

January 1992

July 1992

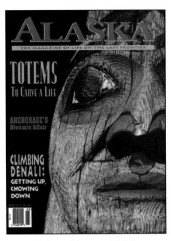

May/June 1994

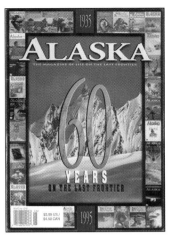

May/June 1995

May/June 1996

September 1996

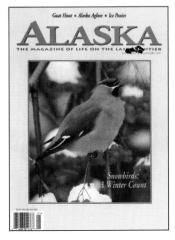

December 1996/January 1997

August 1997

November 1999

April 2001

July 2001

September 2001

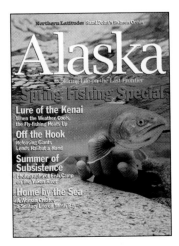

April 2002

February 2002

originally called the Aleutian Livestock Company and was started by a Scot named McIntosh.

My first year on the ranch was full of surprises, not all pleasant. I watched son Randy spread-eagled on a cliffside, chalky faced and terrified, struggling to reach his brother's outstretched hand to be pulled to safety. I saw Milt's horse fall on him, and helplessly watched as he slid into the icy water of the bay, hitting the marine ways when he went under. He had two broken ribs that time, and I was the only medical help. I nearly packed my bags and left after watching Milt and Chuck scramble for their lives when, in a storm, the skipper of a boat misjudged his landing at the derelict military dock they were standing on, waiting to tie catch-up lines. I had to learn to live with constant risk, and it was hard.

We learned to do without much electricity. Diesel generators provide power for shearing the sheep, and for battery charging. Our house is big and comfortable, heated by coal and lighted by kerosene. There are no roads, cars, stores, or television.

The single-side-band radio became our only link with the outside world. Peggy Dyson of Kodiak who, by radio, provides weather and messages for fisherman and others over the vast and stormy North Pacific, gave us the evening weather report, which replaced the news. Fishing boat skippers and crews became familiar friends.

Right outside our front door is a great marine highway. Although we are 80 miles from the nearest village, and we reside amidst 200 square miles of grazing land, we are not lonely because of the Bering Sea fishing fleet. We owe them a huge debt of gratitude. Boats are the only way we get or send mail and supplies. Since the monthly mail plane service was discontinued in 1977, the ranch relies completely on the courtesy of fishermen for mail. I have been here four years, and the longest we have gone without mail was ten weeks—which happened during the no-fishing time between tanner crab and salmon seasons.

There is no airstrip here, and chartering the amphibious Grumman Goose that is stationed at the nearest settlement, Dutch Harbor, is very expensive, so boats also provide our transportation. We go to town very seldom, and then only for medical emergencies or urgent business—like four letters from the IRS in one mail drop.

Once, returning from a medical trip to 800-mile-distant Anchorage, I spent 26 hours on a fishing boat that did not have a functional bathroom. I didn't find this out until I had drunk five cups of coffee and went looking. I have been meaning to write Dow Chemical to tell them I have invented a new use for their Zip-loc baggies.

The biggest adjustment we had to make was for schooling. We managed by taking it by correspondence with an excellent program from Juneau. Chuck finished high school and received his diploma last spring, and now has a job in Dillingham, Alaska. He already had his basics from public school, so it wasn't hard for him.

I have been teaching Randy since fourth grade, and it is a struggle. Instead of hurrying to get him off to school by eight a.m. so I can put up my feet and relax with a second cup of coffee, I have to jump up from the table and get the dishes done while he milks the cow and feeds the chickens. At first I didn't think it was going to be difficult, until I tried to teach Randy how to conjugate verbs.

After what I thought was a precise and understandable explanation of past, present, and future tense, I asked him to write a sentence for me using the past tense of the verb "fly."

He wrote, "The fly died."

I decided there was more to teaching than simply ringing the bell.

We try to have class daily, but it isn't always possible. When ranch activities interfere, we schedule class in the evening or on weekends, or do double lessons. When Randy discovered that Attila the Hun was short and mean, he decided that would be a good nickname for me.

During class time I spin wool. It is a mindless, pleasurable task that leaves me free to concentrate on what Randy is doing. I force myself to correct every assignment as he finishes it, so I can catch mistakes as he makes them. The fact that he and I are still on speaking terms is a testimonial to the quality of our program.

Our livestock year is broken into segments. Spring and summer are mainly filled with working with our flock of about 500 sheep. In 1950 Milt started bringing in Columbia bucks to cross with Romney ewes. Now all our sheep are Columbia, chosen because they produce a good medium grade (54–60) fleece, three-to-four inch staple, are very good mothers and throw an excellent mutton lamb. Being for the most part an open-face sheep, they don't have a problem with wool blindness. They thrive on the wild grasses, lichens, mosses and seaweed of the island, grazing year-round and congregating on the beaches for salt and kelp when the winters are rough.

The biggest lamb killer is cold, wet weather. Foxes and eagles kill lambs, but that toll is nothing compared with the effects of a hard spring storm.

Lambing ideally starts in May, the bucks being put in with the ewes in December. We usually get a few lambs before that, from bucks that have been missed in the roundup.

Last April while on an outing we found an old ewe down. She was trying to give birth and was having a tough time of it. Milt pulled the lamb, and we tried to get the ewe to her feet, but she was too weak to stand. By her earmark, she was more than 11 years old, a real grandmother to be having a lamb. It was a big buck lamb, too. I rubbed him off with dry grass and pumped him on his chest a couple of times. He made a little bleating sound, and the ewe answered. It was love at first sight, but she had nothing for him. Since I am a nurse, my impulse was to interfere.

"Please, Milt, let me take him home and raise him."

I could see him calculating the cans of evaporated milk it would take before that lamb would be on grass.

"Honey, it's a lot of work, and he'll probably die anyway." Milt was very reluctant.

I persevered, and he gave in. We decided to take the ewe also and see whether we could get her back on her feet, because she acted like such a good mother. The boys helped to carry the ewe over the slippery rocks to the boat.

We named the lamb Bummer. He loved canned milk. His mother got better and could stagger around the yard. The boys brought her fresh seaweed to eat. She wouldn't touch grain, not knowing what it was. We put a little plastic coat on the lamb to protect him from the cold. When he stood up against the wind he would have to run to keep up with his coat. He very nearly became the first hang-gliding lamb in history when he turned his tail into a big gust. Everyone enjoyed watching his antics.

We had him three days, and I found him dead in his pen one morning. His mother had rolled on him and smothered him during the night. Milt gallantly refrained from saying, "I told you so."

When the lambs are a month old and big enough to drive, we bring all the sheep in for shearing and tail-docking. It is a slow process, as we no longer hire any outside help. Milt shears 50 to 60 sheep a day. Randy is learning and can manage 12 to 14 head. I used to try to shear, and in a good day once managed 12. When I was shearing, the barn would ring with cries of, "Mom's sheep is loose." So I gave up and now tie fleeces, fill pens and pull Milt's sheep out of the pen for him. Last spring Milt had his second total hip-joint surgery—and he says the "store-boughts" don't work so well as the real thing.

Shearing takes all of June and sometimes part of July, depending upon how much rain we get, for the sheep must be dry before shearing. In October the Bureau of Indian Affairs boat *North Star III* picks up our wool. From Seattle it is shipped to the Santee Woolen Mills in South Carolina. I save 20 or so fleeces for myself, including all the black and gray ones. Sometimes we sell a few fleeces to local hand-spinners.

With our sheep, everything is used but the bleat. We slaughter for both mutton and lamb for a small local market, and for the big Bering Sea fishing boats, and get most of our own meat from the sheep. Each sheep produces an average of 10 pounds of fleece yearly for about 12 years. A fleece will yield four to six pounds of medium-weight yarn for mittens, caps, and sweaters. The bulk of my handspun wool I use for rug making or weave into wall hangings. The hides are sold or tanned for rugs or vests. The feet and heads of the slaughtered sheep make bait for Randy's fox traps.

Milt has gradually built up the cattle herd from 50 animals he had shipped from Kodiak Island, plus a small herd that had been raised here for beef and dairy use. For the last three years, our calf increase has been more than 100. Winters have been mild, and it takes a lot more to kill a calf than to kill a lamb.

The cattle round-up and butchering take up the late summer and fall months. We spent 23 days last summer riding and working about 500 head of Hereford and black bald-face stock. Everything we can find is driven into ranch headquarters for counting, cutting, dehorning, and earmarking.

The cattle graze year-round over a large part of Unalaska Island. We ride horseback for 35 to 40 miles a day, spending as much as 16 hours in the saddle if the stock is badly scattered. There are six line cabins spaced along the range at intervals, but we do not always manage to reach one by nightfall and sometimes have to do with a driftwood shelter on the beach. I have lain under a tarpaulin many times, listening to the wind and rain, wondering whether my horse is going to get loose and step on me.

Most of the terrain of our grazing lease is gentle, grassy slopes, but there are some wicked ridges that nearly bisect the island and cannot be avoided, and several large, boggy swamps we must cross.

The nicest thing you can say about our weather is that it is unpredictable. Sometimes the sun shines, the sky is clear, the hills are covered with beautiful wildflowers, the birds sing and the sea is a placid blue mirror. We can usually count on one such day a year.

At the other extreme, we are compelled to wear a full set of rain gear. Vision narrows to horse's head and saddle horn. Wind drives rain into us with such ferocity that the horses won't walk into it. Most of the time, however, we get just enough rain to make rain gear necessary, enough wind to be chilly, and in between squalls, enough sunshine to make it hot and sweaty under the rain gear.

Fog is the worst weather hazard on our horseback trips. During the summer, warm Pacific Ocean water meets cool Bering Sea water in Umnak Pass, and the result is heavy, low-lying fog. Milt once got off his horse to help some sheep out of a gully. The fog lowered and he couldn't find his horse again. He had to spend the night out with no preparation, huddling against his sheep dogs for warmth. Aleutian weather cannot be taken lightly, even in summer.

Randy's horse, George, comes into his own on our cattle rides. He is a horse who believes in helping and does so by biting anything in his direct line of vision. This keeps the stragglers moving. When he lays his ears back so close to his head that he looks like a snake, you know he is planning something—either biting you on the leg, or your horse on the neck. Maybe he is just trying to lessen his wind resistance, but I never take a chance. I always stay behind him. Many nights we have ridden home in the rain to the music of George's teeth clicking with near-misses as he snapped at something or someone.

Besides being ungainly, clumsy-footed and cross-tempered, he has the bad habit of taking off at a gallop the minute Randy's foot gets into the stirrup. He has more problems with saddle sores than any of our other horses. The cinch strap has to be so loose that balancing the saddle on his back becomes a feat of considerable skill. It no longer surprises me to be trotting along behind Randy and see his head suddenly replaced by his foot as he follows the saddle over the side.

George's worst habit is running off when Randy gets off and drops the reins. Every other horse we own will stand patiently when the reins are dropped.

Not George. Even the quickest call of nature must be accomplished with reins firmly in hand. Randy cannot seem to remember this. George doesn't run off all at once, either. First he walks just fast enough so Randy can't grab the reins. When Randy starts to jog, George trots. Then, when Randy starts running, George gallops, and even if Randy has sworn a thousand times never to do it again, he finds himself chasing a galloping horse on foot. I can't count the times I've seen Randy chase that horse, accompanied by such diverse comments as, "George, you mule, you come back here!" Or, "George, I'm going to kill you!" Randy has George to thank for the quickest reflexes and the finest pair of lungs in the Aleutians.

By late November we butcher beef and mutton for a small local market, and we then come up against the biggest obstacle in Aleutian livestock raising. There is no affordable transportation. We depend upon obliging fishermen to get our beef to town, where Milt's son Stanley sees that it is delivered. Our slaughterhouse will chill and hold 14 beef at a time. The three of us can butcher a beef and dress it into quarters in about two hours. We kill steers two and four years old. Anything older than that is sold to the crab-fishing boats for use as bait.

A few years ago, when the herd was smaller, the 20 to 25 steers that sold locally were enough to utilize all the mature steers. Now that we can sell 75 animals a year, we find transportation out of our reach. Chartering a fishing boat during the height of crab season is impossible, and chartering a refrigerated freight boat is financial suicide.

For the last 30 years this ranch has grown and prospered because it had a hard-working, in-residence owner, a reasonably priced Bureau of Land Management grazing lease, and enough different sources of income to keep it self supporting. We have never had any government funding or grants.

Now we are facing extinction. The grazing land has all been conveyed to the Tanadgusix Native Corporation and the U.S. Fish and Wildlife Service. Our lease expired December 31, 1983, and a new lease has not been negotiated. The ranch headquarters is on five deeded acres, so we will continue to have our home.

When I walk along the beach here, surrounded by simple, primitive beauty, my love for this island becomes an intense physical thing. I hope that the Chernofski Sheep Ranch won't become just another fog-shrouded Aleutian memory.

Chapter 30

ABERCROMBIE'S BARROW BALLET

December 1985

By Robert H. Redding

In January 1956 I went to work for Puget Sound and Drake as a supply expeditor. PS&D was the chief subcontractor engaged in construction of the Distant Early Warning line, which was a series of radar stations in northern Alaska and Canada. The DEW line was built to serve as an advance alarm system in case of surprise air attack from the west.

I flew from Fairbanks to Barrow aboard a Douglas DC-3 and immediately stepped into a different world. Fairbanks was a lively town of grocery stores, automobiles, taverns, women, movies and 50 below zero. The only thing Barrow Camp, as the construction camp was called, and Fairbanks had in common was the 50 below.

To suggest we had none of the amenities of Fairbanks isn't fair; We did, but there were differences. At the camp theater, movies were shown every Saturday night. While the film was likely to be a moldy flicker-flashback, it was better than nothing and offered the men a way to get out of their bunkhouses for a couple of hours. Nearly all of the camp buildings, including the movie house, were Quonset huts of various sizes. The movie was free, but we were expected to drop a few coins in a box to reimburse the volunteer projectionist, who also was a PS&D employee.

If we didn't have supermarkets, we did have a company store that stocked such necessities as shaving materials, tobacco (and the Copenhagen better be fresh), candy, work clothes, magazines and stationery. A man also could purchase beer at the store on Saturday evening. Each customer was allowed two six-packs a week, no more. Those who didn't drink gave their ration to those who did, so few complaints were heard.

There were no automobiles, except for company pickups. However, we did have "weasels" (tracked vehicles). Occasionally, the men were allowed to take a weasel into the village of Barrow, four miles from camp, for a bit of sightseeing. Weasels could traverse the snow-drifted trail without problems. There was never, during the construction phase of the DEW line, a regular road to the village. Each time a vehicle went in, the driver made his own trail along the shore of the Arctic Ocean.

At the height of construction, there were about 2,000 men employed by PS&D on the American sector of the DEW line. In Barrow camp there were 800 men, who were building what was known as POW Main, and in addition to the human population, there were four dogs in camp.

These were the most fortunate pooches in the Arctic. There scarcely was a man leaving the mess hall after a meal who didn't save a tidbit to feed the animals waiting by the door. The four canines were Susie, an old vamp with long, sharp ears and a bushy tail, whose winning ways brought a smile to the most reluctant face; her companion, Bruce, a young husky with a deep chest and bright eyes; Rags, a half-grown pup with feet as big as snowshoes, whose awkward leaps for goodies thrown into the air were always good for chuckles; and Abercrombie.

Nobody knew how Abber, short for Abercrombie, got his name. He should never have set foot north of the Mason-Dixon line, because he was short haired and felt the extreme cold. He had a long body fitted on short, stumpy legs and his ears were floppy and notched from many fights.

In spite of his smallish size, Abber was absolutely fearless. He took on dogs twice his size and weight, which was remarkable, because Abber was totally blind. He couldn't see a flaming blowtorch inches away. He fought by sidling up to his enemy, touching him and then waiting for him to make the first move. The enemy usually was a strange dog from the village. Abber's sensory perceptions were so finely tuned that when the enemy made his move, Abber countered to his own advantage. He had huge incisors, and nobody ever saw him lose a fight.

Abber had an addiction, which was candy. So did the other three camp dogs, and the men, knowing this, bought them sweets at the company store. Maybe this was not good for the animals, but the men were lavishly generous. They liked the dogs and were concerned about them, making sure each was bedded down in a warm place at night. Abber usually roomed with Otto Lombardo, an old Arctic hand who called the dog "Kid."

When one of the dogs sickened, the men worried. I saw tough mechanics, with knuckles cracked open and raw from working in the cold, cradle a stricken dog gently and tell it that all was going to be well. The camp doctor was fetched and medicines purchased. A sick dog was fussed over until he was functioning well on all four feet once again.

Saturday night, however, was the biggest night for the dogs. That was when they received a feast of sweets. Saturday, being movie night, always brought a full house. It didn't matter that the flick was old. Who cared? Most of the men were not movie-goers "Outside," as Fairbanks was called. Whatever they saw was new to them. They arrived at the theater with their pockets filled with rolls of Lifesavers purchased at the store. The dogs were allowed entry, and they climbed at once up the steps to the stage. They knew exactly what was coming, and they watched the audience eagerly.

About 15 minutes before the show started, the rolls of Lifesavers were broken open and the contents thrown on the stage. It was then that Abercrombie's ballet began. It received its name because Abber had been the first of the performers. The other dogs joined the troupe later.

Though Abber couldn't see, he could hear a pin drop in a raging gale. It was he who led the way in the mad chase for the delicious Lifesavers. Around and around the stage the dogs raced, dashing after the candies. Up they leaped, down they dipped. They twisted on their hind feet, pirouetted, dove and slid, until the whole ensemble seemed to be dancing. It was a wild and woolly ballet, created with such joy and clumsy grace that it never failed to amuse its spectators. I worked in the store sometimes during the evenings, and once sold $35 worth of Lifesavers in less than an hour's time.

Lights out signaled that the movie was about to begin. As the silver screen lit up, the dogs filed off the stage one by one. They curled up in corners and snoozed, while their human benefactors either remained silent or hooted, depending on how well the picture was received.

The next Saturday night, Abercrombie's Barrow ballet would be repeated. It didn't matter that outside the Quonset's wall, 50-below-zero temperatures sucked the moisture out of the air. We would think about that tomorrow. For now we watched a great performance that amused both man and beast.

Chapter 31

A MELODY FOR CHRISTMAS

December 1987

By Afton Blanc

When Theresa Jack looked at me and asked, "Will you teach me?" I was silent; I didn't know how to answer her.

She waited a moment and then said, "When Christmas comes, I want very much to play the organ at church. Everyone wants very much to sing the carols on Christmas Eve." And she asked again, "Will you teach me how I can play the organ for them?"

I looked at my friend while I tried to find the right words. I was a language arts teacher in an Eskimo village school, and my musical ability was limited to one-finger plunking.

While I pondered what to say to Theresa, I thought how trusting she was—how confident that one would help another. Helping one another was their tradition; this is why the Bering Sea Eskimos have survived over the centuries. Now one of them was asking me for help, and she expected help in the simplest way and in the least complex terms. How could I tell Theresa that in order to play the organ she would have to study books, diagrams and charts. She would need an understanding of notations, scores, rhythm, timing and treble and bass clefs. How could I explain that she needed a real music teacher and that it would take years of practice to play the organ? Besides, I wondered, why was she asking anyway. There wasn't an organ or a piano anywhere in the village.

"Theresa," I answered. "I—well, I want to—but there isn't even—"
"Eiyee," she said, nodding her head. Her face brightened, and her eyes sparkled in a secretive way. "Come with me, I will show you." She took my hand.

We were in her small plywood house that had only a porch and two small rooms. One room was sleeping quarters for the family. The other room—the one we were in—was for cooking, storage, eating, preparing the seal, ptarmigan and walrus, and for visiting and sipping tea. She led me to the back wall partitioned off with a curtain made of several wolf hides, hanging from twine tied to nails in the ceiling. Carefully, she parted the curtain and held back a large silver-tipped wolf skin to let me pass by.

"Look," she whispered.

I caught my breath. Against the wall was an electric organ, its plastic gleaming and its polished panels of imitation wood shining.

That was in 1967, when life was still primitive in most Bering Sea communities. This village had received electricity only that year. Most of the villagers had never visited another town or city, they had never ridden in an automobile, eaten a banana split, or talked on the telephone. But they all had mail order catalogs where they looked at marvelous pictures and dreamed of the wondrous things on the pages of those books.

For years, Theresa had looked longingly through the catalogs and her eyes always stopped on one page. Her heart yearned for only one thing on that page—an electric organ.

Now, because there was electricity in the village and because there was music in Theresa's soul, her husband had ordered an electric organ for her.

"It came to me yesterday by the airplane," she said, "and Louie fixed for me this music room and hooked up to the electricity."

The "music room" behind the wolf hides was just large enough for the small organ and for two butter barrels to stand on end. The organ was "hooked up" with a cord running from the back of it to a bare light bulb in the double socket hanging above. Theresa dropped the wolf hide, sat down on one of the barrels and motioned for me to sit on the other.

She switched on the power and held her fingers above the keyboard. Then she straightened her back, lifted her head, closed her eyes and touched her hands to the keys. A harmony of sounds filled the little niche we were in. Then, opening her eyes, she touched each key singly—pressing, holding and releasing—as her fingers lingered at first, then flew up and down on both the white and black keys. Each key, pressed at random, played a melody never heard before. But as I listened, I realized there was music in Theresa's soul and music in her hands.

She stopped playing and turned to me. "Now, " she said, "you will teach me. Tell me what names are the keys called."

She opened the hymn book she had brought from the church and pointed to the score. "Tell me where do these notes go to the keys, tell me how to play the right keys to what it says in the book."

I looked into her face, which was lighted from above by the glaring bulb. In her eyes was an expression of natural trust, a confidence that assured her I would help.

"You will give me the lessons," she handed the manual that came with the organ, "and I will pay you for each one." She turned around and reached for a bundle of feathers on the floor.

"Here is for my first lesson," she said, as she gave me a freshly killed goose. "Come tomorrow after school. I will have tea ready."

I walked back to the teachers' quarters in a daze. Theresa believed I could teach her to play the organ, and I felt so helpless. I had only tonight to read the manual and to prepare her first lesson.

On my kitchen table, I spread out large sheets of poster board, felt-tip markers, a yardstick, the organ manual and some basic music books I had checked out from the school. She wanted to know names, so I started there.

The next day, as we sat side by side on the butter barrels, Theresa played the keys, singing their names as I pointed to the notes on the large poster board propped up on the organ.

"SEE, DEE, EEE, EFF, GEE, AYEE, BEE, SEE," she intoned in her soft voice over and over, up and down the scale. Then we went to the bass clef with the left hand.

"I will practice tonight," she explained. "Come again tomorrow for the next lesson," she said. "Louie is out hunting for ptarmigan. We will pay you every day."

And so it went. I sat up late each night, making charts and learning musical notations as I tried to keep ahead of her. Every day Theresa waited for me behind the wolf-skin curtain, eager for the next lesson. Each day she played or sang what she had learned the day before. Then she began putting combinations of notes together and surprised me with her innovation. Once she played a familiar hymn.

"Eiyee, how can I do that?" she asked. "How can I play the music without seeing the notes in the book?"

I told her that many people had the talent to play a keyboard "by ear," which meant they could feel the music and could interpret it on an instrument without knowing what the notes were.

I sighed and relaxed, thinking our lessons were done now that she had revealed this natural musical ability.

But she said, "Oh, I must know what the notes are. When I go to the church with my organ on Christmas Eve, I want to very much put the book on the organ, open it up and turn the pages, then play the notes for everyone to sing." She never again played by ear, except to pick out a melody line or to play along with someone singing a new tune.

As the daily lessons proceeded, she soon went beyond my musical understanding. But she still needed me by her side, listening, approving, correcting, and talking to her about musicians, composers, concerts and great musical works.

Once during a lesson, the village generator stopped and there was no electricity for a couple of days. Everyone in the village frantically ran here and there trying to keep water pipes from freezing and oil-fired heaters going. Theresa sat at her silent organ and played tunes she couldn't hear as she continued to practice. Our daily sessions continued.

The week before Christmas our lessons were over. As I sat beside her on the butter barrel, I marveled at what she had accomplished. She was radiant when I said her music was as grand as any I had ever heard in any concert hall. And truly, it was. I looked around me at the curtain of wolf hides, the bare light bulb in its double socket, the worn hymn book, the diminutive keyboard, and Theresa's delicate hands touching the keys with such intensity.

I was proud of her, and yes, I was proud of myself. We both had accomplished much more than we ever thought possible. My moment of triumph was then and there, but Theresa's was yet to come.

On Christmas Eve she was ready.

Louie took the organ to the church early in the day and hooked it up to the electricity. Theresa spent an hour or two practicing. The villagers waited expectantly in their homes for the evening service to begin. That night an organ would play in their village. The miracle of electricity and the wonder of Theresa's music would bring this gift to the village.

It was time, and the Eskimo families came, walking to the church from every direction with flashlights and lanterns. Theresa was at the organ playing a prelude as we all filed through the door and took our seats.

She was beautiful, dressed in her finest ankle-length *kuspuk,* her black hair shining, her face serene. Gone was the butter barrel and the bare light bulb. She sat on a round stool, and there was a lamp mounted on the organ to light her hymn book.

The minister began the services with a scripture reading, reciting first in Eskimo, then in English. When he read the words ". . . and there was a multitude of heavenly hosts praising God and singing . . ." resounding chords from the organ rolled through the church and echoed from wall to wall.

Everyone opened a hymn book to the carols. Theresa, turning the pages of her own book, lifted her head and once more placed her fingers on the keyboard.

But at that instant, darkness enveloped the church. The generator had stopped.

The first note of the carol dropped off in a low moan.

Here and there flashlights snapped on, but no one moved. I could barely see Theresa's form at the electric organ. My heart was breaking as I left my seat to go to her.

"Eiyee," she cried when I reached her side. Then she whispered, "Give me your light. Prop it up so it shines on the book."

By now, the church was softly lit, and everyone could see Theresa at the organ. She turned to the congregation, her voice rang out, "Hark, the herald angels sing . . ." and her fingers moved over the keyboard touching every key for every note. One by one the voices in the congregation joined in, while Theresa played the silent keys.

I left the church and walked into the night. As I turned to look back at the star-like sparkle of the flashlights through the windows, I listened to the voices— Theresa's above the rest—and I heard the organ playing.

Chapter 32

MT. McKINLEY JOE

November 1989

By Elizabeth J. Fallon

In a small alcove off the main observation room in Eielson Visitor Center in Denali National Park and Preserve is a memorial to one of America's "little men."

His name was Joe, and he was a naturalized American citizen who had worked at hard manual labor for little pay most of his life. He won no state lotteries or sweepstakes before he died in 1975, yet he left to the National Park Foundation the largest single bequest ever received by this nonprofit foundation.

The money came from careful economies, prudent investment and a dedication to the national park system, particularly Mount McKinley. It was a gift from a man who always returned a favor.

I still remember vividly the first time I met Joe. It was the summer of 1965, and I was perched precariously near the top of a spindly spruce tree trying to attach a radio antenna when I was startled to hear a strange voice shouting at me.

"It won't work. The mountain is in the way. You better come down here before you kill yourself."

I grabbed frantically for a firmer hold and glanced below me, where I saw an old man dressed in oversized bib overalls, some dirty, white insulated underwear and a worn out, quilted jacket. His high-topped sneakers had no laces, and his navy blue, fisherman's knitted cap covered stubby white hair. Even from my perch overhead I could tell he wasn't very tall, probably 5-foot-4 at best, and he hadn't bothered to shave for several days.

Since I was secretly more than delighted to take *anyone's* advice who told me to climb down, I hurried to do so. Once on the ground I took a closer look at my uninvited guest. He still looked unkempt, but the ruddiness of his cheeks, the blueness of his eyes and the merry twinkle in them gave me the fleeting impression that I was looking at a wilderness Santa Claus.

A hand was thrust at me to shake. "I'm Joe Hankins," he said. "Your husband shouldn't have asked you to do such a dangerous job."

I had to smile then, since climbing the tree had been entirely my idea. I shook his hand vigorously and asked, "What do you do besides protect ladies in distress?"

He laughed and replied simply, "I enjoy the park."

And no sentence summed up the man's life more completely than that remark. Joe lived for the Denali National Park and its natural inhabitants. He had already been spending his summers near Mount McKinley for nine years by the time I met him in 1965 and was considered by many to be an essential part of the scenery. He arrived in May and stayed until Labor Day, living out of his old panel truck and a small shack at Igloo Creek campground.

While in the park, Joe had a well-established routine. He would get up between two and three every morning, and, if the weather was good, he would drive several miles down the road, park in a turn-off just before the first Toklat River bridge and hike into the mountains in search of Dall sheep. Joe loved all the animals and enjoyed watching them, but the sheep were his special joy.

If the weather was not good, which is often the case near Mount McKinley in the summer, he would take a walk around the vicinity of the campground and then get on the tour bus when it arrived at Igloo Creek around 6 a.m.

He would ride on the bus to Eielson Visitor Center, talking to the tourists and showing them his collection of animal pictures that he had taken over the years. And they were pictures well worth seeing. Joe had an old Leica camera with a couple of telephoto lenses, and he had wonderful shots of almost all the park's mammals and birds.

Since Joe's unkempt appearance surely startled the tourists, I suspect the tour bus drivers were careful to prepare their passengers before Joe shuffled aboard with his unlaced sneakers and ratty Eddie Bauer jacket. Joe was well aware of the initial impression he made, and I came to believe it was deliberate. One day I went over to the campground to give him some fresh biscuits I'd just taken out of the oven, and I discovered him reading *The Wall Street Journal*. I guess my amazement must have shown, because he grinned at me and said, "You'd never suspect a bum-looking guy like me would be reading such high-class stuff, would you? I fool lots of people." I am quite certain I blushed.

As our friendship grew, I discovered many amazing facts about Joe. He had been born in Russia and raised in Argentina. He homesteaded in Canada and then eventually moved to the United States, where he became a citizen. He worked many years as a logger—another surprise for me. "I bet you thought all lumberjacks were as big as Paul Bunyan, didn't you?" he asked me with that merry twinkle in his eye.

On another occasion while we were resting on the top of a mountain near some grazing Dall sheep rams, I heard Joe chuckle as he spotted the tour buses passing far below us.

"If I was on that bus right now, some lady would be trying to give me a tip for showing her my pictures. They all think I'm poor. Wouldn't they be surprised if they really knew how much money I had? I bought IBM stock when they were practically giving it away." Knowing Joe's honesty, I just grinned back.

I learned early that Joe operated on a set of absolutes. Actions were either right or wrong, never justifiable under the circumstances. He judged a person quickly, and if he found you wanting, he put little energy into being polite.

Among Joe's unalterable rules were: You always repay a favor. If I gave Joe some food, he would soon be at my door with a return. His returns were almost always leftover box lunches from the tour bus that the driver gave Joe when he rode the bus. Joe accepted the lunches as just recompense for his services as a tour guide. He ate them all the time, but I came to dread his arrival at the door with another box lunch under his arm.

In addition to the axiom that a favor is always returned, Joe also operated on the theory that you earned privileges; you never just received them because of your name or rank. He didn't care whether you were superintendent of the park or a summer employee—if you didn't know how to behave when out on a hike, you never *never* got the privilege of hiking to "ram country" with Joe. And standards were strict. You never, *never* left any trash, no matter how insignificant. You never, *never* disturbed the animals or their habitat in the interest of getting a better picture or because you were excited. You never hurried anywhere in the park, and you never, *never* walked in front of Joe. This last dictum was particularly hard on my husband, who was much younger and longer legged than Joe and found it difficult to keep to Joe's slow shuffle. I, on the other hand, rather liked hiking with Joe because of that slow gait!

If we discovered rams once we reached the top of the mountain, no one was allowed to approach the rams unless Joe gave the OK. I took many trips to ram country with Joe, and I firmly believe that the rams considered Joe a harmless part of the scenery. They seldom moved out of his way or stopped what they were doing when he arrived. Joe always carried his camera and tripod, and occasionally took a picture or two, but mostly he just came to watch and enjoy.

While Joe's favorite animals were the Dall sheep, he respected all the animals in the park and once he gave me a severe scolding for feeding the ground squirrels who were living under the ranger cabin. "Don't you know, you are reducing their natural defenses when you feed them? They won't learn how to cope for themselves and are easier prey for predators." I stopped feeding the squirrels.

Several weeks later I stopped at Joe's campsite to find him, hands on hips, glaring up into a tree.

"What's the matter, Joe?" I asked.

"That dratted red squirrel has stolen all the prunes I stewed and left out on the picnic table to cool."

I looked up to see a squirrel halfway up a nearby tree, holding the last of Joe's prunes. "Shame on you, Joe, for feeding the animals," I said, unable to resist after the lecture I had received earlier.

The next day when I was hurrying up the little hill behind the ranger cabin to use the outhouse, I was chagrined to see a red squirrel struggling down the hill toward me with the entire roll of toilet paper.

I heard a chuckle behind me. "Bet that's the same squirrel that ate all my prunes," Joe said. "He needs that toilet paper more than you do, I bet!"

The park with its magnificent tundra-mountain scenery and abundant collection of animals was truly Joe's spiritual home. He belonged there and lived for the months spent in the park. Although he came to be near the animals, he also relished the stir he caused among the tourists, enjoying his special status.

In the park Joe was *somebody*. Letters addressed to Joe, Mount McKinley Park (the former name for Denali National Park) were promptly delivered to him. Important visitors to the park often came by Igloo Creek campground to meet Joe, who had great fun looking suitably unimpressed with everyone from U. S. senators to famous scientists, writers and photographers. He made many friends and carried on a large correspondence with people all over the world.

Joe sent out several hundred Christmas cards every year, always adorned with a picture from the park.

I was Joe's neighbor in the park for only two years, and then my adventurous spirit took me to other parts of the world for a couple of years. When I returned to Alaska in 1968, I hurried to the park to check in with Joe. He greeted me as if he had been expecting me that very day. I camped next to him, and we hiked together for a few days. I noticed the shuffling walk was slower and the eyesight worse, but the spirit was diminished in no way.

"I love this park," he told me, "and when I die I am leaving all my money to the National Park Foundation. I want to give back some of what the park has given to me."

How could I tell him that he had already given so much? He had introduced the wonder of the park and all its residents to thousands of visitors for years. He had set an example of how to behave in a park that would be an indelible memory for dozens of people who had been fortunate to hike with him. I knew that as long as Joe came to the park, so would I, and when Joe was no longer there, something precious and irreplaceable would be gone with him.

The last summer I spent time with Joe in Denali was 1971, his last trip there. I brought my infant son to the park to meet him. Joe never commented on his health, but I knew he was finding it harder to get around and see. We laughed together that summer and shared memories. Then for the next couple of years, we were content with letters and notes.

Joe died in 1975 and, true to his word, he left his entire estate of $150,000, just as he told me he would, to the National Park Foundation. To honor Joe, the Park Service sent a uniformed park ranger to Joe's funeral in Chehalis, Wash. In visiting with John Bryant, president of the National Park Foundation, I learned that Joe's gift, put to work in the foundation's endowment fund, has more than doubled in the last 10 years. Joe has truly, many times over, repaid his debt of joy to the national park system. Bryant said that Joe reminds him of the Biblical story of the widow's mite, because he did not give a little of great possessions, but he gave all he had. To many, Joe Hankins may seem to be only a simple, hard-working laborer like millions of other Americans, but I know now that Joe was special and that my second impression of him had been right after all. He was a wilderness Santa Claus.

Chapter 33

DOG TEAM CENSUS

January 1990

By Hana Yasuda Kangas

My new boss sat behind a pin-neat desk in Fairbanks, waiting for a phone call with the answer to his question: Should we take the 1940 census by dog team or airplane?

The Juneau office had deferred the question to Washington, D.C. Arguably, an airplane could do the job in less than a week and at half the cost of dogs. While we waited for the answer, the census supervisor told me, "I'm sure it will be done by dog team; 10 years from now it will be by air." Then he added, as though reading my mind, "The dog team way is more romantic, don't you think?"

I couldn't have agreed more. I was a 24-year-old woman living in Fairbanks and attending the University of Alaska. When I first read and heard about the census, I immediately wanted to go, already certain that my college classes would wait until next fall.

The phone rang. My supervisor listened quietly and then turned to me with a smile. Juneau had received a clear directive from the nation's capital: "Use a dog team!" I was relieved that I would no longer have to hide my fear of flying or relive all those air sickness episodes.

Here was my chance to find out about my heritage. I thought of everything that I, an Alaska Native, had missed while attending school in Washington state for 10 years. I was born in the village of Beaver, but left for school when I was 8 years old. In the early 1900s, my Japanese father, Frank Yasuda, and my Eskimo mother, along with a few Eskimos, traveled from Barrow into the Interior to prospect, eventually establishing a trading post on the Yukon River near the gold fields of the Chandalar River north of Fairbanks. In a few years 15 or 20 Eskimo families had joined them, and the settlement, by then known as Beaver, became the only inland Eskimo settlement on the Yukon River.

My job with the census was to cover the region between the Brooks Range and the Yukon River. The supervisor instructed me on how to record names, birthdays, nationalities and such in the big census book. He also told me how to introduce myself and how to keep a daily time sheet.

Full of excitement, I shopped in Fairbanks for items not found in my father's general store in Beaver: Bobby pins, metal curlers, face creams, and warm gloves filled my arms while I waited for the weekly mail plane to Beaver.

Once in Beaver, I hired a driver with a team and began to accumulate the necessary gear. The first of several trips would be from Beaver to the Little Squaw gold mine in the Chandalar River gold fields in the Brooks Range. To get to the mine, we would drive the dogs on the Chandalar Road, which traveled north for 125 miles and had for years been used for freighting supplies and sledding mail to the gold miners.

In Beaver, Kavik Riley was chosen as the driver, and I began to assemble my supplies. I designed and sewed a fur mask, with slits for my eyes, with scraps of caribou skin provided by my mother. I gladly accepted the loan of her caribou parka and a pair of fur hip boots, visualizing a picture of myself swathed in fur like the early Arctic explorers. When I tried my traveling clothes over my sweaters and long johns, however, I had difficulty moving about, but I was certain I needed the fur garments to keep from freezing.

For four days the temperature hovered around 50 below zero, and we delayed our departure day after day. Finally, on November 29, with Riley on the handlebars and me straddling the loaded sled, we yelled goodbye to our families and slid out of the village.

The Alaska Road Commission had built log cabins 14 to 18 miles apart all along the Chandalar Road, so we hoped to be at the 14 Mile cabin in four hours. I remember thinking, "My, that's awfully slow."

After several miles I dug in my pockets for my fur mask and put it on. It felt good and I knew I had planned well.

About 10 miles out, we came unexpectedly to the end of the dog trail. Riley then told me people no longer used the Chandalar Road because freight and mail had been going by plane for the last six years. This might well be the last overland census, I thought.

We put on snowshoes to break trail for the dogs. With a little practice, I learned to "plop-plop" through the snow like Riley. Riley snowshoed ahead of the team and showed me how to guide the sled by maneuvering the gee-pole, a steering pole attached to the front of the sled. As he plodded out in front of the leader, I considered the layers of clothing I was wearing and wondered how and where I might find the "girl's room." It would have to wait.

With all the physical effort of snowshoeing, the furs I wore became unbearable. The caribou mask clung to my face like a soggy, smelly banana peel. I took it off my sweaty brow and threw it far from the trail.

Fortunately, in college I majored in physical education and had always been active in all sports: basketball, softball, and gymnastics. If it had not been for my good physical condition, I could never have continued that trip.

It was two more hours before we reached our destination and found the cabin already occupied. Riley said it was Nutauksiruq and his grandson, Richard, who hunted and lived away from town. They spoke only Eskimo.

My main concern was finding an outhouse. I glanced around but saw none. Nor would I see one for the rest of the trip. Riley asked the grandfather for me. The old man made a sweeping motion with his arms, and Riley said, "Anywhere."

When I returned, my hands and face pink from washing with snow, Riley handed me a tin plate of hot beans. Pilot bread, butter, and canned peaches completed the menu. Nothing could have tasted better. Within moments, we heard the screeching of sled runners and a driver yelling at his dogs. It was Moses Cruikshank and Tom Sturrock returning to Beaver from Sturrock's gold mine in Hodzana.

While the men were all outside, I rid myself of layers of steamy clothes. In my clothes bag, I found two pairs of sensible fur boots, a pair of slippers, extra socks, and some shirts—items that my mother had slipped into my bag. She knew I was not practical, from my face mask to the bulky, fur hip boots.

We shared our coffee, beans, and crackers with the two newcomers. After Moses ate, he spoke about the deep, heavy snow and the low temperatures. They were lucky to be here. Riley handed him three dried salmon for his dogs.

That night, the little 10-by-12-foot cabin meant for one or two people sheltered six.

Morning came, snappy and refreshing. I filled my lungs to clear out the stale air and watched as Moses and Tom headed south on the well-packed trail. Riley and I faced several days of breaking 100 miles of trail going north. We left some food with the old man and the boy and set out for cabin No. 24.

The temperature was lower and, in fearful anticipation, I again over-dressed. And once more, I faced the urgency of needing an outhouse while we were out on the white open spaces. No trees were in sight.

My mind wandered as I guided the slow-moving sled on the deepening snow. Less than two miles from the shelter, the sled's right runner grabbed the back tip of my snowshoe. Unable to halt the dogs, I fell forward, covered my face with my mitted hands and waited for the brake to tear up my back. Instead, the snow was so soft and deep that my body sank, pressed down by the loaded sled. My "explorer's" clothes further padded me, and I didn't get a scratch when the sled went over me.

But, oh, how humiliated I felt. I'd needed the trees two miles back, and now my pants were wet. A minute of "show and tell" and Riley understood. I found the clothes I needed and changed behind the sled.

At the cabin we threw ourselves into the chores, building two fires—one outdoors to cook dog food and one in the cabin. Riley then started off on his snowshoes to break trail for the next day's trek. As he disappeared, the dogs began howling, one by one, and the sound chilled the back of my neck.

A routine eventually emerged—arise at 4 a.m., attend to personal functions, eat breakfast, wash the tin plates and pack the food box, roll the bedding, gather belongings, leave a meal of frozen beans on the shelf for the return trip, make wood shavings to start the fire, bring wood indoors, load the sled, blow out the candles, nail the door shut, attach boards over the windows and hitch the dogs.

The next three days were dull and dreary. The sameness of the snow, the measured steps and the dragging hours created a monotonous pattern as we struggled northward through more than 3 feet of snow.

After seven days we drew near the abandoned gold rush town of Caro, named decades before for the wife of a U.S. senator. The snow was 4 feet deep. Without our snowshoes, we would have never reached Little Squaw and the seven gold miners whose names I was to enter in my census book.

Later we looked up to see a friendly wing-wave from Jim Dodson, a pilot who was descending on Little Squaw Lake with mail and supplies for the miners.

Riley smiled and pointed to the plane. "Jimmy going to land other side of mountain. You and me have two more days before we get there."

An unbelievable scene of glistening peaks against a sapphire sky overwhelmed us as we closed in on the mountains. We doffed our snowshoes, not needing them in the windswept pass. We were getting close to Chandalar and the Little Squaw gold mine, and we sensed it—even the dogs did. Within minutes we ran into a hard-packed trail, and the dogs sniffed, renewed energy sparking from their coats and tails.

The trail wound around like tiers up the side of the mountain before we came to a long log cabin that had served as a mess hall during the peak of placer gold mining in the Chandalar region. The men of the Mello family called it home.

When I was 5, my father and Manuel Mello were partners. For a year we lived near Mello's camp. Mello attended to the mine, and father supplied the food, clothing, and implements, so I knew all these old-timers.

There at the open door stood my old friend, Mello, still manager of the Little Squaw Gold Mine and as rotund as ever. Upon entering the house, I trotted downhill to the other side of the room. I remember passing a tabletop above eye level. It was like Alice in Wonderland. The floor was terribly out of kilter. At one end of the table, the legs were propped up with unopened No.10 cans of fruit. We laughed as I walked uphill to greet Mello's sons, Frank and Joe.

"Permafrost," Mello said. "Permafrost caused the floor to sink more than 8 feet down at that end of the house."

Before dark Riley and I went to see the old prospector named Anderson on Tobin Creek. I had not seen him for 19 years. Now nearing 70, he ambled around very well. Like many gold seekers, his face still glowed with the dream and hope of his next clean-up. Besides prospecting, Anderson also was postmaster of the small settlement. His three chairs, made with U.S. mail bags, were practical and durable.

When we returned to Mello's camp, nearly everyone was sitting around the different levels of the room, drinking coffee. I found a niche where the men came one by one to be questioned and counted. Despite the close living, isolation and necessity of caring for each other, this little band of men had secrets they would only tell to a census taker.

Dan Murphy did not want to be counted. He disliked government policies and, although civil to me, muttered negative statements from a corner. I remembered Murphy well. He had given his dogs religious names—Reverend, Vicar, Pope, Priest, Padre and others. He yelled, swore and snapped the whip at all of them. As children, we quaked and hid whenever we saw them. Now more than 90, Murphy was the oldest of the bunch in Chandalar, and the six others took care of him.

Mello, his sons, Frank and Joe, Alfred Amero, Red Adney, Carlson and Murphy were counted during that census. Now they are gone—no more to be counted.

Riley and I left Chandalar on December 10 and spent Christmas in Beaver before setting out for the next segment of our mission—a trip to Fort Yukon, about 120 miles up the Yukon River. Still ahead were many dogsled adventures, delicious meals with gracious hosts and one stand-off with a pair of gun-toting sisters. With another driver, Arthur James, I visited Old Man Lake, Chalkyitsik, Shamrock, Old John Village, Burnt Paw, Howling Dog and Old Rampart House. By airplane I flew to Arctic Village and to Owen's Camp on the Coleen River. By late February my work was done.

Back in Fairbanks I reflected on the image of me plodding along in my explorer suit. I remembered returning to Beaver, where I washed and put on fresh clothes for the first time in weeks.

But just then I had another mission in mind and immediately went downtown to the Hollywood Shop and bought a new spring outfit, from hat to shoes.

I had earned it.

Chapter 34

MY LAST GRIZZLY

May 1990

By Nick Jans

I love bears, and I've killed them: two grizzlies and a black in the past six years. I could claim self defense, but that would be a lie; each time I set out with the idea of killing a bear. And though I took away hides and meat, neither a bear rug nor a pot roast explains enough.

There is a picture of me with my first grizzly. The bear is lying on one side, head angling toward the camera. He's a large but not particularly pretty specimen, a mature boar with thick, dark fur and hooked claws.

I'm squatting behind the bear's shoulder, the barrel of my rifle pointing skyward. What most interests me about this picture is my face. You can tell I was younger then, though my skin is weathered from days of sub-zero cold. I look at this face now, and wonder what I've learned since then.

I came to Alaska because of bears. Alaska and bears—the two were the same to me then. I was afraid of bears, eight years ago, so afraid I couldn't keep thoughts of them out of my mind. I gravitated toward the place where imagination and reality intersected; it seemed I had no choice but to go and find exactly what it was that I feared.

Before Alaska, I'd gotten close to bears only once—or rather, they'd gotten close to me. I was 17 years old, camping in northern Quebec. My friend and I fried the fish we'd caught and crawled into our tent. Lying there in the dark, we heard the ruckus of something big coming down the steep hill into camp, rolling stones as it came. We knew it was a bear. Our food was locked in the car trunk, but the bear, or actually several bears, ransacked the unwashed dishes just 10 feet from our tent, and then huffed and sniffed around the edge of the thin, nylon walls. We could smell them. We lay there, stiff and scarcely breathing, as if any movement or sound would guarantee an explosion of fur, teeth, and claws. The bears looted what they could, licked the frying pan clean and strolled off into the night, noisy and unconcerned. We didn't sleep much that night, though they didn't come back.

But bears came back in my dreams, over and over. I know those animals in Quebec were black bears, the dark, doggy animals common all over North America. They really don't tend to attack people. Still, for a couple of years, every noise in the dark woods was a bear. The fear didn't stop me from camping, but it sat on my chest throughout long nights.

In Alaska there were not only black bears, but grizzlies. Grizzlies: As fast as a horse, strong enough to drag off a moose carcass, solitary, curious, aggressive, intelligent. I read everything I could find. They sometimes ran down and ate black bears. They could weigh 500 pounds and up to half a ton. I wanted to see them, to get close to them. I wanted to face a big bear at close range—with a gun in my hands, of course . . . or even better, without a gun. I wanted to set up a tent in grizzly country and learn to sleep soundly.

The first bear I saw in Alaska made a lasting impression on me, and he wasn't even alive. It was the enormous stuffed specimen at the University of Alaska Museum in Fairbanks. He stands upright in a glass case just inside the entrance. I had to lean back to focus on his head, 12 feet off the floor. The plaque gave his live weight as 1,200 pounds. His front legs, at the bicep, were nearly as big around as my torso. He wasn't mounted like a Hollywood bear, snarling, paws raised; instead, he stood in what I'd later recognize as a classic grizzly pose: leaning forward, round-shouldered, squinting like an elderly gentleman, a vaguely puzzled expression on his face. I stayed for half an hour, shaking my head, imagining that bear rising out of the brush 20 feet away. But he just stood staring quizzically into space, as though wondering how the hell he'd ended up there.

Three weeks later, on the Kobuk River in northwestern Arctic Alaska, I saw my first wild grizzly. My traveling partner and I were drifting downstream in a canoe just above the Mauneluk River. The bear was lying on a gravel bar 30 yards away, and at first he was just another driftwood stump. Then the head raised. His fur was matted with rain, his long-lashed eyes almost human in their intense, puzzled regard. Then he burst into motion, bounding off into the willows as if a huge spring were uncoiling inside his chest. We watched him go, and then I realized I'd forgotten to be afraid; there had been no time.

We made camp a half mile below—bravely stacked our plates to clatter us awake if the bear raided camp, and slept with a loaded .44 magnum pistol between us. Later on, a hunting guide told me that if I wanted to carry a .44 for bear protection, I'd better file off the front sight. "Why?" I asked. So it won't hurt so much when the bear shoves it up your ass, the guide said.

Over the next five years there were more bears; I floated past them in boats, watched them from snowmobiles, stalked them on foot—went out whenever my teaching job gave me the chance. I saw many things: a grown grizzly, just out of the den, somersaulting downhill like a kid in snow, then running up to do it again; another big male held off by a wolf protecting her den of pups; one turning to swat a low-flying plane. Every spring a young grizzly (the same one, I decided) would rip my empty wall tent to shreds by the Kugurok River, dismantle my stove and gnaw speculatively on my canoe.

Sometimes shaking, but always bullied by fascination, I followed their grooved trails and poked at their droppings, found signs of infanticide and cannibalism—a cub's perforated skull, a sow's half-eaten body. But even when I got too close—20 yards once—the bears ran, apparently just as scared as I was. I questioned wardens, guides, Eskimo hunters, geologists and hikers and discovered that in the history of the northwestern Arctic, there wasn't one documented case of a bear killing a man, or even of a serious mauling. Everyone had attack stories, but they always ended in narrow escapes or dead bears. Then there were all the bears hunted down over the years. A mountain of dead bears, and not one dead man: The bears had a much better reason to be afraid. And yet, according to state biologists, there are more grizzlies in Alaska now than in 1900. Hunters shoot the big, cub-eating males who hold down the population, and the ironic result is more, if smaller, bears. I heard Eskimos agree about the numbers:

"Too much bear nowadays. Lots more than old times."

I finally shot my first black bear in 1981 after a long, crawling stalk, and got my first grizzly a year later. Hunting then seemed to be a natural part of the Eskimo village lifestyle surrounding me. Looking back, I remember the roar of adrenaline and gunfire, the hollow whunk of striking bullets, the reek of hot blood—and the answering sensation of a strange ecstasy. The heavy-chested flatness I'd expected never came; I forced myself into a few guilty twinges, and that was all. But still I didn't understand, and my fear was still there.

April 14, 1985. Norma and I were out scouting for dens, 20 miles out of Noatak village, into the Kipmiksot Range. We worked up a steep draw, our snow machines straining through deep powder. The sun was warm, though the air couldn't have been above 10 degrees. The draw widened into a sheltered creek valley, the mountains rising sharply on three sides. A pair of wolf trails wound through the willows on the valley floor. A band of caribou climbed over the rim and was gone.

Norma signaled. I followed her point up the valley, and there it was: a freshly dug-out den with a trail emerging. A hundred yards away we pulled up. No doubt about it. A bear—a big one judging from the tracks—had come out in the last day. Digging out, he had come through the den roof, so that there was a deep, narrow trench about 15 feet into the hillside, open at one end. We couldn't see all the way in, but the first few feet were empty. There was a huge mound of soil, rock and willow, untouched by yesterday's dusting of snow.

Norma roared on ahead on her old Polaris, too excited to hear my half-joke about knocking first. But as she dismounted 20 feet above the trench and moved toward the edge, camera in hand, I *knew*. Gunning my machine up the slope, I cut her off 4 feet from the den. A snarling head erupted from the ground, and a broad paw hooked out at me. The roar was drowned out by the machine, but I didn't have to hear it. The bear was thrashing up the 10-foot pit wall, jaws snapping, front paws working cat-quick. Norma stumbled backward and fell. This is it, I thought. He's going to be on us. The world slowed into bright slow motion. I clearly saw a black scar on his snout. Just like a movie, I remember thinking. Could I turn him with the .22? Ten shots from a bird gun? No chance. Norma reached her machine and gunned it, spinning the track. Stuck. "You're not going to make it," I shouted as I pulled alongside and dragged her on behind me. I didn't look back, braced almost calmly for the slamming impact, the hot breath, the teeth.

When we did look, he was already 100 yards off and moving fast in the opposite direction. Though just 10 feet away, harassed and cornered, he'd charged out of the den entrance and kept going downhill. He'd had us both dead and let us go.

May 10, 1986. A year later. Midnight. I'm alone on my snow-camouflaged Arctic Cat, 25 miles back in the Kipmiksots. In the past few weeks I've made a dozen trips, covering hundreds of miles with my machine, hundreds more with my eyes. I'm looking for a bear, a particular bear. I know where he denned last year, and I know what he looks like. A huge brown male with a scar down his snout. If you want an explanation, I don't have one, even for myself. An old time Eskimo shaman (if there were any left) might say that I'm looking for my *kila*, my animal healing spirit, so that he might give himself to me and make me strong. But this isn't enough; in fact, it's evasion. The part of me that knows looks down bitterly and hopes for failure as the rest of me pushes on. Fear flutters in my gut, but I can no longer pretend it's anything external. I know it's my last bear hunt.

The last few days have been warm; the spring thaw is right on schedule, the Noatak Valley floor a patchwork of brown and fading white. Even in the cool of the evening, the going is slushy and the creeks run with overflow. But once above 2,000 feet, the snow is solid and the wind stings my face as I ride into it. I travel the ridgelines and drop down into the same little creek valley, though I know he wouldn't den there again. I recognize the spot, but it's unmarked, drifted in. That was another year. Gone, like Norma. I've been hunting hard all spring to keep away from the village, from the empty cabin, from another man's wife. Hunting hard, but only for a certain bear. Is this how I repay him?

It's been four weeks of looking, and the snow machine season will be over tomorrow, or the next warm day after that. I've crossed two bear trails tonight and half-heartedly followed each one, knowing they weren't what I was after. One trail led to a winter-killed caribou. All that was left were a few bone shards, trampled snow, hair and wrist-thick scat. Probably the work of a young male. I lost the other trail in a wind drift.

Two a.m. I haven't slept in 28 hours. The light throws all internal clocks off. Even now it's not dark—the light is gray and flat, faint, but enough. My fuel gauge shows just over half a tank. I'll cut across the mountain into the next watershed, ride along the creek for a few miles, then loop home. Am I discouraged or relieved? He'll be safe from me if he can last another two hours.

I bang across a stretch of rock-hard drifts and then a patch of bare tundra, and finally drop down into the next creek. I know it well. Four years ago I shot my first grizzly here. It's good denning country, and big bears seem to favor it. A light snow is falling, tiny flakes like dust. The heavy ache of fatigue sickness has set in, and my eyes play slight tricks. I look again, straining against the near whiteout of snow on snow. No depth perception. But yes, that's a bear trail in front of me. I've been riding right over it, not seeing. I stop and dismount, run my fingers over the fresh prints. No snow in them yet, the outlines sharp, but feather-soft. The rear foot is more than 12 inches long, 8 wide. It's his and he's less than five minutes ahead. I unsling my rifle and check the magazine. Why pretend the odds are equal?

I ride slowly, as quietly as I can, the gun across my lap. The wind is in my face, and the falling snow muffles the sound of the machine. I leave the creek, clear a low rise and there he is, the dark, wide rump shuffling along, less than 200 yards off, bigger than I'd remembered. He can't see me, hasn't smelled me, must not have heard. Is he deaf?

I cut the engine, swing my rifle up, brace off my seat. The crosshairs fix on his rolling shoulder hump. The best way to put him down fast is with a spine shot. I take a deep breath, let half out, and tighten on the trigger. Why don't I at least hesitate?

Whump. A hit, but I've missed the spine. He lurches into a heavy-footed lope. I work the bolt and touch off a second shot. He staggers and turns toward me, charges. He's coming in, head low, determined, moving on blind rage. Another round into his chest and he's dead on his feet, but still coming, mouth open, jaws working, spraying blood. He stumbles down on the fourth round, biting at his chest as if his own failing body is the enemy. Thirty yards away I can hear the last heavy breath sigh out: resignation, disappointment. All these seasons have come to this. My gun slides from my gloved hands; I rock back and forth, crying as if he were my brother, the valley quiet and white with new snow.

Chapter 35

MEDICINE WOMAN

June 1990

By Marilyn Savage

Her shiny, silver hair was parted neatly down the middle and pinned up in back, with brown combs on each side of her head. In her living room made overly warm by a crackling fire in the woodstove, she sat knitting gloves with her favorite Redheart yarn. Bending over, she quietly spit her Copenhagen snuff into a coffee-can spittoon on the floor. Straightening, she resumed telling her life experiences as a medicine woman.

A full-blooded Gwich'in Athabascan Indian, she stands tall, even though inches shy of 5 feet. Most of her grandchildren call her "Granny," which suits her just fine. Granny turned 84 in December. But even though she's raised 16 children, beginning when she was 14, Granny looks and acts like a woman in her 60s.

Fort Yukon, her home, is located 150 air miles northeast of Fairbanks. Located on the confluence of the Yukon and Porcupine rivers, this Gwich'in Native village is close to the Canadian border village of Old Crow, Northwest Territories.

Gwich'in, one of 11 different Athabascan languages in Alaska and also spoken in Canada, is in the same family as Navajo and Apache. White fur traders first made contact with the Gwich'in people about 150 years ago, and although many things have changed for these Alaska Natives, some of the traditional culture is still valued and practiced, such as the medicine skills of my grandmother, Julia Peter.

Speaking only in her native language, Granny shared with me stories about her medical practice of 50 years ago. I am fortunate enough to be able to translate this story from her.

On the day before she is to perform a medical procedure, Granny explained, she cannot drink any hot liquids, such as tea or soup. "So that's why when I heal people; they must be good people. That's why they heal."

One of the first stories she told me was how she healed her father's back. At the time the family was living in Beaver Creek, where they were trapping. Then, as now, a family living out on a trapline had only itself to rely on for survival. There were no doctors, dentists or emergency numbers to call when medical attention was needed.

"Around Christmas time in 1940, my father, Paul Solomon, Sr., hurt his back by pulling frozen fish from underneath ice and snow," Granny said. "When my father hurt his back, my husband, Abraham Peter, my son, Walter, and my younger brother, Sambo Solomon, were checking their daily traplines that kept them away for days at a time. I stayed home tending to our children and housework.

Granny's son, Simon, helped out with chores around the cabin. Although old enough to be out on the trapline with his father, Simon was confined to home by a partial paralysis of his left arm and leg that had afflicted him since childhood. To keep busy, he cut wood and tended a small trapline with his mother.

"We set rabbit snares near our cabin," Granny said. "We mostly needed to do it for dog food supply. Usually we fed them fish my father caught. Jack fish was plentiful that winter, and the frozen fish piled up under the cache. That's when he hurt his back and could barely walk."

"He came in the house holding his back and explained his injury. He sat down and sharpened his knife." Granny smiled as she remembered how he peeled two willow sticks that he would ask her to use to heal his back.

"I watched what he was doing without saying a word. That is how we learn: by observing carefully and silently."

"Simon came in from cutting wood. He noticed the sharpened knife and two sticks lying on the table. At this time my father told me to cut his back. 'You'll have to show me how,' I told him. Right there he bared his back and showed me how to squeeze the flesh of his lower back between the two sticks. The sticks, called *liiglaat*, are used to squeeze the flesh to keep it still.

"You just gash the flesh between the sticks quickly to let it bleed," he said. "This is done to both sides of the spine with the sharpened knife." About this time, Simon bolted for the door. All I saw of my son, Simon, was the door slamming behind him.

"So there I sliced his back quickly and put a clean towel to catch the blood. This being my first time, I gave him a big scar." With her fingers about 1½ inches apart, Granny showed me the width of the scar, laughing at her mistake.

"Then what did you do to him, Granny?" I asked, my curiosity increasing.

"I bandaged him with a clean baby diaper after the bleeding thinned out. You can tell when it slows up. We only had white plaster then. That's what I fixed him up good with. Oh, there was a lot of blood that flowed out from his back."

Wanting to know more about this incident, which took place nearly 50 years ago, I asked Granny how the procedure was supposed to help him.

"His blood was not good where he pulled his back muscles and the pressure of the blood gathered, causing him much pain. After his blood was released, he ate and went back to his own cabin close to ours.

"At 6 the next morning I got up as usual. Simon got up with the news that he had seen his grandfather walking down toward the big lake and carrying his rifle. Simon reported excitedly that his grandfather had a bounce to his walk.

"Simon came in again from cutting wood. 'Ma, Ma, I hear Grampa shoot his gun at the big lake. Ma, could I go down to Grampa?' Simon asked pleadingly. He was dressed warm, and I let him go. He disappeared down around the bend from the house.

"Oh, he made his Grampa happy. Here his Grampa shot a cow moose and its young calf. With Simon's one strong arm, he helped his Grampa skin, cut up moose parts which are heavy and difficult for one man, especially when his back had been operated on just the night before."

Granny had been keeping an eye out for Simon and her father, and spotted them as soon as they came around the bend. Simon, beaming with pleasure because his grandfather needed his help, was pulling a makeshift sled of tree branches lashed with rope. The sled was loaded with heart, kidney, stomach, and fat. It was for Granny.

"This is quite a gift for Gwich'ins. It is a delicacy and is taken first from the animal for eating," Granny explained.

Daisy Stevens recalls how Granny healed her abscessed tooth in Fort Yukon, where dentists were not available.

"I remember my front tooth had abscessed and swelled. I could not eat for three days, only suffered. It was 60 below zero outside. No planes, and besides I didn't have the money to see a dentist.

"I went to your grandmother. This was when my husband was alive. So he helped by holding my head in place for her to do the operation. Granny boiled her instruments, a needle, a razor blade split in half. She wiped them with alcohol. While sitting rigidly in a chair, she drove her needle into my front tooth. I screamed and stood up. Afterwards she sliced the top gum to drain the pus. I passed out from pain and slept all night and day. When I woke up there was nothing wrong with me. No after effects. No swelling. It was as if nothing had happened. Strange, huh?"

Daisy, a stepsister of Granny, now lives in Fairbanks, where she recently had that very same tooth capped by a dentist. As if in confirmation, Daisy proudly flashed me a beautiful smile.

Granny continued with another story. "I fixed the eyes of both Ruth Martin and Margaret Solomon. Their eyes were infected—swollen and painful. They couldn't see out of them." I listened spellbound as Granny detailed how she cut the blood capillaries on the inside of the eyelids.

"I broke a razor blade in half and boiled it, and when it cooled, I barely nicked the tiny blood vessels. On Ruth I had a hard time opening her eyes. I did the right side and then the left side. There was a lot of blood draining from her eyes. I put a clean towel on her face and had her lie on the pillow, face down. While she was lying down, she fell asleep. While sick, she had spent all her time behind the curtain in bed. That evening, she suddenly came out from behind the curtain by herself. From then on, her eyes never got red or infected. I did the same to Margaret."

"How did they get eye infections, Granny?"

"I don't really know how, but their eyes just got so painful that they couldn't see daylight and were restricted to bed with curtains," Granny replied. "Back then, we didn't have bedrooms, only cloth curtains partitioning the room into sleeping areas.

"I myself had an eye infection when I was a child. My grandmother, a medicine woman named Chi'kyaa, cut my eyes, but it didn't help." Another child had thrown sand in Granny's eyes when they were playing. "There was a hospital, and they gave me medicine for my eyes, but it didn't work.

"Lucy Dirtynose's uncle, named Raggedy Simon, was a great medicine man in the Indian way. My father paid him to fix my eyes. I heard him tell my mother, 'When he comes here, don't let Julia resist his aid.'

"Well, I didn't know what was going to happen to me, so I was scared. While in bed, I lay face down on the pillow. I couldn't go beyond my curtained bed. I heard Raggedy Simon come in the door. 'I heard that young woman's eyes are bad,' he said. My mother explained the situation to him as she led him to my bedside. He told me to turn over, while he took my pillow away and spread my eyes open, and then before I knew it he put his own spit into one eye."

"What! His spit?"

"Yes, his spit from his mouth. Then he did the same to the other eye. He was doing that because he was a shaman. I fell into a deep sleep. It was nighttime when I woke up. My eyes were wide open. I made it to the table on my own and ate for the first time in months. 'I can see you good,' I told my mother. That's how my eyes were fixed."

I asked her if she ever worked on my mother, Charlotte.

She said, "Yes, I cut both sides of her temples to free her headache. She had meningitis. She had pain in her head. They thought she had tuberculosis, but she didn't. She almost died."

"I heard you fixed your youngest daughter, Mae, too," I said.

"Yes, after she had Bonnie, she had an infection in her womb. Mae was bedridden for one whole month. The nurse came every day to give her shots. Then they sent her to Fairbanks." This occurred in 1973.

"So I was taking care of her, and she was too sick for too long. I went to Louise, an elder, and told her about Mae. My daughter has been sick, and she can't walk. What can I do to help her?"

"Louise said, 'You boil water with Pine-Sol and you put it in a clean honey bucket and make Mae sit on it with blankets around her, like a sweat bath.'"

Granny continued, "So Mae sat on the honey bucket that was sterilized. She was uncomfortable and wanted to get off soon. But I told her to sit a while longer. Nothing came out of her. Finally, I took her off and put a clean flannel nightgown on her and put her back in bed. As soon as she lay down, she said, 'Ma, I need to go use the honey bucket.' I put her back on the pot, holding her. She said something discharged from her. A white tissue, about a foot long, came out of her. I put it on a piece of cloth for the nurse to look at. The nurse said it was a piece of afterbirth that had been left inside her. She would have died from it if left much longer. After two days she could walk on her own."

I asked Granny to tell about the time she healed her friend, Martha, of what Granny thinks was high blood pressure.

Pointing to the two large veins under her tongue, Granny said that Martha had asked her to cut them and take her blood. Granny had never performed this surgical procedure before, although her grandmother had told her about it.

"What if I kill you?" Granny asked. "I won't tell on you," Martha replied. So Granny got ready for the surgery.

"I boiled my little knife. I have a special little knife I use. With a clothespin holding her tongue out, I cut under her tongue on the vein. As soon as I did that, her blood splashed on my blouse. Even with the little nick, the blood splashed. The other vein, too. She spit into a bucket. All night she had blood in her mouth.

"My grandmother, Chi'kyaa, taught me these skills when I was young, and I didn't know what it meant then. She told me in the future I would need these skills."

"How old were you when she told you this?" I asked.

"About nine or 10. At first, I just delivered babies. All the women I have helped deliver their babies know me and are good to me, because they know I delivered them."

Granny said that the most common baby illness was diarrhea. She would make a juice from wood ashes, which she forced the babies to drink. It was horrible tasting, this charcoal juice, but the next day the babies would be well.

Usually medicine women don't do surgery on themselves, but on one occasion Granny had no choice. She asked other people to do it for her, but they didn't know how and refused.

"I couldn't walk. My knees swelled up. I used a cane, and my daughter helped me go to the store and post office. I asked Solomon Flitt to make me a *liiglaat*. I put my leg on a box and cut my flesh on both sides of my knees where it was swollen, one at a time, and let it bleed into a nearby bucket. Afterward I wrapped and bandaged it in a baby diaper."

Today, Granny is a healthy, active woman. I am proud of the way she looks, with her silver hair parted neatly down the middle and covered by a paisley kerchief. Her face is serene. There are five generations alive in Granny's family, including nine living children and dozens of grandchildren and great-grandchildren. Granny takes life easy now, but she still gives advice and help whenever she feels it is appropriate.

Chapter 36

ADVENTURES IN NIGHT FISHING

April 1991

By Ken Marsh

Water isn't as crowded at night, and some fish seem to bite just about as frequently once the sun sets. But I've discovered an even deeper attraction to night fishing.

For me, the allurement of night fishing lies in its intrinsic suggestion of naughtiness; a lusty, adventurous zeal probably left over from childhood when curfew and bedtimes were strictly enforced. Also, it's illegal in some places, but not here. I suspect all night anglers delight in the sensation of freedom immortalized by tales of the great Huckleberry Finn who, along with going barefoot and smoking a pipe, enjoyed nothing more than sitting on the banks of the Mississippi River, hand-lining for catfish long after Tom Sawyer and his cronies were banished to bed for the night.

I see the night, its domed canvas a universal bolt of cloth cut from Merlin's cap and gown, as a magical time. For me, sundown hails a period of dormancy for the known and familiar, and is marked by the resurrection of things strange to me and my diurnal world. And therein lies the promise of adventure, which I sought last fall when I took my first taste of night fishing on a lake in the Matanuska Valley.

Tom and I saddled up our float tubes and pushed off into the still waters of the lake. The day had been warm and bright, and the rainbows at first were reluctant to rise. As we bobbed along, waiting for the sun to set and the water to cool, we watched muskrats paddle passively on the lake's surface.

Gradually, like grains in an hourglass, tiny pieces of night fell from the sky until dusk engulfed us within its murky shroud. Visibility waned, our eyes nearly useless. I began relying on my other senses—sound, smell, touch—and discovered a plane of awareness and appreciation of my surroundings long neglected.

I listened for the gulping sounds of rising fish as I paddled along the alder-fringed shoreline. Dragonflies on cellophane wings made soft, rattling noises as they fluttered among the lily pads and sedges. I cast by feel, forearm cocked, ready to respond to the strikes. The autumn air smelled of ripening cranberries, a bittersweet liqueur.

Tom and I fished just a few feet apart, yet we couldn't see each other. We talked quietly, chuckling when a frenzied splash marked a fish hooked. There was something strange about our hushed conversations. In broad daylight, we had talked boldly. But, once the sun went down, our voices fell in gradual diminuendo until we found ourselves whispering. The power of darkness, it seems, simply commands an implied reverence.

A great horned owl called out on the ridge above the lake. Tom didn't say a word. I thought of something ol' Huck once said through Mark Twain's pen:

"The stars was shining and the leaves rustled in the woods ever so mournful; and I heard an owl, away off, who-whooing about somebody that was dead . . . and the wind was trying to whisper something to me and I couldn't make out what it was, and so it made the cold shivers run over me. Then away out in the woods I heard that kind of sound that a ghost makes when it wants to tell about something that's on its mind and can't make itself understood, and so can't rest easy in its grave and has to go about that way every night grieving."

As we fished in the darkness, I saw the window of a single cabin glowing on the lake's southern bank and mused how nice it would be to live there. Why, I'd be out here fishing every night, I said to Tom.

"For me, part of the fun of fishing, is trying out new places," he countered.

I couldn't dispute that. And for me, fishing the little lake at night for the first time was new. In the blue light of the stars and the moon, the lake had become mysterious and deliciously forbidden. I had entered a new frontier.

Following that night on the lake, I felt compelled to try other forms of nocturnal angling. So, later that week, I went with another friend to spend a night chasing silver salmon.

We walked for 25 minutes on the rim of a bluff covered with dense black spruce to reach the spot. Even in the light of early evening the trail was gloomy, a moist brown rut in the green sphagnum, sheltered by the canopy of the forest.

Ducking our heads under low branches, snagging our rod tips in the brush, we finally descended the bluff to the creek mouth below.

Creek water the color of strong tea met and mixed with the thick, milky-brown, glacial waters of the Susitna River. The creek appeared stagnant where it joined the swirling current of the Su. The river roiled, churned and tumbled away, a living highway for salmon—kings, pinks, reds, chums, and silvers. The fish move blindly up the Su, feeling and bumping their way in primitive desperation through scores of muddy, braided channels.

Greg scanned the water, his eyes intense. Even before he had a chance to open his pack, I lobbed a prune-sized gob of cured red salmon roe into the mousse created by the mixing of the two streams. Perfect cast, Greg said. I worried aloud that my ultra light pack rod lacked the muscle to handle the fish that lurked in these waters. Give 'em lots of drag, Greg suggested. He seemed skeptical.

Soon we were both fishing. Greg used a light bait-casting rig. It was a sweet outfit.

Greg caught the first fish—a bright chum. The 8-pound salmon fought bitterly, and, for a fish saved as dog food by many, died with honor. Greg smiled. The chum would barbeque nicely, but it wasn't a silver.

In the next hour I caught several rainbow trout up to 10 inches long, which I released. At 11:00 p.m. my rod tip bucked. I snatched the rod out of its forked stick brace and yanked sharply. The hook set deeply, and a shiny 15-pound salmon sprang into the cool night air. I applied just enough pressure on the rod to keep the fish moving so it would tire out. The silver jumped three more times and made several surging runs toward the main river. Luckily for me, he never made it, for with the help of the powerful current he would almost certainly have snapped my line, if not my rod. Each surge became weaker until he eventually surrendered, turning his flashing side to the surface. The size of a late-run Kenai coho, it was the biggest silver I have ever caught in the Susitna drainage.

When the night became so murky that we could no longer see our rod tips, Greg and I built a fire on the bank and relaxed. We watched a meteor shower etch the sky with gold and silver and saw the moonlight dance on the river. We heard coyotes bark, and listened to a beaver munch birch twigs on a nearby gravel bar. We sat by the campfire, inhaling its acrid spruce pitch smoke, and telling untold stories of personal coups. All the while we dipped snuff, snickered, and generally acted like delinquents. Yes, naughty as we were, we became part of the wild nocturne. Our presence seemed no less natural than the song of the coyotes or the murmuring river.

When morning arrived, it came in tones of pink and yellow, carefully and steadily following a night's deliberate retreat. And I noticed that there was something in the pale light of dawn that seemed almost apologetic, though for what I couldn't fathom. However, I knew the humility of the newborn day would progressively evaporate with the rising sun. And the light would eventually strengthen and become harsh, until night recaptured its rightful post 15 hours later, no apologies accepted.

Chapter 37

ZAPPED ON RAINBOW MOUNTAIN

October 1991

By Yvonne Lindblom and Ruth Moulton

The Chugach Range sparkled in a cloudless spring sky as I drove into town to pick up Ruth for our hike. We had climbed many mountains together through the years and were looking forward to another refreshing outing high above timberline on Rainbow Mountain.

Rising 6,700 feet above Cook Inlet, Rainbow Mountain lies 18 miles southeast of Anchorage. We had driven past it for years going and coming from other hikes in the mountains along Turnagain Arm, but only in the past few months had we considered it as a possible climb. We wondered if the valley behind it was linked to Rabbit Creek valley, which we'd explored on previous hikes. The view it promised was reason enough to make the trek.

We did not follow a trail, although we've since learned there is one, and it looked like our route up its slopes would be steep. By 9 a.m. we left the car beside the dirt road into Rainbow Valley and started hiking through sparse cottonwood growth that quickly faded to scrub and then to sharp rock slopes.

The day was unusually warm for late May in southcentral Alaska. The hot weather made each boot seem just a bit heavier than it was. We soon learned that conquering Rainbow's summit is an exercise in patience and stamina; the mountain's steep slopes seemed to go on forever, its peak beckoning just out of reach.

After a lunch stop about three-quarters of the way up, the brilliant sunshine surrendered to dark clouds that had crept suddenly over the summit. A few raindrops fell. There was a swift drop in temperature, and we put on our jackets. We heard thunder in the distance, and Ruth commented on how rare that sound is in Alaska.

We continued climbing, and as I neared the top I felt cobwebs on my face. This wouldn't have been unusual down among the bushes; I was used to running into them there. But cobwebs on this rock mountain? I brushed at my face and continued to climb toward the summit.

I topped the peak first. As I waited for Ruth, I stood by a tall rock that looked like a giant thumb. Oddly, a constant humming sound came from the rock. It wasn't the familiar fluctuating *ZZZzzzZZZzzz* of a bumblebee that I knew from my prairie childhood, but just a steady *ZZZZZZZ*. This surprised me, and I wondered if bees buzzed like that when they couldn't get free.

I looked down the mountain to check Ruth's progress. She was swatting at her head, and I figured she was probably fighting a heavy dose of the same cobwebs I'd encountered.

Later I learned that Ruth thought she was fighting an invisible swarm of insects that bit and crawled through her hair. When she took her glasses off to brush the bugs away from her face, they seemed to swarm around the frames, humming; but she couldn't feel them or squash them when she wiped the frames with her fingers. She had begun wondering if her mind was playing tricks when she noticed me standing by the rock. Feeling as impatient as I to see what was on the other side, she dismissed the insects and started up to join me.

Now, I found that every time I moved my arms I heard a *ZZZttt*, and I thought there must be ants or some other insects caught in my cuffs. At the same time, I was excited about reaching the top. When Ruth caught up, the first thing she said was, "Something keeps biting me. There are bugs in my hair." She leaned over, and I parted her hair in several places, searching, but I didn't see any insects.

We started along the ridge, eager to look down into the valley we had wondered about. I raised my arm to point, started to say something, but heard that ZZZttt again and stopped in mid-sentence. Ruth glanced at me sharply and asked if my cuff had just made a noise. I said there must be a bug caught in the Velcro. She said her cuffs were making noises and there were no bugs caught there and . . .

Suddenly Ruth's hair again swarmed with "insects." She tried to comb them out with her fingers and asked me to help her, but I still couldn't find them. Then she felt something bite her temple. Ruth snatched her glasses off her face.

She held the glasses in front of her with one hand while she swatted with the other, and the frames started to hum loudly. She straightened and looked at me with wide, frightened eyes. Suddenly I knew. "Ruth, it's electricity!"

We ran down that steep mountain faster than I ever thought possible. We picked up our packs where we had left them after lunch and dumped our pop cans and sardine tins on the ground. We wanted to get rid of everything metal and get off the mountain.

In the midst of my frenzied sorting, Ruth spoke, her voice quiet with fear. "Yvonne, your hair is standing on end." I looked at her. "Yours is too," I said, horrified. Not only was her hair standing on end, but the curl in it had been pulled almost straight.

As we frantically shouldered our packs, I wondered: Should we flatten ourselves on the mountainside, or run until our hair fell limp again?

We chose the latter and raced down the mountain. It was not time to misplace a boot and break an ankle, and seldom have I concentrated as intently—or as briefly—on the contour of the rocks I was choosing as a route. Finally, we realized our hair had fallen and that we were out of the charged area. Still we ran a bit farther to be certain. It was a tremendous relief to sprawl on the mountainside and let our adrenaline return to normal.

As we hiked out, we analyzed our ordeal. Of course, Ruth's metal frames and small gold earrings had made her the better target and had caused the "insects" to concentrate on her. And there was only that one tall rock—the humming thumb—near the top. Otherwise we were the best lightning rods available. Most of the way down, we walked in silence, now and then looking at each other, shaking our heads and laughing nervously.

We have since asked many questions and have learned a bit about electricity and lightning. We know now that we are fortunate to be here to ask the questions. Of course, we still haven't seen the valley on the other side of Rainbow, and we mention that to each other from time to time.

Chapter 38

FORGOTTEN PIONEERS

February 1992

By Lael Morgan

Deep in a stack of 1943 war records from the national archives is a note by a black soldier on what working on the Alaska Highway was like.

"It's miles and miles of nothing but miles and miles!" he said.

The Alaska section of the road was built by the all-black 97th Division of the Corps of Engineers over the protests of the U.S. Army commander for Alaska, Gen. Simon Bolivar Buckner, Jr.

He was placated only by the promise that black troops would not be allowed near any settlements.

Buckner's objections were echoed by top brass in Washington D.C. until a desperate manpower shortage caused military planners to chance sending them north for the strategic Alcan mission.

It proved to be a good decision. However, the brutal winter of 1942–43, the coldest in recorded history, was a setback. The majority of the men were from temperate climes of the Deep South.

A confidential report from the war department noted during a field inspection at 63 below zero that the clothing of Delta Junction's black regiment was found to be in "abominable condition."

The warm confines of a newly built air base at Delta were off limits to blacks. Most wintered in tents.

Despite this, Walter E. Mason's "A" Company built 295 miles of road through stunted forest from Slana, across the Tanana River, and then south into Canada.

"We made about five miles a day . . . had to move camp every two or three days," the Lexington, Va., engineer recalls. "Ours was the first cat (bulldozer) to cross the border, and everybody climbed on. We were supposed to meet the (all-white) 18ᵗʰ coming up from the south. When they didn't show up, we kept on going."

"The morale was good, as every man accepted the conditions and lived with them," says Howard Garber of Richmond, Va., who headed Company "E" of Alaska's 97ᵗʰ Second Battalion.

The Alcan assignment offered opportunity for many blacks who, for the first time, received the same pay and benefits as white workers, notes the Rev. Edward G. Carroll, a black officer who served as chaplain.

"Yes, there were discrimination problems, " concedes the veteran who later went on to become the bishop of the Methodist Church for New England. "The race you don't know is the race you suspect, but our men proved themselves."

During the formal dedication of the road, Brig. Gen. James O'Conner, head of the Northwest Service Command, singled out the black troops who comprised roughly one-third of the work force.

"Some day the accomplishment of these colored soldiers . . . will occupy a major place in the lore of the North country," he promised.

Ultimately, the military became the first U.S. agency to integrate. But the only tangible tribute to the black builders of the Alcan is the remarkable road they left behind—still in use and the sole land link to Alaska after 50 years.

Chapter 39

BIG TROUBLE ON THE "WIDELOAD"

September 1994

By Chris Schelb

I was in an air pocket beneath a capsized fishing boat off the coast of Alaska, surf crashing over the hull above my head. I had already given myself up as dead, but I was alive. And now I was determined to survive.

I had made my living from the richness of Alaskan waters for years. It was May 1986, and my longtime friend Tom Tomrdle and I were fishing out of Cordova. Tom was the owner and captain of the fishing vessel *Wideload*. I was the deckhand and cook.

The *Wideload* was a 28-foot gill-net boat, built for speed with a shallow draft to fish the surf-pounded waters of the Copper River flats, just east of Cordova. The early sockeye salmon were running, and the Alaska Department of Fish and Game had given us 24 hours—from 6 p.m. Thursday to 6 p.m. Friday—to catch all we could.

The "flats" are home to sudden, fierce storms that affect weather throughout all of North America, but today the weather was beautiful, and the sea was calm. For now, we were enjoying ourselves. The sockeyes were running slow, but the incidental catch of 40- to-60 pound king salmon was good.

As night fell, Tom and I decided the weather was nice enough to allow us to fish close to shore in the midnight sun. Usually the sea conditions dictate that when night comes, it is time to run out into the open sea and deeper water. But tonight the radio chatter suggested we were doing better than most by staying in close and picking up stray kings.

During the night, the forward gear of the boat's transmission went out. Though we couldn't maneuver, we weren't worried. The weather was still good, and plenty of boats were close by. We planned to fish until the end of the fishing period and then get a tow home from one of our friends.

About 4 p.m., two hours short of the end of fishing, sea conditions started changing fast. Within an hour, the ocean had gone from a glassy calm to rolling lumps of green that rose and fell 10 to 15 feet. When fishing closed, we got a towline to another boat and headed toward protection and repairs.

First we would need to cross the Softuk sandbar to open water, wait for a large tender vessel to take our fish, then cross the bar again to get back to port. At about 7 p.m. we arrived at a buoy to wait for the tender. The surf was rough, and the seas were 15 feet and rolling in toward shore.

I made dinner of fried pork chops, fried potatoes with onions, and vegetables. After 30 hours awake, I was tired and hungry. A dozen or so boats had gathered. Tom and I enjoyed our meal, knowing we had a better catch than those around us. After eating, I crawled into my bunk in wet, dirty clothes and instantly fell into a deep sleep.

About midnight, I awoke to radio chatter. The fleet of a dozen or so small boats was circling around as it waited for a 55-foot steel tender to cross the bar and buy their fish. All of the boats in the group were anxious to get rid of their catches. The tender would assure the quality of the catch. More important, the small boats would handle much better in heavy weather without all of the extra weight of the fish on board.

The radio squalled: "What are we going to do?". . . "Did you see that guy (the tender) come out over the bar?". . ." He's going to lose that boat if he keeps that up around this neck of the woods."

Apparently, the tender had set his autopilot to a course that kept him in the channel and just plowing through the surf. Some of those who saw it said that a couple of times the entire boat was covered with breakers. This was the path we needed to take to get back to protected waters.

The tender's sodium work lights revealed a frightening scene. The seas were rolling in at a height of 18 to 20 feet, crashing over the bar as surf. Though the night was clear, a foglike mist rose above the surf. I started to worry. I wanted to be over the bar in calm water and fast asleep.

Skippers talked over the radio about what to do. The weather was supposed to kick up and blow 40 knots. No one wants to be out in the Gulf of Alaska in those conditions. One option was to head east, down the coast approximately 20 miles, for protection behind Wingham Island. The other choice was to wait until slack high water and attempt a bar crossing. At high water the channel would be the deepest, and the current would briefly slow or stop. We hoped this would be the easiest time to go across the bar.

Since we were being towed, the tender would unload our catch last. But before that could happen, the time came to cross the bay. By group consensus, we decided the tide had stopped running; we had to move. With the small boats around us, Clyde Woods on the fishing vessel *Meri-Dee* began towing us into the mouth of the Softuk bar.

The waves were steep and close together, coming up behind the boat and shoving us forward with the bow down and the stern high in the air. We were in danger of broaching, which meant a wave could force the boat forward, out of control, and toss it sideways in the trough of the wave, where the wave would break over it.

When our little fleet got into the Softuk channel, the seas stacked up. All of us were in broaching conditions. Thirty-foot boats seemed to stand on their noses. Without power, the *Wideload* would lie sideways in the trough of the waves until the towline snapped taut and jerked us forward. Our nerves were as strained as the towline. We silently waited to see if we would make it.

A wave broke behind us. Tons of white foam came over us. We were out of control. The *Meri-Dee* pulled hard. The slack in the towline tightened, ripping two cleats and 15 feet of gunnel from the *Wideload's* deck. The chunk of deck shot out into the ocean along with our lifeline to the *Meri-Dee*. We were adrift in big surf and big trouble.

Clyde brought the *Meri-Dee* in close and made a pass around us, throwing a line. I caught it, but before I could make it fast, the sea ripped the line from my hands. The waves were bucking Clyde's boat completely out of the water; I saw its propeller spinning in the air. His windows were blasted out by a wave. Tom radioed for Clyde to get out ofs there.

Out on deck I saw a wave that was about to crash over us. Just as I staggered back inside the cabin, the breaker caught us broadside, driving the boat over so far that the windows were in the water. Everything in the cabin was being thrown about. The top of the stove came off and flames shot up. I struggled to close the fuel valve.

It was survival suit time. Tom and I helped each other zip up as we bounced around the cabin.

For the next 45 minutes, we rode the surf. Giant waves crashed over us. Each time they hit, I thought it was the end. The boat would roll over until the windows were touching the sea. The big, forward work deck was buried in water. Although the boat was listing heavily to starboard, we miraculously stayed afloat.

But I never really felt scared. I didn't have time. Tom and I stayed positive. On each wave, we shouted to each other, "We'll make it! We'll make it!" I had no doubt that we would survive. I didn't know how, but I thought we would end up safely on the beach.

Finally, things seemed to calm down. We figured we had drifted over the bar. Joy swept over us. A call came over the radio that a boat from inside was coming out to rescue us. We told them that we were OK and to go after another boat that was still in the surf.

Then, out of nowhere, a giant wave hit us. We were in the surf again. I got on the radio and told the Coast Guard the name of our boat and our names. We weren't going to be able to take many more hits like the last one, I said.

We looked up to see another monster wave breaking right at us. Tom sat in the captain's seat. I sat with my back against him and my feet braced against the galley table.

It was like being hit by a speeding train. The wave crashed over us. We capsized immediately.

Water was all around me. It was dark. I was dizzy. The water was cold on my face. The floor was now the ceiling, and the survival suit kept me floating there. I couldn't find my way out. I held my breath, but it was hard with my heart beating out of control.

Finally, I had to swallow. Water filled my lungs. I began to relax. A second breath of ocean, and my thoughts turned to death. "This is it," I thought. I had never felt such loneliness. I wanted to live, but figured I had seen and done more than most people in my life. I thought this was an honorable way to die, a fisherman going down with his boat.

I decided to try to escape one last time.

I reached back and pulled myself up into a completely dark place. There was air—about an 18-inch pocket. I began throwing up seawater through my mouth and nose.

Everything was out of place. On a 28-foot boat where I had lived through four fishing seasons, I had no idea where I was. I pushed my feet down and touched nothing. Dead salmon were hitting me in the face. I finally decided that I was in the fish hold.

I heard Tom yelling and pounding on the hull from the outside, "Are you in there? Are you in there? You've got to get out!" Then I heard the sound of a wave crashing over the boat and silence from Tom. I was alone and helpless.

I started breathing hard to the point of hyperventilation. I kept screaming, "Think! Think! Think! Relax! Think! Relax!" I kept this up until I was exhausted. At that point, panic was replaced by a feeling of calm, and I was ready to use logic.

"You're in deep trouble," I said to myself. "You're alone, and no one is here to help you. So you're going to have to help yourself."

I tried to push myself under the side of the boat to escape. No way. The buoyancy of my survival suit wouldn't allow me to go deep enough. Mentally, it was even harder to push my head under the water. I was afraid that I might get tangled in the net and lines that were hanging down. Besides, the boat was still in the surf, being tipped from side to side and going up and down 15 to 20 feet at a time. From the crashing noises I heard, it seemed safer inside the boat. Though I was not happy here, I had to stay.

I propped my back and legs against the bulkheads in order to sit and think without being thrown about. It was dark, but phosphorus in the water gave everything a sparkling glow. The waves were still tossing the boat around, and me inside it. The roll of the boat would trap me, submerged, swallowing water, drowning again. Then I would rise back to the air space for a breath.

Pieces of boat and dead fish kept hitting me viciously in the darkness. I realized I had to secure them. As pieces of wood and fish came flying by, I grabbed them and worked them under and out of the hold until the area was clear.

I thought of survival. I thought of telling Tom's wife Kathy what had happened; I was certain at this point that he was dead. I thought of my friends. I knew that, even if I had to carry this boat to shore, I would make it. I was completely confident and positive.

Suddenly, there was a loud explosion. Pieces of boat came flying through the fish hold. The boat had hit the beach. The cabin and its contents were gone.

More boat pieces banged and bruised me. Pain shot through me as I was struck by the heavy galley table.

The boat bounced down the beach. I tucked myself in as tightly as possible. Finally, the boat stopped. I felt the ground beneath me, but for fear of quicksand, I still kept myself wedged between the bulkheads in the fish hold. The Copper River region is known for bottomless quicksand pits. Slowly, I got up enough courage to feel the ground for firmness. It was solid!

While the boat was pounding in the shallows, the roar of a helicopter intensified. I heard knocking on the hull of the boat. I was kneeling in the sand in about 18 inches of water. I pounded back with all of my strength. It was then I noticed severe pain in the right side of my upper body and in my right arm. It was hard to return the signal through the pain and the clumsiness of the survival suit.

The knocking stopped, and the noise of the helicopter faded away. My only thought was that Coast Guard rescuers had heard my reply, but someone else nearby needed their services more than me, and the rescuers would return shortly. Later, I found out that they never heard me and planned to return later to recover my body.

One of my main fears was that a rescue ax would splinter through the hull and break my air pocket. I had nearly drowned, and now I was scared of anything that might bring back that threat. What would happen if a hole was made in the boat? I felt sick to my stomach at the possibilities.

Moments later, my fears came to life as the water level plunged in the fish hold and then, just as quickly, came rushing back in. And just when it reached the point where I thought I was going to drown, the water ran out again.

An intense pain shot through my ears. The action of the water sucking out of the hold had created negative air pressure in the overturned hull. Later I found out that I had ruptured my right eardrum, either from the pressure drop or from the pressure of my fear-clenched jaw.

And then there was fresh air. With the water below the level of the fish hold, the clean, cold air rushed in and filled the compartment. Until then, I hadn't noticed the stench of the air pocket in which I had been held captive.

The next wave hit the boat and half-filled the fish hold again. But as fast as the boat filled, the water ran out. After half a dozen waves of diminishing volume, I was left lying in a pool of sandy water.

I needed to dig my way out from under the boat. It was like being in a little cage with no windows. The cabin and deck machinery were leveled off at the gunnels. With my face in the cold, wet sand, I could see the sun rising behind the mountains to the east. The majestic pinnacles had never looked so pretty.

But my arm and shoulder hurt more and more. The first few times I started digging, the hole filled itself as fast as I could move the sand with my one good hand. Though it was hard to be patient, I had to wait for the ocean to run out farther so the waves wouldn't backfill my escape route.

Meanwhile, I looked for a digging tool. I would need a passage approximately 24 inches wide and 48 inches long. For a shovel I found a piece of bin board, used to keep dead fish from shifting from side to side.

After digging for 15 to 20 minutes, my body in intense pain, the sound of the Coast Guard helicopter returned. It was good to know that help was there, but I had already decided I was coming out of the boat with or without help. I saw two bright orange legs and a pair of leather combat boots. Then a face loomed in under the overturned boat.

I said the only thing that came to my mind: "Top of the morning to you." It was a great day. I was on the beach, and I knew I was getting out of my tomb.

The guardsman's eyes grew as big as saucers. He asked if I was OK. Then he dropped to the sand and started digging. He seemed even more excited than I was. He got help digging, and the passageway to freedom was soon completed.

I lay on my back and reached my good arm through to my rescuers. They pulled me out from under the boat. When I stood, I realized how beat up, weak, and cramped I was. I felt like I'd gone 15 rounds with a professional boxer, and lost every one.

The first steps I made were to walk around the boat. The guardsman motioned me toward the waiting helicopter, but I kept circling the hull nestled in the sand. I pointed toward the surf and said, "If you rode through that, you'd want one last look, too." I gave her a friendly pat. I never saw the *Wideload* again.

Boarding the helicopter, I met the shivering, blanket-clad, smiling face of Tom, strapped in one of the passenger seats. We simultaneously said, "Good to see you." I put on a seat belt and kept my survival suit on. If boats can go down, so can helicopters, and I wasn't taking any chances. Ten minutes later, we were landing in Cordova, where ambulances were waiting.

At the Cordova Hospital, Tom explained that when the boat flipped, he was tossed over me and through the side window. He struggled to get on top of the boat to talk with me, but a wave pitched him off the hull. For the next few hours, Tom was thrown around in 35-degree water, sucked under by vicious undertows, and nearly drowned many times.

The Coast Guard found him staggering on the beach. It was Tom who had encouraged the Coast Guard to go back to the *Wideload* to see if my body was still in the boat.

I'm glad they did.

Chapter 40

POLAR BARE SWIM

December 1994/January 1995

By William L. Earl

There are many advantages to living in a small town. The ability to remain anonymous is not one of them. Allow me to offer an example.

Polar Bear clubs exist in Oslo, Stockholm, Juneau, Seattle and other cities that grow on the shores of an ocean. Such clubs gather on the shortest day of the year and swim (or dip) in the cold waters available to them. My hometown, Kodiak, is in the North Pacific. Why not join the ritual? I thought. At least it would be good for my cardiovascular system. Little did I know, at the outset, exactly how this new activity would affect my heart.

So, around midnight of December 31, I drove to my favorite beach, which is well beyond the traffic flow. Away from the streetlights and yard beacons, I stripped down and waded into the rolling surf. The moon winked behind clouds as I waded through the incoming tide, holding my undershorts high and dry above the waves. Not a sound reached my ears except my own splashing and laughing.

As I hit chest level, the need for dry shorts seemed excessive. I dove in and splashed a little with that hyperventilation-style breathing that one gets in nearly freezing water. The sound of my hoots echoed in the silence. Proud of my achievement, I started for shore, giddy and moving fast. I whooped a little and waved my wet garment like a lasso over my head.

Suddenly bright lights swept over me. I paused, blinded. My heart stopped!

Then the red-and-blue rotating lights switched on.

Fight-or-flight juices were pumping hard and fast throughout my body.

Something crisp moved from under my naked foot.

The Alaska State Troopers aimed their brights in my direction.

Adrenaline hit the mainstream. Whatever it was that moved from under my foot could be waiting. Was I going to put something besides myself into my shorts?

Bobbing and hopping, I tried to get a foot up, slip the collapsed leg hole around my toe and draw thin cotton between myself and the law.

More than once I bobbed below the waves, trying to synchronize the momentary opening of the leg hole with my raised limb. The struggle could have been no more terrifying than if it had been with the giant crab that I imagined underfoot, waiting to get at portions of my anatomy I have come to cherish. Just then, a voice swept over the churning surf.

"Are you all right?"

Bobbing and dancing, waist deep in the churning surf, I managed to wave. "Everything is fine! Just out for a swim!" I laughed and waved and hopped and blushed.

"Dr. Earl?" another voice called. "Is that you?"

Damn!

"Well, yes," I answered, blushing so hard I thought the water around me would begin to boil. I could imagine the report that the troopers were making for every curious radio nut on Kodiak Island, 99.5 percent of whom listen to the police calls religiously:

Stopped at Mission Beach. . . Old Dr. Earl is up to his belly button in the surf and it looked like he's been swimming. Alone. Do we bring him in?

While I hopped and splashed and blushed in shame of what might be happening, and what might occur as the whole town heard about my indecent exposure, the older trooper called again.

"Doc? You sure you're all right?"

Then the sound of the dreaded car radio intruded, informing them of a real emergency elsewhere.

"Positive!" I called back, trying to sound calm, cool, and sane. I had no desire to walk any straight lines in my unclad condition, even though I don't drink. Further, I dreaded more radio communication about slurred speech or anything that would have to be lived down in the harsh light of day.

"I'm fine!" I yelled. Cold, splashing to keep my feet safe from whatever I thought might be down there, worried about being exposed, so to speak.

"If you're sure that you're all right, we've got another call!" The second officer yelled.

A couple of muted laughs, a gear shift, and they were gone.

Blessed darkness returned. I was safe. Safe from call but my own imagination and dumb luck. I knew the moon was giggling behind the clouds, but it didn't matter anymore.

Chapter 41

THE LAST SPEAR HUNT

September 1995

By Sidney Huntington

As told to Jim Rearden

In the spring of 1943 I mushed a dog team from the Yukon River village of Galena to the headwaters of the Huslia River, a tributary to the Koyukuk, where I planned a lone hunt for beaver. On the way, at the village of Cutoff, I encountered Louis Golchik, a Koyukon Indian elder who was dying of tuberculosis.

"Let me go with you, Sidney," he requested. "It will be my last hunt, for I don't have long to live. I promise I won't be in the way."

"Sure, Louie," I agreed, for he was a wonderful old man. "If you'll take care of camp, I'll do the rest."

During that hunt we lingered over many evening campfires when I should have been hunting, because the failing Louis wanted to share his memories. Among other stories, he told me of the last Koyukon winter spear hunt for grizzly bear. He had been one of the hunters.

I have hunted with several other Koyukon elders who also sometimes talked about the old ways. Many aspects of the early Kuyukon cultures are almost unknown because of a taboo against talking about them. Many elders are reluctant to talk because they don't want to be considered superstitious, for some of their beliefs would be so labeled today. Other compelling reasons for silence were the cultural mores that celebrated humility. Because he was dying, Louis Golchik was willing to talk about forbidden subjects.

To the early Koyukons, killing a grizzly with a spear was the supreme test of a man. Their respect for "the big animal," as the grizzly was always obliquely referred to, was, understandably, close to fear. Hunting a grizzly bear with a spear required detailed planning, from the construction of the spear to the selection of the time and place to confront a bear.

Early Koyukon hunters never talked about big game animals in the presence of a woman. This cultural taboo was particularly true of the grizzly bear. The hunt was ruined if a woman learned about it; that put a curse on the hunt that could cost the hunter his life. Sometimes a woman, learning of a planned hunt, warned the man, "Don't go. We've heard of your plans." When that happened the hunter canceled the hunt.

In summer or fall the hunter usually went alone, for more than one hunter could distract a bear, making the animal more unpredictable. The bear was sought on hard ground atop an open ridge with ground on which the end of the spear would not slip. To entice a bear to charge, the hunter taunted it by shooting it with blunt arrows. The angry bear would charge, and at the last moment it would rear on its hind legs. It was then that the hunter plunged the spear point into its chest. He then jammed the end of the spear into the ground and held it there, literally for dear life. The bear pushed forward—it never retreated. Front paws beat upon the spear handle. Sometimes the bear pivoted on the crossbar, circling as it tried to reach its tormentor. The harder it tried, the more damage the spear did to its lungs or heart, and soon the grizzly toppled to the ground, dead or dying.

A winter hunt for a grizzly in its den was more complex, for it required cooperation of at least three skilled, strong and agile hunters. To kill one or more grizzlies at a den tested a hunter for speed, quickness and character. His actions determined whether he could control fear, if he was a liar, whether he could keep his mouth shut, and whether he was a braggart.

The hunt that Louis Golchik described for me occurred about 1917, and I belive it was the last Koyukon winter spear hunt for grizzly. Here is his story:

Austin Joe and Chief Paul, Koyukon hunters from Koyukuk Station, decided to make a winter hunt for grizzly bears with a spear. Both had helped take bears from a den about 10 years earlier. This was to be their last great test, for they realized that no Koyukon was likely to make such a hunt again. The tradition, and the knowledge of how to make these hunts, had nearly died out.

That fall Chief Paul told Tom Patsy and me (Golchik) that we had been chosen for the supreme test of a Koyukon hunter—to take a "big animal" from its den with a spear.

"You are the fastest and strongest young men on the Koyukuk and lower Yukon," Chief Paul said, "You will be the fast men for this last great spear hunt for the 'big animal.'"

I had never been so honored, but I couldn't discuss it—that would have been bragging. I knew stories of famous hunters who had speared the "big animal" both in the Koyukuk Valley and in the nearby Nulato and Kaltag areas, but no traditional Koyukon hunter ever admitted that he had taken, or helped take, a "big animal" with a spear.

"When the time comes, two of us will teach you," said Chief Paul. That surprised me. "Where is the other hunter?" I asked him.

"You know him. You will meet him this winter before we try to take a 'big animal,'" Chief Paul answered.

Chief Paul told Tom and me to keep in shape by running. "I want you to secretly practice the pole vault, too," Chief Paul instructed. We were to constantly think about what we had to do to beat the "big animal" in order to be real men and proud Indians like our forefathers.

In December I met Chief Paul and four others at Chips Island in the Koyukuk River. They were Tom Patsy, Austin Joe, and Andrew Paul, Chief Paul's son. I will not mention the name of the other man, because it could embarrass relatives who are still living. He had bragged about taking a "big animal" single-handed with a spear.

Chief Paul said, "Austin Joe has found the den of a female 'big animal' with two almost grown cubs. We'll practice at an old bear den and you will learn what must be done." Austin Joe had prepared the metal-tipped spear for the hunt.

We reached the old den in a day and a half, and rehearsed our hunt. Each of us had a role, and each of our lives depended on the quickness, bravery and ability of the others.

To test Tom's and my pole-vaulting ability, a big fire was built, and each of us had to vault through the flames while wearing a fur parka. A scorched parka would have disqualified us for the hunt. We were both quick and strong; I was in the best physical shape of my life. Each of us weighed about 135 pounds, and stood 5 feet, 11 inches.

Both of us qualified.

From a distance we studied the den of the three bears, planning the routes each of us had to follow to reach our positions.

The evening before the hunt we told traditional stories of ancient Koyukon hunts, tales that had been handed down from generation to generation. Some were stories about hunters who had died when their spear hunt for the "big animal" went wrong.

At daylight next morning a light wind blew from the north, and the temperature was about zero. We didn't eat breakfast. Chief Paul gave last-minute instructions, and the six of us swiftly moved to the occupied den.

Tom Patsy, who was the fastest, dashed to the den entrance, vaulted over it with his 8-foot pole of dried birch, and drove the pole across the den mouth. I followed and quickly drove my pole in place so that the two poles formed an X across the den opening. "Big animal" dens usually have loose, dry soil at the entrance, which permits poles to be driven into the ground so they won't slip.

The two poles Tom and I held kept the "big animals" in the den until the man with the killing spear was ready. The commotion we caused by vaulting into position and closing the den with our poles brought the old female to the den mouth. She pushed against the poles, but we held firm. In front of the den, while the old bear raged against the crossed poles, Austin Joe cut a hole in the ground into which the handle end of the killing spear could be planted. Meanwhile, Chief Paul talked to the "big animal" in a language unknown to me. I was later told it was bear talk.

While Austin dug the hole, Andrew Paul and the other man joined Tom and me in holding the gate poles. Austin Joe finished the hole, and Chief Paul set the spear handle into it and braced himself.

"Let the first one out," he called. We pushed our poles back and the big female rushed directly onto the spear held by Chief Paul. The point entered her chest, and the crossbar held the roaring and struggling animal off so that her powerful claws and teeth could not reach him.

Chief Paul held the spear handle firmly in the hole in the ground, and with a mighty heave, using the momentum of the charging "big animal," threw it right over himself. The big female, her chest ripped open, flew about 25 feet downhill. She landed with a thud, rolled a few feet, and lay dying.

The instant the big female left the den, Tom and I jammed our poles back into the ground to re-form the gate. Two nearly grown cubs remained. Now the test: Chief Paul handed the spear to the man who had bragged about spearing a bear single-handed. Chief Paul spoke, "I helped take a 'big animal' once with a spear. I never talked about it before. I know this is my last 'big animal'—the one you see lying there, dead. This could be your last one, too. Now you try, because I don't believe you ever took a 'big animal' with a spear.

"We didn't tell you that we were going to try to take the 'big animals' with a spear because we were afraid you would talk, or perhaps you would refuse to go with us. I want to demonstrate to these men how not to brag, and why no Koyukon should talk about taking 'big animals' with a spear, trying to make a big man of himself."

The man accepted the spear. He tried to get the young "big animal" at the mouth of the den to accept it. To test the "big animal," he placed the point of the spear under its mouth, near the throat. The "big animal" slapped the spear aside. This meant he sensed fear in the man holding the spear. If the "big animal" had not slapped it aside, it would have meant that the man holding the spear was brave enough to handle that "big animal."

The "big animal" pushed the blade aside not once, but twice, indicating that the man was afraid. Then Austin Joe grabbed the spear, saying, "You lie. You never took a 'big animal' by yourself with a spear. This one tell us. I never took one either, but I never lie. Now watch this."

With that, Austin Joe called, "Open the den." Tom and I pulled our poles clear. One of the "big animals" charged. Austin Joe set the spear and the charging "big animal" impaled himself upon it. As with the old female, the growling and struggling bear was thrown through the air to land far downhill.

Austin Joe handed the bloody spear once more to the braggart, with the same results. The last "big animal" in the den pushed the blade aside.

Then the spear was handed to one of the younger men. The third "big animal" charged and impaled himself, and the spearman tossed it down the hill to join the others.

"One of the younger men," was, of course, Louis Golchik, who refused to brag, even though he was near death.

The 18-inch long metal blade from the spear used on that hunt was displayed for many years in the home of trader Dominic Vernetti at Koyukuk Station. With lingering belief, Louis told me, "That spear point would not be good for another hunt. Too many women's hands have touched it. Too many people have seen it."

Louis Golchik died a few weeks after our beaver hunt.

Chapter 42

WITH TRUSTING EYES BEHIND ME

February 1996

Story by Ellen Paneok

Barrow, December 21—winter solstice. It is 8 o'clock on an arctic morning swathed in darkness. Today we will have maybe two hours of twilight.

I am an Eskimo pilot from Kotzebue but have been flying out of here since 1987. I consider this my home. My people keep bringing me back.

At 27 degrees below zero my breath freezes to my eyelashes as I walk out to the airplane for my first flight of the day. I am headed for the village of Wainwright, 86 miles southwest.

Hoarfrost covers everything standing in the wind's way. Every antenna on the Cessna 207 bristles with whiteness and the wings need to be swept clean of frost.

My flashlight bobs as I walk in the silent darkness. The wind sucks my breath away, whips my hair about my face. I wonder what brought me back to this cold, desolate place. Why would anyone settle here in the first place? Are humans that desperate for space? Then I think of the people here, my relatives, and realize that I am doing something for them, my aunt in Point Lay, my great-uncle in Wainwright, my great-uncle in Nuiqsut, my cousins in Barrow. They are the reason I put up with the cold and the harshness.

The village awakens, lights glow brightly from windows. In the darkness, the village generator hums, enabling work-a-day life to go on. Dogs let out for the morning bark greetings to each other. They know that with their protection, polar bears won't trudge into the village. Cars startled to life grind their engine bones together to wake up.

The airport comes alive with activity, too, as the bush air taxis prepare for their daily mail and passenger runs. The airline forklift shuttles mail to the commuter carriers, a cloud of exhaust following it, pushed by the wind. The airport beacon signs its hello to open tundra; blackness answers.

I request the weather and turn over the engine. I have no passengers, just an airplane full of freight and mail. It takes awhile to thaw my trusty bird, even though it has been plugged into an engine heater all night. The engine pops to life grudgingly. My seat is hard from the cold. The instruments fog up, and it will take up to a minute before the oil pressure rises.

I do not touch the throttle or the control wheel with my bare hands, lest my fingers freeze. The ink in my pen has congealed in my pocket, forcing me to warm it with the palm of my hand before writing. I carry two flashlights to ward against the dark in case the cockpit lights fail.

After the engine is warm, I rev up, taxi and take off into the black sky, knowing that exhaust billows in my wake betray my flight path. I don't expect to see any sign of human life for another half hour in this black Twilight Zone.

Soon enough I will have a little puff of heat down by the side of my knee, but the rest of the airplane will remain cold. Navigation needles direct my path. Occasionally, my flashlight searches the wings' leading edges for ice buildup. I would have to return to Barrow if I saw any ice, for it adds weight and dangerously changes the wing shape.

In the many hours I've spent in the sky, I've often thought back to the days of exploration and the early period of aviation in Alaska. As in the 1930s, when Wiley Post and Will Rogers visited the Arctic, planes remain the main source of transportation and communication among the villages. But I was born too late for that era, when it seemed each day brought a new discovery.

Years ago, the fuselages of dusty airplanes were covered with notes and salutations roughly scribbled-out between people in the villages. I still carry envelopes containing love letters or deliver checks to wives for shopping money. Sometimes, by special request, I bake and deliver birthday cakes for my friends or relatives who live in other villages.

In the old days, when airplanes flew so slowly, women were proud to say that their children were born between destinations. People with broken bones or sickness were flown in and out of remote sites. All of that still goes on today, only with more sophisticated equipment and, of course, the planes now are much faster.

When aviation was young in Alaska, a whole village—the young, old, working and sick—would rush out to see the strange bird land as they anxiously awaited the pilot and cargo. Often the pilot would throw out candy to the children, which they scrambled over like ravens on a feast. Furs were carried out and love notes carried in. The airplanes were held together dubiously with putty and bailing wire from numerous unplanned contacts with the ground. Now the modern engine is so reliable it is rare to have any real trouble while flying.

The trust was great in the eyes of the Eskimos as they trundled onto these venerable birds for the next destination. I used to own and fly antique airplanes, and can imagine what nightmares it took to keep those airplanes running. Early pilots had to drain out the engine oil every night and figure out ways to heat their aircraft each morning. I must remember that every time I complain about the need to plug in the engine heater. I must remember to be more thankful.

Thirty-five minutes into the flight, I start looking for signs of human habitation. The only thing I expect to see is the faint glow of Wainwright's lights in the far distance. Sometimes the ice fog blots out the lights until I am right over the village. In the blackness I click the microphone seven times, and a runway suddenly appears with ghostly, fuzzy lights directing my landing path. I feel powerful. I made those lights come on.

On final approach for landing, the bright lights flash past me in a whir as I feel for the ground. Watching the gauges and gauntlet of runway lights, I touch down. The hard-packed snow squeals in protest as the tires come to a halt. My temperature gauge reads 35 degrees below zero.

The welcoming committee consists of the village's trucks and cars. They hunker down, headlights on, billowing exhaust caught in the ramp lights. As my engine ticks down to a stop the villagers drive up to my plane. I climb out into the cold in the blaze of their headlights. A truck backs up to the cargo doors, which I open with gloved hands.

Greetings are fast and frantic as I grip the frosted cargo net and slide it off. Dark shapes of people bustle around, boots squeaking as we hurriedly off-load mail onto the truck.

A glad cry exudes from the crowd. The fog is dense, and nobody expected any flights that day.

Baggage materializes, and I recognize it before I even see the passengers. I think to myself that I've been in the Arctic too long when I can distinguish one bag from the next. The airplane is unloaded and hands extend greetings—gloveless, as is the custom around here. Then everyone climbs into my plane and the gloves snap back onto cold hands in a hurry.

An old Eskimo couple is going to Barrow for the week's shopping. There will be bright city lights and shopping treasures—fresh fruits and vegetables and presents for grandchildren—that aren't available in the villages. Another Eskimo lady who I have known for years journeys to Barrow for her weekly chemotherapy. I have been taking her there every Friday for two months now. She is doing fine and improving. It looks hopeful that she will win over the cancer.

A man approaches importantly, expecting his company's paychecks. I wonder where in this village they could be spending it. Another awaits a little box of snow machine parts. He has been on foot for a month and he grins in anticipation of having transportation again. His snow machine broke down 40 miles out on the tundra, and he'd had to walk back to the village, the aurora lighting his way.

Another box holds Caterpillar road grader repair parts, so the runway can be properly cleared of drifting snow. His beard and mustache are caked with frost, but he doesn't seem to notice or care because he is thinking about the parts. An old, old Eskimo man comes up to me and tells me I have owl eyes, meaning I can see in the dark. The young Eskimo men furtively glance in my direction when they step up with their baggage, not saying a word. A little girl, barely 2 years old, knows my name and wants to be a pilot when she grows up. Her mother smiles. Another woman brings me a bag full of whale muktuk to take home. Here, the skin and fat is considered a delicacy. I hug her and tuck it away in my bag to eat later.

I am numbed with cold as I load up the passengers and instruct them on the safety features of the airplane. A passenger tells me that my cheeks are turning white—the onset of frostbite. I tighten my face cover and still feel the stinging bite of the frost. I turn back in my seat to face my passengers, and to make sure that they are comfortable and seat-belted. I see faces like my mother's. She was born here in Wainwright. We gossip and joke, despite the freezing air.

I can see the trust in the silent eyes shining in the darkness, the same trust given to pilots before me. I have seen this trust before, even as I've struggled to land on snowblown village runways with only a little visibility and a lot of luck. And yet the passengers always eye me in mute certainty that I will get them to their destinations.

Cold steam emanates from everybody, the windows frost up, and as I crank up the engine, another arctic sojourn begins, the black morning sky before me, the trusting eyes behind me.

Chapter 43

CLUTTER

October 1996

By Carol Sturgulewski

"You've got a pretty nice place," my dad admitted, visiting our Aleutian home for the first time. "But isn't it a bit . . . cluttered?"

That's not clutter, Dad. That's a decorating scheme. Books, food, laundry detergent piled in every corner—that's what you call Bush Décor.

We live in rural Alaska, where the nearest interior decorator is 850 miles away by plane, and the price of his airfare runs into even higher figures. By the time you work in the cost of shipping furniture out here, those dreams of an Ethan Allen grandfather clock have degenerated into a Timex.

Because lumber and other building materials are expensive to ship to our treeless island paradise, the cost of housing is extremely high. The same is true for just about anyplace in Alaska off the road system. As a result, builders try to use as few materials as possible, which leaves one with smaller spaces. The most popular architect for the Bush would be someone with previous experience designing sardine cans.

Unalaska was a major staging area for World War II in the North Pacific, and many wartime buildings are still in use. Military "cabanas"—16-by-20 foot frame houses—are home to lots of folks. These tiny abodes bring new meaning to the phrase "breakfast in bed;" one need only roll over in the sack to open the refrigerator door. And be sure to knock loudly before stopping by Captain Dave's cabana: The bathtub is in the entryway.

When a single man wound up living in a three-bedroom duplex next door to us, my friends and I were appalled at the wasted space. We mumbled about posting his address at the airport as a shelter for stranded travelers, until he redeemed himself by taking in boarders.

Recycling is not a new concept in the Bush. One popular building block is the container van off a semi-trailer truck. Once they've been retired from service by shipping companies, container vans make dandy utility buildings. Stack a couple on top of one another Leg-O style, install another pair a few feet away, slap a roof over the whole thing, and you've got a mechanic's shop, a small seafood processing plant or a warehouse—to name just three of the commercial ventures that have capitalized on this idea in our town. The fire department frowns upon them as housing, citing some pesky details about doors and windows and ventilation. But they're just the right size for the Bush version of the "mini-storage warehouse."

In the suburbs back on the mainland, people use their garages to handle the overflow of living. Here, a garage is a rare luxury, and when you do find one, it's probably stuffed with deflated buoys, ragged crab pots, torn netting and other precious commodities that no true fisherman could ever part with, but somehow never gets around to repairing.

This lack of space causes a problem in dealing with such minor incidentals as food storage. Most of us do a lot of our shopping in bulk, buying six months' worth of groceries at a time and shipping it out from the big city. This is where elastic walls become an exciting architectural concept.

In my kitchen, sacks of dog food are stacked in one corner, buckets of laundry detergent in another, and cases of pop in a third. The pantry shelves are groaning, the washer and dryer buried under giant-sized cartons of cereal, and rolls of paper towels and oatmeal boxes line the tops of cupboards. (Homeowners' Hint from "Ring of Fire": Use those high shelves for light stuff in case of earthquakes.)

The list isn't finished. There's a 50-pound sack of sugar under the bed, two 25-pound sacks of flour on top of the freezer and 18 pounds of margarine in the neighbor's freezer next door. Making cookies can be a real scavenger hunt.

Outside the kitchen, the pileups continue. Books and videos overflow from shelves to boxes to heaps. Our oldest son has no interest in wearing anything that needs to be placed on a hanger, so his closet is devoted to the family's winter clothes and hunting gear. The middle child, who currently refuses to wear anything but Batman pajamas (day and night), shares a tiny room with two filing cabinets, the computer, bookshelves, canning jars, laundry baskets, and the dog. The baby's bassinet is in our room, sitting on a box of family photos and letters. He's outgrowing it, which means he'll need a crib, which means moving the computer into our room, which means moving out my dresser, which means . . . well, maybe we'll just burn the photos and put the baby in the empty box.

What makes all this livable is the fact that nearly everyone we know lives the same way. We adapt. If opening a cupboard brings down an avalanche of macaroni and cheese mix, I just assume that's what God wants me to make for dinner tonight.

At least I don't have to order all my groceries a year in advance. In many remote villages, especially those in the far north, the barge comes in only once or twice a year. All of life's necessities are ordered once a year. When the huge order arrives, putting away the groceries becomes a creative activity. I've had reports of using cases of food as the basis for more Bush Decorating: A few pillows and throw rugs placed artistically over your stacks of canned goods, and you've created a couch, table, etc. By the middle of winter when the cabin walls seem to be closing in on you, your furniture starts shrinking, too.

Of course, at my house, things seem to expand while the walls shrink. We've added two children to our household since Dad made that comment about clutter. We'd invite him back to compare the place, but I don't know if we could squeeze him in.

It could be worse, though. We have running water and electricity, which isn't always taken for granted in rural Alaska. A friend once told me her ultimate fantasy isn't a romantic rendezvous on a Caribbean beach. It's taking a hot bath in her own home three times a day.

I can revel in that luxury anytime I want. But, of course, the towels are stashed behind three cases of toilet paper, a gallon jug of hair conditioner, six boxes of toothpaste . . .

Chapter 44

KINGDOM OF CLEAN-ENOUGH

May/June 1997

By Leslie Leyland Fields

At fish camp, I hang out my wash in the rain sometimes. With rubber boots, orange slicker, I haul the water-soaked clothes down the back steps and piece by piece drape the limbs and torsos, the empty feet, from the dripping line. I gave up on waiting for sunny wash days years ago. The dirty clothes would multiply in their designated corners while I played the meteorologist, hand out, head up to the sky, forecasting the future of our wardrobe: Clearing to clean or continuing to pile and darken? The goal back then was to wash the eight or 10 loads and get them hung out, dry and back in, all in one day.

This seldom, if ever, happens now. I'm pleased with whatever wet falls upon my wash as it hangs. This is what we call the second rinse, more than a simple euphemism for rain. We mean the term quite literally as the clothes hang and sway between various stages of wet, damp, cool, nearly dry, then wet all over again, through three, four, even five days, which is the current record. This is where the real cleaning comes, the purification. It is badly needed. For a great domestic irony is that on an island, in a place of such water, there is so little for our clothes.

I do the wash here for seven people in two stout old women called Ms. Maytag and Sears Kenmore. They are wringer washing machines both of them, one nearly 20 years old. One washes, one rinses. They are my lady friends, these two, my servants with iron muscles and tight foam lips that clamp and squeeze out the most conspicuous waters. I work them hard, and their agitation and ardor is admirable, but the task is muddied by our well.

My husband and I hand-dug the 20-foot pit the fall we moved here. The water that filters in is clear enough, but there is simply not enough. I can fill the machines only once, then I must nurse and strategize my way from the cleanest clothes to the dirtiest, from towels to socks, running usually eight loads through those same two drums of water. After the first load, the wash water turns a light gray, the rinse water has a skim of suds. By the time I finish with the socks, roiling now in a murky soup, I am watching for rain.

At the end of last fishing season, even this compromise of cleanliness was stretched. Tragedy (of an admittedly domestic sort) struck. I had just begun what was to be a day of washing—10 loads heaped in the room waiting for their own brand of redemption, when smoke began coiling delicately from the cord of the old Maytag. The room soon filled with the smell of electricity gone bad, and sure enough, she was gone. In the midst of her duty, with a belly full of water and clothes, she died, an inglorious but fitting end after 20-some years of service.

There was no time to mourn, however. We were out of clothes, all of us, and the washing had to go on. Within minutes, as I rearranged the washroom, I was back to more primitive days, to the one-machine system I used for 10 years. The one machine, S. Kenmore, washed, and I took over Ms. Maytag's job and acted as agitator and de-soaper. After I fed the washed clothes through the wringer, they peeled through, sliding into the laundry sink, where I lifted them up and down in the water as though making smoke signals—in, out, plunge, slop, then back through the wringer and into the basket while I began filling the machine for the next load. Though I could often see froth on the fabric the last time through, I pronounced them done in successively shorter times.

Several hours later, I issued an edict to my four young children in the patient voice of exhaustion: "You must wear your clothes two days now. The second machine has broken and it is much harder to do the wash, so we'll wear our clothes longer, OK?" They had no problem with that, despite the fact that it summarily reversed an earlier edict: "You cannot wear your clothes two days in a row—they're too dirty."

My husband had no need to alter his fish camp dressing habits, however. A child of a mother who washed on a scrub board, he had full appreciation for the labor of washing. He can jury-rig a T-shirt for a week, a sweatshirt for four days, jeans for five, and still look reasonable. I seldom complain, but nor do I compliment, because what do you say, exactly—"Thank you for not putting clean clothes on this morning?"

I could wish for another machine, a modern automatic gal who could foment, agitate, sudsify, wring and centrifuge completely dry. And while wishing, I could wish for a well with more water, but I don't. I am reconciled to the labor of washing, to this darker shade of clean. I discovered years ago that one is not injured, maimed or otherwise damaged by wearing jeans still stiff with soap, grayed socks, or whites blushed with assorted dyes.

Though a prime candidate for rescue by a white-steeded knight or a white tornado who would lift me from my relative squalor into a well-scrubbed kingdom, I refuse to live by the rules of such a zealous place. They are the make-believe rules of a fantasyland where resources pretend to be infinite. Not so in my kingdom. Here everything is finite; here, everything costs. I could pack more water for the washing machine, use it a little more liberally, but that costs water that pools in the well on its own schedule. We could bathe more frequently in our wood-fueled sauna, but it costs more water, and wood that must be gathered, cut and packed in armloads up the hill. There is a formula for all of this: Reasonably clean costs this much; very clean costs this much more; dazzling television-commercial clean costs all of this. No. Name me Reasonable, a willing subject in a land ruled by Economy and Frugality, twin princesses who stand in stiff-knee'd jeans ruling with lavish wands, wands that crown us all clean-enough and good.

Chapter 45

JESS'S ARK

September 1997

By Carol Knight Copeland

D ad was in a restless way. By 1948, he figured we children had experienced one
Alaska winter too many. A better future, he and mom agreed, was in store Outside, especially for my brother and me. They would take us to Kansas City, to
live with our grandmother and attend school. Well, they had the desire to go, but
doing it would be neither simple nor easy. While Eagle had air service, he could not
afford the fare. And while Eagle had roads, none of them went anywhere. The regular steamboat service that had for almost 50 years connected the upper Yukon with
the rest of the world had been discontinued.

So while other Eagle residents pondered nothing more serious than the
coming of the Spring thaw, Dad pondered what he saw as the only option to
making an escape. Build a raft substantial enough to float a car and then "sail" it
down the Yukon River to Circle. From there he could drive the Steese Highway
to Fairbanks and then the still-new Alcan to the Lower 48. Easy as pie.

When he mentioned this plan to the hangers-on at the Northern Commercial Co. store which he managed, there was much polite shaking of heads.
Dad, they assumed, had a particularly bad case of cabin fever, common in these
parts, and once a wildflower bloomed and the ice went out, he would come back
to his senses. Sail a raft with a car on it down the Yukon River? Talk about a
dumb idea.

But my Dad, known as Jess Knight to everyone except my brother and me,
was not a man who did a lot of talking and when he did talk, seldom was what
he said dumb. Added to that, he was an expert welder, skilled mechanic and experienced riverman, not to mention an accomplished inventor. So he gathered what
would become known as his "planning committee" around the toasty-warm barrel stove that was the wintertime centerpiece of the store and set his plans to paper.

Dad had one of the village's three autos in mind, an ancient 1926 Oakland which belonged to long-time customs agent Jack Hilliard, who enjoyed riding around the 20 miles of Eagle road with his dog, Ramona. When the car was not set to the business of riding Mr. Hilliard and Ramona, it was set to the business of helping the local kids learn to drive. In fact, my brother Billy, at age 10, had begun using the car to help Dad deliver groceries. It was a deal made in heaven, because that was about the last place this old car had to go. But it was a car and that made "The Ark" possible. No, Dad didn't call it The Ark. Everybody else did. In many ways, it was the Knight family version of the Biblical ark. On it, the four of us, our dog and as many household treasures as we could safely carry would make the 160-mile trip to Circle. With the days lengthening, Dad got to work in earnest next to the company warehouse on the riverbank. He fashioned together a raft of heavy timbers, each bolted firmly one to the other, and then welded together 16 empty drums that were fastened to the underside of the logs to supply the necessary (he hoped) buoyancy. This was all done by the use of the "figure" gauge. In other words, Dad figured that each drum would support approximately 400 pounds, which would give the raft enough strength to carry the Oakland, us and whatever else was necessary for the trip.

By mid-July all the bolting and welding had been done and the monstrous raft was ready to launch. A dozen of his most ardent supporters helped Dad slip The Ark over the riverbank and into the glacial waters of the Yukon. And it floated perfectly. High, wide and handsome, its barrels well above the waterline, a veritable master of the seas . . . well, master of the Yukon at any rate. There was much congratulating of Dad but his smile was tight. There was still that business of the car.

His helpers pulled the raft, which was really a jury-rigged barge when you think about the size of the thing, up against the riverbank and Dad pulled the Oakland slowly onto it. Everyone took a deep breath as the ton of automobile swished the raft this way and that before finding true center. And they did not exhale quickly, because the weight had driven the drums almost completely underwater.

But this was Alaska . . . in mid-July. To start from scratch would mean one more winter and Dad did not intend to put our Outside educations off for that long. He stood on the bank a long time, looking at the raft with its drums almost under water and then said, "If the paddles work, it can go."

The "paddles" were actually wooden affairs bolted directly to the rear wheels through slots at the rear of the raft. The idea was simple: Crank up the car, put it in gear and Presto! You have a motor raft.

Again, Dad had a great disappointment. The raft just would not go up river and would not buck the six-mile-per-hour current. But, again, this is Alaska where the best made plans work whether they will or not. It's that winter situation. Dad's smile returned and he announced that since Circle was downriver, there was no need to go upriver. The Ark is plenty stable for downriver so we are going.

The Day of Departure

Mother couldn't sleep the night of August 18, though she was exhausted from packing. We kids could not know the worries that can go through a mom's mind, about how that river was going to handle us, where ultimately it would take us, what dangers lay ahead: drowning topping that list, but being marooned in the trackless lands of the Yukon, even in August, had dangers not far behind drowning. And then there was Alberta Stout, my best friend, who would be going with us, at least as far as Fairbanks, where she would visit her grandmother. It was one such thing to keep your own children safe during an adventure such as this, adding another's child must have compounded things tenfold.

Mother was also sad thinking about leaving her home of the past 10 years. She recalled arriving in Eagle in 1938, when Billy had been two months old and I only three. We had flown in from Circle where my dad had managed the company store for four years. She fought away the tears, but we knew leaving was painful. These had been happy years.

The entire town stood along the riverbank waving good-bye as The Ark was pushed into the current and began to float, lazily at first, downstream. Dad started the Oakland and used the power to turn the paddles for a short while to let the well-wishers know the system worked: It wasn't long until the little town of Eagle disappeared from view. The river was gentle in these first few miles. We had breakfast at Calico Bluff and as we floated slowly on down Billy and I were allowed to row the small lifeboat around the raft and even to the shore to give our dog, Cookie, some relief. While this trip was a problem for Dad and something of a sadness for mom, for Billy, Alberta and me it was really big adventure.

We played "pirates" and "attacked" the raft as we brandished a hand-ax we found in the rowboat.

We continued in this playful spirit until we reached Trout Creek where the idea of adventure took a meaning none of us children had truly contemplated. First we felt a perceptible surge as the current narrowed and grew stronger. Then, too late, Dad realized we were being swept into a fast, narrow channel behind an island. Hanging over the now charging current were huge "sweepers," massive spruce trees that had fallen into the river, but were still rooted to the banks. Sweepers are the scourge of every riverboatman, from the Mississippi to the Yukon. Hit just one and it can destroy a vessel, large or small. This was no pretend danger here. The water was fast and shallow, our raft was large and unwieldy. To make this passage safely, all hands would have to work and work hard. While Alberta and I rowed against the current with our paddles, Mom, Dad, and Billy pushed on the pike poles with all their might to keep the raft from being caught—and possible destroyed—by the trees. Finally, The Ark passed the trees, only to bump ominously on the rocky bottom several times before, finally, floating into the main channel. Our first crisis was behind us, but Dad didn't let the congratulations last too long. More rough sailing was to come below Nation City.

This old town, by then abandoned, was an early day settlement of trappers and miners. Even so, it was here Dad decided to make camp that night. He took a chance and chose not to put the tent up, but before midnight it began to rain, so we hurriedly put our bedrolls in the car, ate a light breakfast and pushed off at 5 a.m.

Rolls, Boils, and Whirlpools

August 19. A short distance downriver from Nation City lurks the Nations Rocks where the river changes it character completely, from a long, generally slow glacial stream into a hard, driving section of whitewater that rolls, boils and spins out whirlpools. It looked like an awful place for any boat, but we were committed. Mom and Dad grabbed the oars and, like a couple of accomplished white-water rafters, rowed hard to keep the raft between the rocks while we kids held on to whatever was secure. Waves splashed onto the deck and water rolled all around, but was of little concern since the rain had already wetted us to the core. And the rains were a gift, as we all came to appreciate, since they raised the water level and that helped us float safely over that dangerous place.

Six miles past Nations Rocks came the Chain of Rocks, which Dad hoped to avoid by going through a narrow slough once used by the steamboats. But the current and the big raft had other ideas and, even with power, he could not get The Ark out of the strong current. Recognizing his plight, he quickly cut the engine, jumped from the car and, with Mom as his only helpmate, manned the oars. Two human beings matching their strength against that of a rushing river and a ton of raft. We passengers again endured a hard ride as the raft rolled through the rough water, the little lifeboat banging against the deck with such force that green paint and even wood chips were splintering off. Luck was again on our side; we missed the rocks themselves though it seemed some of that water was very "hard." Mom and Dad were visibly relieved by our close call on the Chain, but we kids were delighted by the whole adventure. And, Dad said, with the Chain behind us, the worst was over . . . or so he thought.

If there was a real danger on that raft, it was water across the bow. Dad had said that water crashing over the front could sink the raft or throw it off center, causing the car to slide off. But none of us had given that danger much thought until about 4 p.m., just after we passed the mouth of Coal Creek, when a brisk headwind suddenly started blowing, causing waves to wash over the deck. Mom was scared. Really scared and Dad's face was a study in serious concentration. The headwind was so great, the raft began to swing ponderously in the river, hardly making any progress at all. To stabilize the bow and get some forward motion, Dad started the Oakland and—very slowly—turned the paddle wheels to give us some progress downriver. A half hour later, the river widened into what I can best describe as a lake and the waves continued to grow, beating against our raft. We all knew we were in serious danger. We kids were put into life jackets and Dad was looking for a port, any port. An island was nearby, off to our left, so he hoping to find shelter from the wind and waves, drove the raft slowly in that direction.

At this point, the current was fortunately stronger than the wind and we made it safely to a channel between the island and the main bank. We were out of the wind, but landing was not going to be easy. The motor was turned off and as we approached the shore under a dead drift, a gust of wind and a push of the current caused The Ark to make a complete 360 degree revolution. This could have been ticklish as well, if The Ark got caught in shallow water and grounded. Quickly, Dad gave Alberta and me the two lines, we got into the rowboat and headed for the beach. Dad and Mom used the oars to slow down and guide the raft. Once ashore, Alberta and I scampered for a dead spruce and tied the lines to it. Mom jumped into the knee-deep water to stabilize the bow and Dad pushed us on in with the pike pole. And thus ended day two, 50 miles from Circle and one more crisis behind us.

In spite of the day's adventure, we kids took to exploring the beach as Cookie, glad to have four legs on solid ground, ran right along with us. Mom changed out of her wet clothes and got to drying all our wets as best she could on the campfire, which almost consumed one of her tennis shoes. Dad put up a tent to insure the rain would stop and not come again and, after a good supper, we all went to bed. Sleeping was difficult for the adults since this day had been a series of scary moments, but for us kids, it was just the end of an exciting day. We slept soundly, Cookie curled up between us. Tomorrow, Circle.

The Home Stretch

August 20. That morning we found a world dazzling in its benevolence. The river here seemed like a great smooth lake and on it we would travel, slowly and lazily, for the first eight miles. Billy was sleeping in the bedrolls in the back seat of the car and Cookie got so excited about not having to deal with water splashing against her that she was again her happy self, running and barking back and forth on the raft. She got so carried away in her unbounding happiness that we were no longer facing storms, rocks and sweepers that she fell off the raft on several occasions. Even Dad and Mom were making small talk and the optimism was palpable.

But we had one more major challenge ahead of us. Actually two, and both could turn this thus-far successful adventure into a catastrophe.

On our approach to Circle, the channel splits—one part flows straight, while the other, which leads to Circle, makes an almost reverse bend. If we missed that channel, The Ark would float past Circle, we would be unable to drive upriver and none of us wanted to think about the bad things that could happen past that.

Dad realized he needed maneuvering power, the only hope was Cornelius Roberts, who ran a fish camp some six miles north of Circle and owned a skiff with a kicker. But Dad couldn't take the raft to Roberts' side of the river for fear of running into the fellow's fish wheel. So he instructed me to row the lifeboat to the Roberts camp and ask for help. It was somewhat of a scary trip, at least for Mom and Dad, since from their vantage point, it seemed I was going to run into the fish wheel, but I got past it and down to the Roberts landing where Jennie, Cornelius' wife, came down to speak with me.

I nodded that I understood and pushed off to paddle back to The Ark, an island now between me and it, so I couldn't yell my message. I paddled hard and was making good time when I ran into a sandbar. I pulled the rowboat off, paddled hard as any 12-year-old girl can and finally reached Mom and Dad.

"What'd she say?" Dad asked.

"Mr. Roberts gone bear hunting," I answered.

Dad looked crestfallen, so I hastened to add, as the raft moved quickly toward decision time, "She expects him back any time."

I don't know why, but Dad decided not to wait. He started the car and was attempting to get into the channel that would take us to Circle when we heard a motorboat. We turned and there was Mr. Roberts. Within minutes, the raft and the motorboat were tied together and slowly, with the motorboat pushing us like a tugboat easing an ocean liner into safe harbor, The Ark moved into the Circle channel.

By now, many of Circle's residents were lining the riverbank. Many had heard of Dad's crazy scheme and few had believed he would actually do it. But there he was: Raft, Oakland, wife, kids and dog chugging slowly toward the Circle dock. Within minutes, The Ark was secured and there was much laughter, handshakes, backslaps and some tears of joy shared between people who knew what Alaska was really about and how one had to make do to live in it. For Dad, this was his shining moment. He had made it to Circle. Next stop, Kansas City. Well, maybe. Remember, there were two final challenges? The second and most important was getting that Oakland off that raft and onto a road.

There was some chin-scratching on that one until Eddie O'Leary offered to lift the car with the bucket of his Caterpillar tractor. Nobody had a better idea and truth be told, there was some worry there for a while that our ride to Outside might become rip-rap on the shores of the Yukon. But Eddie got the job done and soon the Oakland was ready for one more ride, this with a loving family inside heading for the home of friends in the town of Central.

And that night, as they were to tell later, Mom and Dad slept very well. Family safe and sound. A "dumb idea" that had captured the imaginations of an entire region proved good.

Epilogue

Postscript. My brother and I were enrolled in school in Kansas City, where we lived with our maternal grandmother; we never returned to Alaska as permanent residents. Mom and Dad drove the Oakland to Seattle, where it was sold for about $75. This completed the circle, since the car had been shipped to Alaska from Seattle in the '20s. They then flew to Fort Yukon to manage the Northern Commercial Co. until the fall of 1950, when they returned to Kansas City. In 1967 they returned to Eagle to manage the Biederman General Store. After retirement in 1974, they spent summers in Eagle in the old N.C. Co. store, which they had purchased. Ill health prevented their return to Alaska after 1988; Dad died in 1992 and Mom in 1996.

Chapter 46

RAVEN

September 1997

By Sherry Simpson

Every winter morning, just as the sun's uncertain light washes across the Tanana Flats, ravens fly over my log cabin on their daily commute to town. Perhaps, like me, they would prefer to remain here in the hills above Fairbanks, where temperatures are a little warmer. But town is where the day's work lies, where ravens and people earn their daily victuals. The birds crest the ridges alone, maybe in pairs, sometimes strung out in groups that punctuate the sky like ellipses.

When the light drains from the sky several hours later, they return the same way, arrowing toward the twilight gathering at the northern edge of the world. Alaska Native myths say Raven—the Creator, the Transformer, the Trickster—tossed the sun into the sky and had the power to plunge the world into night. This is how it appears to me, too, as the ravens appear with dawn and depart at dusk.

Where they go is only one of the raven's mysteries. There are other, new-fangled scientific puzzles, such as how these birds perch on metal light poles at 40 degrees below zero without freezing their feet solid, and why creatures that are technically migratory stick around these chilly provinces all year round. When the sun stalls just above the horizon and the cold makes me feel sorry for myself, I stop asking what I'm doing here and start wondering what they're doing here.

Rod King spends his winters wondering, too. A pilot and a biologist for the U.S. Fish and Wildlife Service, he studies ravens by relying on tags, radio transmitters and an ability to drive while peering out his windshield at the sky. He captures ravens when they come into town to pick at the carcass of civilization, having discovered that eating *moo goo gai pan* out of the Chinese restaurant's garbage is much easier than locating a moose carcass in the forest.

At nightfall, the ravens return along the same flight paths so faithfully that, as King notes, you can almost take a compass bearing to their roosts outside Fairbanks. My house falls underneath one such route. Another winter roost lies about 40 miles away. Why would a raven fly 80 miles every day when it could sleep in perfectly good spruce trees closer to town?

"The mystery of the raven," King intones, half-joking. Then he thinks of a better answer, "So they can hide the sun and bring out the moon and stars." Just as I suspected.

Ravens are enigmatic for other reasons. They are the largest passerine, or perching songbirds, but their eloquence emerges in syllables, not notes. One Fairbanks researcher identified more than 30 distinct calls he described with such words as *kukwik, kikkoo, kulkulk, kowulkulkulk,* and so on. I grew up with ravens' voices in my head, but I always thought of these calls as "the sound like a water drop" or "the sound like I'm being laughed at." What unnerves me in a raven is not fluency but silence, the silence of a bird that has fixed you with a knowing gaze and is thinking things it chooses not to say.

Ravens seem equally charming and vexing. One year I helped hide colored eggs for an Easter hunt in Juneau; the ravens discovered the eggs long before the children did. When ravens inexplicably began poking holes in the covering on a giant satellite dish at the University of Alaska Fairbanks, technicians tried jiggling the dish mechanically to shake them off. When that failed, they sent out a "ravenator," a man armed with a firecracker gun to scare them away.

Probably it is too easy to see something of ourselves in ravens, to identify with the show-off vocabulary, a braininess unparalleled in the bird world, a complicated personality that serves as both ally and adversary in many cultures. Folklore tangles with facts. In Alaska, many people insist that ravens show wolves where to find moose and caribou so the birds can share the kill.

Science underpins most raven mysteries: heat exchange systems in their feet are known as *rete mirable,* or "miracle nets," and hyper-efficient internal combustion warms them in winter. Still, even King appreciates the appeal of a good raven story, if only because it stokes our own curiosity.

I witnessed the uncanniness of ravens when King attached a mouse-sized radio transmitter to the back of a bird he'd captured with a net gun. I wore leather gloves to hold the raven, but it flexed powerfully beneath my grasp, clamping its ebony beak on my fingers and twisting until I winced. The feathers gleamed with greens, blues and browns, unexpected sheens in a creature so black. The bird did not call out.

Glimpsing my reflection in the raven's fierce and glistening eye, I began feeling a little uneasy. No one wants to get on Raven's bad side; he did create mosquitos, after all. Sometimes, King says, he goes outside after work and finds ravens waiting—or so it seems. Sure enough, when we carried the indignant bird out in a dog kennel, a raven perched in a nearby tree took flight and passed overhead, uttering a derisive cry I didn't need a glossary to translate.

Last winter, I tried to be more watchful, like ravens. Once I saw a score of the birds plunging into updrafts roiling off the edge of a building and then tumbling out again. What else would you call this foolishness but play? I listened carefully to the hollow *kawws* echoing through the birch forest (or was is *kowah?*). When courting season arrived in February, the birds abandoned purposeful flight for barrel rolls, aerial filigrees, high-speed chases. Nature does not exist to teach us lessons, but, nevertheless, I learned something about how to survive winter with spirit intact.

There are worse things than to be caught in the eye of a raven. Late one afternoon, as I walked my dogs along a snowy trail, a raven swept overhead bound for its roost. The swoosh of feathers eddied in the still air as the bird looped around for a closer look. The failing light of the sun gilded its breast. Twice more the raven circled us and then flew on, darkness falling from its wings.

Chapter 47

FISHING THE COMBAT ZONE

April 1998

By Les Palmer

Slumped on the riverbank like a boxer collapsed in his corner late in a losing fight, I watched the scene before me with punch-drunk wonder.

The shore was choked with anglers, subway tight, their rods a mad, waving thicket of cast, retrieve and cast again. Here a ferrule dove for the roiling water in a strained, trembling bend; there a rod whipped back, all pressure gone, line heartbreakingly limp as a salmon broke off. The air rang with yelps of joy, groans of disappointment, the atmosphere as frantic as the swirl of a grade-school playground. And suddenly I found myself grinning like a kid.

Alaska, you see, has tranquil wilderness waters aplenty but it also has *combat fishing*.

The crowds surprise first-time visitors to the state. The reason for these clusters of casters, of course, is that Alaska's salmon runs remain healthy. When fish migrate up streams, they attract anglers. And when great schools of salmon congregate in small areas near paved roads, fishermen go into a feeding frenzy.

My introduction to combat fishing began one June morning with a phone call from a friend.

"The reds are in at the Russian River," he said. "Let's start early and beat the crowd."

That crowd was exactly why I had always shunned the Russian. This time, caught off guard, I agreed to go.

Blame it on red fever. Each summer, sockeye salmon—"reds"—migrate up the Kenai River to spawn. Where the Russian River joins the Kenai, tens of thousands of reds sometimes hold, finning near the bottom, a few feet from shore. Reds average 6 pounds, and some weigh twice that. Acrobatic as steelhead, they're great eating, too. Even people who don't fish for anything else get red fever.

I'd never before angled *en masse,* but had always been curious about it. While driving to the lower Kenai Peninsula, I'd often stopped to watch and wonder at the throngs fishing the confluence of the Kenai and Russian rivers, where Alaska combat fishing began in the 1970s. Now I was joining the crowd.

We took our places in a long line of anglers waiting to board the ferry that crosses the Kenai. On the far shore stood what appeared to be a solid wall, a veritable phalanx of fishermen. They lined the banks of the river for as far as I could see.

More disconcerting, I noticed that everyone around me was packing heavy-caliber outfits loaded with 30-pound line. Holding my spindly 8-weight fly rod, I felt like a moped owner at a Harley meet.

On the other side of the Kenai, the scene was enough to set the most jaded meat-fisherman's heart to pounding. Rods flailed. Salmon churned the water. Cries of "Fish on!" rang in the chill morning air. Above all could be heard the blood-chilling *cr-r-rack!* of breaking lines, rods, and for all I knew, bones.

We moved up, warily eyeing the fracas from the top of the 10-foot bank. In the skirmish line below stood people of every age, sex, race and shape. At any given time, about one in 10 had a fish on. Behind them, others untangled lines and tied on new gear. Stringers of salmon lay about like battlefield casualties.

A hundred yards from the ferry crossing, we entered the fray. The angler nearest us gave us a look that said, "No room here, pal." But my friend, a hardened veteran of combat fishing, just waded in right beside him, grinning a cheery, "How you doin'?"

I rigged up. The area where the Russian meets the Kenai is "fly-fishing-only waters" but real fly-rod fanciers pass it by. The preferred fly, the "coho," is typically affixed to a sturdy spinning rig and sports a hook that could tow trucks from ditches. One-ounce sinkers are commonly used to drag this bushy, deer-hair streamer to the bottom in swift current. Leaders, when used, are 20-pound, minimum.

I walked behind the line, watching for an opening, scanning faces for any trace of human warmth or other exploitable weakness. But people were intent on fishing, their faces hidden under hats and behind sunglasses. I felt like a kindergartener on the first day of school. I must have looked pathetic, because a woman turned around and took pity.

"If you promise to be good, you can fish here," she said, making room.

I laughed and promised. The man downstream from her moved over a couple steps, and I was in.

As it turned out, I'd blundered into a family group. In no time, we were swapping banter like close friends.

And I do mean "close." Fishing was like casting from inside a phone booth. I learned to synchronize my casts with those of my neighbors, and to jerk my line from the water when someone yelled, "Fish on!" Every move required cooperation.

The first red I hooked launched into the air in a silvery arc, crashed back into the river and streaked off downstream. In a heartbeat, it ran across 20 lines, some of which were hooked to fish. My fly line and 100 yards of backing zipped away before I could break off the manic sockeye.

Hands trembling, I tied on new gear. All about me was mayhem. Now I knew why everyone had industrial-strength outfits. You didn't "play" these fish, you *fought* them. In what other angling setting is the ultimate demonstration of skill the ability to hook and land a fish in one motion?

Every few minutes, a fly would come unstuck from a thrashing salmon and zing back, sinker first, and hit something, or someone—thock! Women shrieked. Dogs barked. Babies cried. Strong men cringed on the beach, beaten and humbled by a fish with a brain the size of a pea.

Call me crazy, but in the midst of all this chaos I was having fun. With 40 years of angling behind me, I was experiencing fishing as I had never imagined it could be.

My next cast was a repeat of the first fiasco, except that I scorched my thumb and bloodied my knuckles on the reel handle before breaking the fish off. A few casts later, I hooked up again. A slab-sided rogue of a sockeye leaped toward the stars and shook like a wet dog. The fly snapped back and wrapped around an overhanging spruce, joining several other rigs fruiting its limbs.

I eventually retreated to watch from a safe distance, *hors de combat*. Several people nearby caught their limits of three reds and headed for home. Some, like me, hooked and lost fish, then sat watching, dazed. A good Samaritan offered me one of his salmon. Another handed me two coho flies and said, "You look like you need help." And so it went.

Months later, I was still telling people about that day. Not about the fish I caught—none—but about the sheer joyful *wackiness* of it all. And since that time, 10 years ago, I've been drawn back to the Russian many times.

Hey, once you've seen combat, everything else seems tame.

On the subject of combat fishing, misconceptions abound.

People use the phrase to describe any crowded spot. Trouble is, these can include places like Allison Point, where anglers cast for pink salmon from the shoreline of Port Valdez. Comparing this relatively serene experience to the Russian River run is like comparing the invasion of Grenada to World War II.

And somewhere along the way, combat fishing has gotten a bad rap. Fact is, lots of people kind of *like* having others around when they fish. By way of explaining this human trait, Kenai River fishing guide Joe Hanes reminds us, "Nobody goes to an empty bar."

Real combat fishing, the frenzied, shoulder-to-shoulder kind, occurs only during the peaks of salmon runs and lasts but a few days. For the remainder of the year, "combat zones" belong to the bears and eagles.

Of course even when a salmon run is peaking, not everyone joins the crowd. Anchorage resident Phil Cutler says he combat-fished at the Russian only once. After that, he walked upstream until the people thinned out.

"It's amazing," Cutler says. "If you walk a half-mile, you can be virtually alone in an almost pristine wilderness. People are so lazy. They just don't want to walk."

Some fear that "combat fishing" implies an atmosphere of animosity. In fact, most anglers are polite and helpful to others. Take Kenai resident Dan Patton, who makes the combat zone at the Russian sound like a love fest.

"I like people," says Patton. "They'll see me catching reds, and ask me what I'm doing. I show them how, and next thing, they're catching fish and having a great time. I love watching people catch fish."

Interestingly, the better the fishing, the more competition anglers will tolerate. When it's excellent, they sometimes fish three-deep.

Anglers say that they fish to fill their freezers. However, when pinned down, most will admit that their main goal is to have fun. Thousands of people can enjoy themselves in a small place, if they cooperate, says Chris Degernes, Kenai area supervisor for State Parks.

"Considering the number of people fishing at the Russian River, there are almost no problems," Degernes says.

Willow Creek, north of Anchorage, sometimes rivals the Russian as a combat zone. During the peak of the king salmon run, more than 400 people and 15 or 20 boats can jam a 400-yard stretch.

"It can be a real zoo," says State Parks ranger John Wilbur.

All things considered, though, these crowds of fisherfolk get along pretty well, Wilbur says.

Anglers sometimes claim that adding more fish or providing better access will eliminate the crowding that leads to combat fishing. Not so, says Kevin Delaney, director of the state's Division of Sport Fish. More fish would only attract *more* anglers, and better access would simply create additional high-use areas. Aside from limiting the size of parking and camping areas, the only other way to limit use is by a permit system. And people aren't ready for permits, Delaney claims.

Some streams, though heavily fished and often called combat zones, don't see much serious combat fishing. Take Ship Creek, so near downtown Anchorage that businessmen fish it on their lunch hour.

"It's the neatest thing," says Phil Cutler. "You take your tie off and put your hip boots on."

That "downtown" salmon fishing, both convenient and productive, does draw crowds. In 1996, some 15,000 people put in 55,000 angler days at Ship Creek, catching 6,000 kings and 7,000 silvers.

Ship Creek fishing has a special flavor, says Wayne Carpenter, "derby master" of the creek's salmon derbies. Compared to the Russian River, it's more mellow and not quite so "bumper-to-bumper," he says.

"When people go to the Russian, they drive a hundred miles or more," Carpenter says. "It seems like it's incumbent upon them to catch a fish, no matter what. At Ship Creek, it's a more relaxed atmosphere because they live nearby and can come back the next day."

Fishing guide Jeff Varvil, who has worked many Alaska rivers, calls Ship Creek "one of the state's best salmon streams."

"There's lots of camaraderie, lots of fish, and they're chrome-bright, fresh out of Cook Inlet," Varvil says.

David Eagle can look out of his office window and see the action at Ship Creek, 100 feet away.

"Last summer, I saw five guys hooked up with kings at one time," he says. "I haven't tried for kings there, yet, but I've done real well with silvers."

Finally, it must be admitted that combat fishing attracts a few anglers for the very reason most dislike it—the chance for some free competition.

"I'd rather combat fish than anything," says Ken Wardwell, of Anchor Point. "I want to catch more, quicker and bigger. I want to be the hero. It's really not much different than being addicted to something like poker."

In addition, when fishing is slow, a friendly crowd keeps things from getting boring, Wardwell says. He also notes that someone else's catch can help keep your spirits up when the hits are slow in coming.

As much combat fishing as he does, it's not surprising that Wardwell does occasionally have arguments. He even admits to having started a few. Taking someone's spot is the main cause, he says.

Still, instead of solitude, Wardwell purposely seeks out people—the more the better.

"That's where the fish are," he says. "Bunched up people are like a flashing neon sign that says, 'Fish Here! Fish Here!'"

Chapter 48

A FEW MOSQUITO BITES

October 1998

By Jim Rearden in the voice of Frank Glaser

During the 12 years I lived alone in the Savage River wilderness, I was constantly aware that, if I became injured or ill, I was on my own. My closest neighbors included bear, caribou, and moose—but no people. As a result, I was always careful not to fall when I was on my trapline or traveling in the mountains. I used an ax with great caution. I guarded against fire at my cabins. I handled my traps and guns with special care. I was cautious on river and lake ice. In short, I was always aware that I could not expect help if I got hurt or became seriously ill, and tried to conduct my affairs accordingly.

But I couldn't guard against everything.

In late May of 1932, I needed some babiche (rawhide) to repair one of my dogsleds. I soaked a moose hide in water, rolled it up and left it in a warm place so the hair would slip. After a few days, when it was slimy and smelled pretty strong, I scraped the hair off before nailing one end of the hide to a tree so I could cut strips from it.

Using a sharp knife, I walked backwards as I sliced nice long straight cords from the big hide. As I worked, mosquitos worried the back of my neck. I noticed a little blood on my fingernails after scratching the bites, but I paid no attention to it. I didn't think about the slime on my hands from the moose hide, either.

After all, they were only mosquito bites, common and minor annoyances.

But that night my neck started to swell. The glands under my jaw and in my armpits became hard and hot. For days my condition worsened. Finally, my jaw became so swollen I couldn't eat. My neck ballooned to about twice its normal size. I couldn't even hold water down.

After nearly two weeks of this, I became desperate. I cut deeply into the back of my swollen neck with a razor. It was terribly painful, but I kept cutting. When I felt I had cut deep enough, I stopped. By then I was bleeding heavily.

My large bottle of iodine, on hand for eight or nine years, had thickened to a syruplike consistency. I dumped some of this on my hand and rubbed it into the cuts. I immediately tasted iodine. Within 10 minutes the cabin began to whirl around, and I passed out, falling hard to the floor. A doctor later told me that the concentrated iodine was a strong poison.

When I came to, I realized I had to go for help. Unfortunately, it was breakup time and water was running bank-full in many creeks, while others were still covered by ice with water running over it. Worst of all, Savage River, which I had to cross first, was high. To compound my difficulties, I had seven big wolf-dogs to take with me.

I turned all the dogs loose, which I rarely did, because I always worried about them fighting. I left my rifle, which was almost like leaving my right arm, but I was so weak I couldn't have carried it. And, with my wolf-dogs accompanying me, I was in no danger from grizzly bears. I cut a strong cane to help me walk and to use if any of the dogs started a fight.

It was early in the morning when I slogged upstream on Savage River until I found a place where the water appeared relatively shallow as it flowed over the ice. I waded up to my waist, skidding on the slick ice, fighting to stay upright, the frigid water taking my breath away. I finally reached the far bank, only to face an 18-mile walk to Healy and the nightmare of crossing streams that were bank-high with water. On some of these I had to walk upstream for a mile or two to find a safe crossing. As I trudged on, I had to stop to rest frequently, and because of my swollen, sore neck, I could only lie face down.

My wolf-dogs realized something was wrong. There was no fighting, and during my frequent stops, they all gathered around me whining, wanting to help me. None strayed far from my side. Their behavior touched me.

With frequent rests on soft tundra moss, I walked all day and all night. While crossing over one mountain, I forced myself to climb nearly 2,000 feet; I'd go a short way, lie down and rest and, when I could, I'd go at it again.

I must have been a sight as I staggered into Healy, wet and bedraggled, with a grossly swollen neck, and surrounded by the pack of seven big wolf-dogs that walked quietly beside me.

John Colvin, a trapper friend, tied up my dogs, promising to take good care of them. Luckily, a coal train was ready to pull out for Fairbanks. The conductor, a good friend, put me in his bunk in the caboose, then gave me two

Anacin tablets, the first medicine of that kind I had ever had. The pain stopped and I went to sleep, not waking until we arrived in Fairbanks.

Once there, my conductor friend helped me walk the short distance to St. Joseph's Hospital. Dr. Aubrey Carter consulted with two other physicians before he operated on my neck to clean out and drain the poison. Just before giving me ether, one of the Roman Catholic sisters asked, "What is your religion?"

I was so sick that I wanted to get it over with. "Sister," I said, "I have no religion right now. Just let me have the ether and the operation." She insisted on an answer, but I repeated, "I have no religion right now." One big sniff of ether and I saw a black, spinning funnel. My last thought was, "Well, I'll get away from all those questions, anyway."

I awoke five hours later. Dr. Carter told me that the poison had been nearing my spinal cord and it probably would have killed me in another day or two.

I slept most of that day and night and awoke the next morning hungry as a spring bear. When a sister brought breakfast, I wolfed it down.

"Had enough?" she asked.

"I could eat more," I told her. She brought me another breakfast, and I ate all of that. It was the first food I'd had in more than a week.

Four days later I left the hospital feeling fine.

"What do I owe you, Doc?" I asked Carter.

"I'll make a deal with you," he offered. "If you'll promise to take me hunting next fall out at your place, we'll call it even."

That suited me fine.

He came to Savage River that fall and I helped him kill a nice bull moose and a couple of big bull caribou. He was very good company. When we talked over the disaster that had caused us to meet, we could only shake our heads in wonder.

Alone, I've survived charging grizzlies, dangerous climbs, violent rides on a bucking dogsled, breaking through river ice at 40 below, terrible mountain blizzards and months of deep cold.

But a few mosquito bites and a rotten moose hide almost killed me.

Chapter 49

SOCIAL CLIMBER

August 1999

By Martha Black (edited by Flo Whyard)

We left Dyea on July 12 at noon, to walk the dreaded trail of 42 miles over the Chilkoot Pass to Lake Bennett: first to Sheep Camp at the foot of the Pass, then to the summit, down to Lake Lindeman, round the shores of that beautiful lake, past the rapids and finally to the little village of Bennett.

With staff in hand, at last I had taken my place in that continuous line of pushing humans and straining animals. Before me, behind me, abreast of me almost every man toted a pack of 60 to 80 pounds, in addition to driving dogs and horses harnessed to sleighs and carts, herding pack ponies and the odd cow, while one woman drove an ox-cart.

We were lucky enough to be traveling light. We had let out a contract to a company of packers for the transportation of our clothing, bedding, and "grub," which weighed several tons. After much haggling we had secured a "reduced" price of $900 spot cash—this, in the words of the packers, "a damn low figger." After I got over the pass I agreed; it was a super-human effort to transport those thousands of pounds up that narrow, slippery, rocky trail of the pass, through boulder-strewn canyons, across swampy bottomlands. It meant changing every box and bundle from steamer to wagon, to horse, to man, to sled, and finally to horse, before they were landed on the shores of Lake Bennett, where we were to wait for the building of our boat, which was to take us downriver to Dawson.

A quarter of a mile from Dyea we crossed a toll bridge, and after the attendant had collected our toll of $1 each, he abused us because we would not buy a $5 steering paddle to use on the lakes and rivers on the other side of the pass. Fancy paying this price for it and carrying it over the trail too!

For five or six miles we followed a good wagon road, through cool, shady woods. We forded several clear mountain streams by stepping from stone to stone, and now and then I was carried across pick-a-back (I weighed only 110 pounds in those days). The trail became rockier, and we scrambled over tons of enormous stones and boulders, through four miles of a valley, with hardly a tuft of vegetation. It might have been the playground of the gods, so wild it seemed! My bulky clothes made the walking hard. My pity went out to the beasts of burden carrying their heavy loads. At three o'clock we stopped a half-hour for refreshments at a wayside cabin, kept by a widow and her little son. She brewed us a cup of strong tea and, as we ate substantial ham sandwiches, told us grueling stories of the rush of the year before.

Refreshed and undaunted we continued, soon reaching the little settlement of Canyon City. Here we struck the mountain trail which led to Sheep Camp, at the foot of the pass, where we planned to spend the night. As we traveled we began to realize that we were indeed on a trail of heartbreaks and dead hopes. On every side were mute evidences—scores of dead horses that had slipped and fallen down the mountainside (so few got over the pass) and caches of miners' outfits. We looked into a deserted shanty, where lay a mildewed ruined outfit. "Home of two brothers who died from exposure last winter," they told us.

And was I glad to call it a day when we arrived at Sheep Camp, the small shack and tent village of one street huddled between precipitous mountains. There seemed nothing permanent about it save the isolated glacier that glittered and sparkled in the sun above our heads. Before us was a huge pile of snow, ice, and rocks, the debris of the snow slide that had happened at Easter, and had crushed to death 30 such adventurers as us. We were greeted with the news that several more bodies had been discovered that day. They were buried under a large cairn of stones, which was pointed out to every newcomer. As I looked at it I could not help but feel that such a sudden end—to be snuffed out without a chance to make one's peace with one's Maker, and in a mad search for gold—was surely an ignominious death.

I looked up the pass. I can see it yet—that upward trail, outlined on an almost perpendicular wall of ice-covered rock, alive with clinging human beings and animals, slowly mounting, single file, to the summit.

We stopped at the Grand Pacific Hotel. In writing home a description of this to Father and Mother, I said, "Look at your woodshed. Fit it up with 'standees,' and you have the Grand Pacific." But I had no such uppish attitude when, weary and footsore, I staggered in, and when I left, my heart was warm with gratitude to the elderly couple who kept it. In addition to the regular supper bill of fare I had half a canned peach. I was given the only "private room" in the house—a cubicle partitioned off by a wooden wall, two-thirds the height of the room, with a built-in bunk filled with hay and covered with two pairs of gray Army blankets and—comfort of comforts!—a real feather pillow!

After a wonderful night's sleep, a hearty breakfast of cornmeal mush, bacon, and cold-storage eggs, condensed milk, prunes, and a whole orange—the last one in the camp—and settling our hotel bill (meals and bunk $1 apiece), with high hearts that glorious July morning we started to climb that 3,000 feet of steep, narrow, icy mountain trail. The Indians said there was a curse on all who attempted it in summer, as the hot sun melted the winter snow, and it came crashing down—crushing everything before it. These avalanches had already taken a total of nearly 100 lives.

For the first hour we walked over the trail of the recent slide. In the melting snow I saw a bit of blue ribbon. Bending down, I tugged at it and pulled out a baby's bootie. Did it belong to some venturesome soul who had come to seek a fortune for wife and baby? Would those who were waiting for him wait in vain? Was this one of the hundreds of tragedies of this mad stampede?

I did not dare look round at the magnificent mountain scenery nor drink in the beauty of the tumbling torrents, for every minute the melting snow was making it more slippery under foot. The greatest of care was needed in crossing the dangerously thin ice that was often the only bridge over a mountain stream, which had paused a few moments on a narrow ledge, to drop over a precipice, hundreds of feet below.

As the day advanced, the trail became steeper, the air warmer, and footholds without support impossible. I shed my sealskin jacket. I cursed my hot, high, buckram collar, my tight heavily boned corsets, my long corduroy skirt, my full bloomers which I had to hitch up with ever step. We clung to stunted pines, spruce roots, jutting rocks. In some places the path was so narrow that, to move at all, we had to use our feet tandem fashion. Above, only the granite walls. Below, death leering at us.

But soon, too soon, I was straining every nerve, every ounce of physical endurance in that ever upward climb. There were moments when, with sweating forehead, pounding heart, and panting breath, I felt I could go no farther. At such times we dropped out of line and rested in the little snow dug-outs along the way. But such a few moments of rest! Then on with that cursing procession of men and dogs and horses, pulling sleds or toting packs.

Mush on . . . Mush on . . . It beat into my brain . . . Cracking of whips . . . Wild screams of too heavily loaded pack horses who lost their footing and were dashed to the rocks below . . . stumbling . . . staggering . . . crawling . . . God pity me!

Mush on . . . Mush on . . . Another breath! Another step . . . God give me strength. How far away that summit? Can I ever make it?

Mush on . . . Mush on . . . or die!

"Cheer up, cheer up, Polly!" I hear my brother, George, break the long silence. "Only a hundred feet to go now." One hundred feet! That sheer wall of rock! Can I make it? In some inexplicable way the men of our party get round me. They push and pull me. They turn and twist me, until my very joints creak with the pain of it. "Don't look down," they warn. I have no strength to turn my head, to speak. Only 10 feet more! Oh, God, what a relief.

Then my foot slips! I lose my balance. I fall only a few feet into a crevice in the rocks. The sharp edge of one cuts through my boot and I feel the flesh of my leg throbbing with pain. I can bear it no longer, and I sit down and do what every woman does in time of stress. I weep. "Can I help you?" "Can I help you?" asks every man who passes me. George tries to comfort me but in vain. He becomes impatient. "For God's sake, Polly, buck up and be a man! Have some style and move on!"

Was I mad? Not even allowed the comfort of tears! I bucked up all right and walked triumphantly into the broker's tent—an ancient canvas structure on the summit. I had made the top of the world, but "the wind that blew between the spheres" cut me like a knife. I was tired, faint, hungry, cold. I asked for a fire, and was answered, "Madame, wood is two bit's a pound up here." George, who was really concerned about me, spoke up: "All right. All right. I'll be a sport. Give her a $5 fire." One heavenly hour of rest. I took off my boots, washed my wounded shin and poured iodine on it. I dried my wet stockings, had a cup of tea, and got thoroughly warm.

We then went through customs, as we had now entered Canada. Around us, shivering in the cold wind, were many waiting people, their outfits partially unpacked and scattered about them in the deep snow. It was here that I met for the first time members of the North West Mounted Police, and I thought that finer, sturdier, more intelligent-looking men would be hard to find.

Then the descent! Down, ever downward. Weight of body on shaky legs, weight growing heavier, and legs shakier. Sharp rocks to scratch our clutching hands. Snakelike roots to trip our stumbling feet.

We stopped at the half-way cabin for a $2 supper of bean soup, ham and eggs (of uncertain age), prunes, bread and butter—the bread served with the apology of the proprietor, "The middle of it ain't done but you don't have to eat it. I hurried too much."

I had felt that I could make no greater effort in my life than the last part of the upward climb, but the last two miles into Lindeman was the most excruciating struggle of the whole trip. In my memory it will ever remain a hideous nightmare. The trail led through a scrub pine forest where we tripped over bare roots of trees that curled over and around rocks and boulders like great devilfishes. Rocks! Rocks! Rocks! Tearing boots to pieces. Hands bleeding with scratches. I can bear it no longer. In my agony I beg the men to leave me—to let me lie in my tracks and stay for the night.

My brother put his arm around me and carried me most of the last mile. Captain Spencer hurried into the village, to the Tacoma Hotel, to get a bed for me. It wasn't much of a bed either—a canvas stretched on four logs, with a straw shakedown, yet the downiest couch in the world or the softest bed in a king's palace could not have made a better resting place for me.

As my senses slipped away into the unconsciousness of that deep sleep of exhaustion, there surged through me a thrill of satisfaction. I had actually walked over the Chilkoot Pass! I would never do it again, knowing now what it meant . . . Not for all the gold in the Klondike. And yet, knowing now what it meant, would I miss it? No, never! Not even for all the gold in the world!

Chapter 50

THE BEAR AND THE BRIDE

September 1999

When a 13-year-old boy kills "the big animal,"
he finds that his troubles have just begun.

By Sidney Huntington as told to Jim Rearden

The bear raided our fish-drying racks during the night. Our sled dogs lunged on their chains and yammered into the darkness, but when we rushed from the cabin with a lantern we saw only the downed racks and our scattered, partly dried fish.

At daylight I found tracks where the bear had prowled. "A black bear, Dad?" I asked. "I don't think so," he answered, peering. "Black bears are eating berries, getting ready for den-up. I think it's a grizzly."

A grizzly. The strongest, most dangerous animal in the region. I had briefly seen a swaggering, hump-shouldered grizzly a few weeks earlier. It could have been the same animal.

It was 1928, and I was 13 years old. The previous year my Caucasian father, in ill health, had yanked me and my 11-year-old brother, Jimmy, out of the Indian Service Eklutna Vocational School so we could join him and his partner, Charlie Swanson, at their remote trapline in northern Alaska. While he was still able, our father wanted to teach us how to survive in the wilderness. Our Koyukon Indian mother had died when we were both babes.

So now we lived in a riverbank log cabin, and most of our food came from the land. That fall we picked 40 gallons of blueberries and preserved them with layers of sugar in wooden kegs. We picked another 10 gallons of low bush cranberries, plus an assortment of a dozen less common berry varieties. We dried mushrooms and killed many fat ducks and geese and dried the meat for winter use.

We were still catching a few pike, whitefish, and worn-our salmon in the gillnets we set in eddies of the Koyukuk River. We split and hung them to dry, planning to feed them to our sled dogs during winter. The dried fish also made good bait for marten and mink sets. The fur we caught brought dollars for ammunition, tools, sugar, flour and other basics we couldn't get from the land.

So the loss of our dried fish was serious. Without enough to feed them, we might have to kill some of our dogs, which we needed to run our trapline. The grizzly had to be stopped. He'd found easy food, and he'd be back for more.

"I'm going to catch the bear, Dad," I declared.

"Go ahead," he replied, knowing that doing things ourselves was the best way for us boys to learn. He didn't have much time left to be teaching us.

I made a snare from a length of airplane cable that flying game warden Sam White had given me, and set it between two trees on the raider's trail. That night we listened for the fish stealer to return as we read and worked at domestic chores in our lantern-lit cabin. All remained silent though, and we bedded down.

We were awakened at dawn by a chorus of roaring grizzly, screaming dogs and snapping brush. In bare feet and long johns I streaked from the cabin, grabbing Dad's .30–40 Winchester lever-action that was propped by the door. I'd fastened the cable to a stump, and the bear was bulldozing a circle around it, mowing birch saplings like grass. Its bawling raised hairs on the back of my neck.

I fired into the bear. The .30–40 kicked like a mule, but I didn't notice. The rampaging animal slowed, and I fired again.

"Shoot again, before he charges!" Dad yelled.

After several more shots, the bear fell and I ran toward it.

"Stop! Sidney, stop! Keep back!" Dad shouted.

He then lectured me on carelessly approaching a freshly downed bear. "Dead" bears are the ones that get up and kill you.

The animal looked huge to me, but Dad said it was a small grizzly. It was old, with worn teeth and a scarred face. We skinned it, and after aging it, tried to eat the meat, but the flavor was so strong we couldn't handle it. Even our sled dogs wouldn't touch it, so we tossed the unused meat into the river.

Near freezeup my uncle, Little Sammy, a brother to my mother, arrived from his distant cabin to spend the night. He spotted the grizzly skin. "Where did you get it?" he asked Dad.

"It's Sidney's bear," Dad explained, relating how I had snared and shot it.

"Pretty foxy, Sidney," Little Sammy said. "You use head. You slow big animal down so you can shoot. You pretty young to get big animal already. I was much older before I killed one. That's when they said I could have a partner—a woman to live with."

Not once did he use the words "brown bear" or "grizzly bear." No respectful Koyukon Indian ever spoke directly of a "grizzly" or "brown bear." It was always obliquely, "that big animal."

I didn't know what Little Sammy was driving at, but I think Dad suspected. After much talk about the skill I had built, salmon I had caught with a fish wheel on the Yukon River, furs I had trapped the previous winter, and finally the "big animal," Little Sammy came to the point: "You are young, but I have to say you have earned the right to have a woman partner."

My jaw dropped, and Dad and Charlie grinned. Little Sammy had made his point and dropped the subject. For weeks after Little Sammy left I was needled about my wife-to-be. "Ya got your lady partner picked yet, Sidney?" Charlie might ask during a quiet evening when we were reading. A rip in my clothing brought a sly smile from Dad, "Better get your wife to fix that, Sidney." I was making breakfast once when Jimmy wised off, "I bet you'll be glad when your wife gets here so you won't have to cook."

Girls were a mystery to me, and I didn't appreciate the teasing.

On a cold winter day a few months later my Uncle Weaselheart, another of my mother's brothers, arrived from Hughes by dog team with our mail. His brother, Little Sammy, had told him about the grizzly.

With Dad, Charlie Swanson, Jimmy and me sitting around the cabin with the stove glowing and cups of coffee, Weaselheart asked me about the bear. After I'd recounted the incident, he asked, "Have you ever caught a black one?"

I had, in fact, killed two black bears, one in its den during the winter when I had stumbled onto it while setting marten traps, the other while blueberry picking. "Two," I told him. "Good," he said.

Then Weaselheart broke the big news he had brought. "The family (meaning my mother's Indian relatives) has found a 12-year-old 'woman' for Sidney to marry," he said.

I was dumbstruck, and Dad exploded. "Sidney's just out of diapers. How in hell is he going to support a woman, let alone himself? Let's at least wait until he's dry behind the ears."

"But Jim," Weaselheart said patiently, this is the Indian way. Besides, I've paid $5 to the girl's parents for Sidney's right to marry her. He has proven himself to be a man."

The custom of granting the privilege of marriage to a young man when he killed a "big animal" was an ancient Koyukon tradition, going back to when bears were killed with bow and arrow or spear—a far cry from what I had done.

I stuttered a bit, and blurted, "Thank you, Uncle, but I think Dad is right. I'm not ready to support a woman."

For years after, the girl would hardly speak to me. She was forced to marry an old man, and she blamed me because I hadn't accepted her as my partner. When I snared and shot that grizzly, I had no idea I would get myself into such a stew.

Chapter 51

THE EELS ARE HERE

December 1999/January 2000

By Frank J. Keim

We were in the middle of an Alaska Studies class when a running figure paused at the open door to whisper excitedly to one of my students. His news spread rapidly, developing into a general hubbub before I was able to make out these words, "The eels are here!"

That was the end of class.

We'd known for some days that lamprey eels were on their way upriver, because people in town were in constant touch with friends and relatives in the downstream villages of Pitkas Point and Pilot Station. With excitement fueled by anticipation, I grabbed my coat and camera, and away I went, following my students. By now, there was a mass exodus from every schoolroom, as elementary and kindergarten teachers joined their children to watch the action by the river.

This run was particularly thrilling because the eels hadn't passed through Marshall for the last four or five years. Some winters they simply had not shown up at all, during others they'd used the south channel of the river and bypassed us.

Everyone had his or her own theory to explain the dry spell. The Elders said it was because people had left some eels on the ice after catching them and had wasted the food. The spirits of the lampreys had been offended by this, and they were teaching us a lesson by not coming back. The returning run might, the Elders thought, mean that the eels were ready to give us another chance.

When we got to the Fortuna Ledge overlook, it seemed as though the whole village had shown up to welcome the returning lampreys. It was a radiantly clear day, with the last of the season's sun just peeking over the mountains to the southeast, and I could see people lined up along the riverbank for half a mile. Everyone was busy dip-netting; slicing the water with eeling sticks; or putting on rubber gloves, grabbing up writhing knots of captured eels and tossing them into large containers. Since the river was not yet frozen over, the men were stationing themselves along the fringe of shore ice that had formed during the previous two weeks. They thrust their long-handled dip nets deep into the strong current, pulling them first downriver, then back up again, then abruptly out into the waiting hands of relatives who helped dump the nets, each heavy with a frantic tangle of eels, into nearby containers or onto solid ice.

As soon as the lampreys were shaken loose, the nets were dipped again. The routine was repeated with dogged determination, time after time. Very few dippers allowed themselves to take breaks, since no one could predict when the run was going to end.

Many of the men grew tired, but they took pride in, and continued motivation from, the enormous (and still growing!) piles of eels. Tens of thousands of lampreys were writhing and churning and slithering and sliding like giant worms all around me as I walked along the edge of the river.

The only other time I'd ever seen anything approaching this harvest was back in 1991. But then there was almost a foot of ice on the river when the run came through, and instead of nets nearly everyone had used eeling sticks.

These traditional tools are long and thin and made of straight-grained wood, measuring about 8 feet long by 3 inches wide by a half-inch thick, and toothed with nails on both narrow edges. After cutting a slot in the ice about 12 feet long by 1 foot wide, both men and women slashed the sticks deep into the water from side to side, throwing the impaled eels out at either side of the narrow hole. There were huge piles of lampreys then, too, but nothing compared to this year.

The scientific name for the creature causing all this excitement is *Lamprey japonica*. It's a snakelike fish that breathes through gills that are located under seven holes on each side of its body, beginning just behind its circular, toothed mouth. The adult lamprey is a parasite, attaching itself like a suction cup to the sides of larger host fish, including salmon, and feeding on their blood and other body fluids.

Every November these eels migrate up the Yukon River beyond Russian Mission to spawn in the sand and gravel beds of the river's clear-water tributaries. After spawning, the adult eel dies. Come spring the eggs hatch into small, red, wormlike creatures called ammocoetes, which are both blind and toothless. These young eels (also called elvers) live in the sand and mud at the bottom of streams and rivers for two to three years. During this time they mature, developing eyes and teeth, after which they are ready to begin their journey downriver to saltwater.

In a curious case of turnabout, as the young eels enter the Bering Sea they sometimes become a rich food source for the year's first run of king salmon. "That's probably why our early kings smell and taste so much like eels," a fisherman told me. Once out in the open ocean, the adults feed and mature at least three years in preparation for their own long migration back up the Yukon. During their time at sea some of them grow to be quite large. One of the men on the banks held up an eel that he said, grinning, was "the world's champ." It must have measured almost 3 feet long and 2 inches thick.

By 11:30 a.m. the main part of the run had passed the village, and the dippers were catching few eels. The many clusters of fishermen and their families gathered at the edge of the shore ice were beginning to pack up their catches and wait for the next pulse of eels, which they expected within a few hours. The lampreys on shore had started to freeze. This made it easier for the fishermen to pick them up and put them in their storage containers, which, in addition to large plastic totes, included freighting sleds, barrels, and even an old wringer washing machine.

When they got their catches home, the fishermen would store some away for themselves, share some with Elders and others who weren't able to participate in the work party, and eventually feed the remainder to their many dogs. As I stood by, one of the local mushers tossed a few freshly frozen lampreys to his team before leaving the riverbank. Since eels have a lot of oil in them, one per day is all the dogs get, he said. Otherwise they'll suffer from diarrhea. People, too, have to be careful. It's best to either bake or boil the lampreys to render out most of the oil.

Eels are most commonly preserved by freezing, although some villagers who own pressure cookers can them. I've eaten them myself, and think they taste a little bit like anchovies.

Frozen or canned, the harvest is enjoyed throughout the winter and, with luck, will last until another run of eels wriggles past Marshall.

Maybe next November. If there weren't any lampreys left on the ice this year.

Chapter 52

AN ORCA REUNION

February 2000

By Mark S. Decker

During 10 years spent fishing near Unimak Pass in the Bering Sea, I've become friendly with a large group of killer whales. The huge mammals always seem to be waiting to welcome my boat, *Rebecca Irene,* when our search for bottom fish takes us to the pass (and readier, still, for the feast of fish heads dished up through the discard chutes of the trawler).

I've gotten to know individual whales in the Unimak Pod well enough to name them. The group is led by a huge, dominant male I call Bent Fin. Other prominent members include a female with two babies in tow and a piece of her fin missing (we call her Chunk); Bumps, a playful calf covered in lumps that look like orca acne; Goofy, who seems to spend more time swimming upside down than right side up; and old Hook, too elderly to challenge Bent Fin for leadership of the pod, but the largest of them all.

If I were a longline fisherman, I'd almost certainly not have such a friendly relationship with these whales. Orcas learn to eat sablefish and turbot right off the longliners' hooks, and such vessels can lose an entire catch to the thieves. *Rebecca Irene* is a factory trawler, however. The orcas don't bite through the meshes of the nets we tow behind us, and seem content to sup on the leftovers from our onboard processing plant.

The floor of the Bering Sea is like an undersea plain that gradually rises into shallows near Bristol Bay. Just north of Unimak Pass is an area called the Horseshoe, which lies on the eastern edge of deep water. The Horseshoe is a very productive fishing ground; it's also the summer home of the Unimak Pod.

My boat trawls for ground fish there, harvesting various species of sole, flounder, cod, and turbot. The orcas that follow us have become picky eaters.

Turbot heads are their clear favorites, with sablefish (also called black cod) running a close second. The whales will actually spit out an arrow-tooth flounder head if they spot a turbot snack within easy reach.

Before the whales can eat, of course, our nets must be brought on board and the fish sent below deck for processing. Between haulbacks, when the factory runs out of fish to process, the flow of whale treats stops. The Unimak Pod responds immediately to this outrage. This usually takes the form of about 10 minutes of tail-slapping (each one cracking like a rifle shot) and spy-hopping, which involves raising the front halves of their bodies from the water to look on deck or peer at me in the wheelhouse. They honestly seem to be trying to figure out what the hold-up is.

If the chutes still don't spit out any fish following this display, the whales will pull away about 100 yards or more and lazily keep pace with the boat. As soon as they hear the hydraulics kick in to raise the net, though, the whole pod comes charging back, and the tail-slapping and spy-hopping begin again. Goofy will commence swimming in circles upside down, and old Hook will take up his traditional position in the stern, patiently waiting for lunch.

When I returned to the fishing grounds in April of last year, the Unimak Pod was already there, as usual, having arrived at the Horseshoe from wherever it is they spend their winters. I stood at the rail and waved to the ones I recognized, feeling only a little foolish. Old Goofy came close to the boat, spy-hopping so high that only her tail remained in the water, and seemed to look me right in the eye. She repeated this greeting five times before backing off and returning to the peaceful monotony of her upside-down patrols.

All was not well, however. After I'd been in the pod's territory for more than a week, I had yet to see old Hook. Each day new members of the extended orca family turned up, but the ancient patriarch didn't show. Since he's the largest of the seven or eight mature males that are the pod's "big bucks," I knew he was well into orca senior citizen status. Maybe, I speculated, the long trip to the summer grounds was too much for him this year. Perhaps he decided to hang out in the Southeast and entertain the cruise ships.

Or maybe he had gone to that great fishing ground in the sky.

Each morning, with my first cup of coffee in hand, I'd go to the rail to greet the pod and welcome any new arrivals. "Still no Hook," I'd mumble to myself before heading back to the wheelhouse, worry nagging me. But then, on

April 26, I woke to sunshine and a light southeast wind. Latte in hand, I stepped outside just in time to see Hook glide by the ship's starboard.

"Hello, old fellow," I said, grinning despite myself, "glad you've finally arrived." I lifted my mug in a toast, and Hook rolled on his side in seeming acknowledgment, huge brown eyes looking into mine.

Hook was clearly hungry. He took up his rightful prime feeding spot at the bottom of the chute. The other whales seemed to back off, as if consciously giving him, for this one day at least, first choice of the groceries. He was, I thought, looking a bit thin, as if suffering the effects of old age and a long, difficult swim from somewhere. But for the moment, at least, he was done with hardship.

"Your worries are over, old boy," I whispered, "it's haulback time."

Chapter 53

TRACKED BY A BEAR

February 2000

By Dana Stabenow

OK, folks, you want to be real quiet now," Gary Porter said in a low voice. Since a grizzly sow and two 1-year-old cubs were at that moment 10 feet away, I wasn't about to argue. The sow was in the lead, rolling up the narrow path, dragging the backs of her paws along the ground, big, sharp claws hitting first when she put them down again. Her dark brown fur was thick and wet. Her head, lowered beneath powerful shoulders, was constantly in motion, swiveling between the fish in the creek and the 14 of us reclining in camp chairs on the bank. Her eyes were little and mean. She didn't look the least bit cuddly.

Bringing up the rear, looking wet, cold, and hungry, the cubs were major whiners. It was one long continuous moan, Mom, I'm hungry, Mom, feed me, Mom, I'm starving, Mom, do I have to stay starved, M-o-o-om!

The sow glanced our way. I felt like I'd wandered into the middle of Jurassic Park, and tried not to look like protein.

Gary Porter is the owner and operator of Bald Mountain Air in Homer, Alaska, and was our pilot, that day, of a deHavilland Single Otter, which, Gary said with a grin, used to belong to the Nicaraguan army. With that grin, you never know if he's telling the truth or trying you on, but it's a good story, and, if you're like me, that's partly why you fly with him. It's guys like Gary who make books like my *Fire and Ice* possible (In 1998 Stabenow launched a new mystery series with *Fire and Ice*, in which the female protagonist, Wyanet Chouinard, runs an air taxi operation in the Bush).

Gary's been flying since he was 12 years old, and flying bear watchers to Katmai National Park for the last seven. Going bear-watching with Gary is not like going bear-watching on McNeil River; you don't have to try for a permit in the Park Service's lottery and maybe you win and maybe you don't. You just make a reservation at Bald Mountain Air with Gary's wife, Jeannie, drive to Beluga Lake in Homer, and climb on board. You don't have to camp out, either, it's over and back the same day, always a plus for me, since I did my share of moose hunting when I was a kid and have sworn an oath never to sleep beneath a fly tent again.

It's a 90-minute flight, and on the way we saw no less than five pods of gray whales. There were spectacular views of the Barren Islands, Cape Douglas, Afognak, Shuyak and Kodiak en route. We landed in a delightful little bay, on the southern shore of the Alaska Peninsula, protected by a miniature archipelago and steep mountains still layered with ash from the explosion of Mount Katmai in 1912. We ate our lunch on board a 65-foot yacht, piled into a skiff and headed for shore . . . and bears. Grizzly bears, the undisputed mammoths of the ursine world. Lots of them.

I did kind of wonder what I was getting into. When I was a kid growing up in Alaska, my mother said that bears were cantankerous animals that would just as soon eat you as look at you. Stay away from bears, she said. OK, Mom, I said, and I did, too.

Now here I was, sitting down (to make sure I wouldn't run), in hip boots (so I couldn't run very fast anyway), armed only with a camera. It didn't help that one bear tracked us from the skiff to where we would sit. He was a young bear, Gary said, recently kicked out by his mother, and he looked skinny. And hungry.

Another sow with two 3-year-olds could be seen far up the curving beach, steadily approaching. A boar was napping, a mountain of fat and fur sprawling on the sand. Others fished the creek, rearing up on their hind legs and splashing down hard on their front legs, startling the fish into moving so they could see them and catch them. And eat them.

Goldie, the bear who had followed us up the beach, was a pitiful fisher. He chased after everything, never caught anything: The salmon simply snapped their tails in scorn. One collared bear, on the other hand, was so obliging as to catch and eat a salmon right in front of us. She ripped that fish apart like it was Kleenex—there were salmon eggs flying everywhere. The seagulls, hovering hopefully nearby, were pleased.

The bears had a routine, a path they walked regularly, up the creek in front of us and down the dry creek bed in back of us. Sometimes we were surrounded by bears, few of which I am relieved to report paid us much mind.

"If you're in the same place at the same time every day, acting the same way," Gary said, "pretty soon you're part of the scenery."

Of course he also told stories about boars tearing into cubs the moment a sow's back was turned. "Why do they do that?" someone asked. Gary replied, a thoughtful crease in his brow, "Well, you know, I think the boars just think the cubs taste good."

Right.

There were eight bears converging on the creek mouth as we left. It was an experience like no other I have ever had, and I wouldn't have missed it for anything, but I wasn't sorry to go. Lessons learned young are the ones that stick. Stay away from bears, Mom said.

OK, Mom.

If you decide (despite my mother's warnings) to join Gary on a bear watch, you'll be in Homer at least two nights, as the trip to Katmai is an all-dayer. Stay at the Driftwood Inn, the closest thing Homer has to a historical building. A one-room schoolhouse in the '30s, it has since been reincarnated as a hotel. You can't beat the location on Bishop's Beach, where you can walk for miles and there is always enough driftwood to build a fire. Owner Merlin Cordes and his roommate, Carol, a University of Alaska classmate of mine, set up a table next to the fireplace in winter and invite guests to play board and card games. (Be careful, Carol and I used to win all our beer money at school paying pinochle.)

And as long as you're in the area, there are two things in town you shouldn't miss. One is the Facing the Elements forest trail in back of the Pratt Museum. I can't tell you what you'll see there because it changes every year, a show of work by local artists in accordance with a common theme. This year my favorite was the McDonald's sign mounted on spruce bark beetle-killed stumps, accompanied by a poem that began "In this hollow-graphic age . . ." Homer artists have strong opinions, and aren't shy about expressing them.

And then there's the sperm whale exhibit at the Homer High School. A local fisherman found a dead whale washed up on one of the Barren Islands in 1988, and—with the combined efforts of the U.S. Coast Guard, the Pratt

SAVINGS CERTIFICATE

SAVE UP TO **45%** OFF THE COVER PRICE!

YES! I want to subscribe to Alaska magazine.

- ❑ 3 year subscription (30 issues) $49.95
- ❑ 2 year subscription (20 issues) $34.95
- ❑ 1 year subscription (10 issues) $19.95

Name _____ Address _____

BVLF02

City _____ State _____ Zip _____

E-mail _____ Phone No. _____

❑ Payment Enclosed   ❑ Bill me later   Charge my: ❑ Discover   ❑ Visa   ❑ Master Card

Card Number _____ Exp. Date _____

Signature _____

FOR FASTER SERVICE CALL TOLL FREE 1-800-288-5892 OR VISIT OUR WEBSITE AT WWW.ALASKAMAGAZINE.COM

Alaska is published ten times a year. Regular cover price is $30.50. In Canada, add $6.50 and $10.00 for foreign subscriptions. All payments in U.S. funds. Please allow 6-8 weeks for delivery of first issue.

GIVE Alaska TO A FRIEND

SAVE UP TO **45%** OFF THE COVER PRICE!

- ❑ 3 year subscription (30 issues) $49.95
- ❑ 2 year subscription (20 issues) $34.95
- ❑ 1 year subscription (10 issues) $19.95
    - ❑ New   ❑ Renewal

My Name _____ Address _____

BXLF02

City _____ State _____ Zip _____

Gift Name _____ Address _____

City _____ State _____ Zip _____

❑ Payment Enclosed   ❑ Bill me later   Charge my: ❑ Discover   ❑ Visa   ❑ Master Card

Card Number _____ Exp. Date _____

Signature _____

FOR FASTER SERVICE CALL TOLL FREE 1-800-288-5892 OR VISIT OUR WEBSITE AT WWW.ALASKAMAGAZINE.COM

Alaska is published ten times a year. Regular cover price is $30.50. In Canada, add $6.50 and $10.00 for foreign subscriptions. All payments in U.S. funds. Please allow 6-8 weeks for delivery of first issue.

BUSINESS REPLY MAIL
FIRST-CLASS MAIL   PERMIT NO. 512   MARION, OH

POSTAGE WILL BE PAID BY ADDRESSEE

Alaska

PO BOX 2036
MARION, OH 44306-2136

BUSINESS REPLY MAIL
FIRST-CLASS MAIL   PERMIT NO. 512   MARION, OH

POSTAGE WILL BE PAID BY ADDRESSEE

Alaska

PO BOX 2036
MARION, OH 44306-2136

Museum staff and the high school student body—it was recovered and the skeleton assembled to hang from the ceiling of the school's lobby. Look for student Jared Fisher's cartoons, which compare Charlie Sperm Whale to a school bus (Charlie = 41 feet long, school bus = 34 feet) and show Charlie's refrigerator filled with squid, octopus, sharks, and eels.

Chapter 54

CRISIS OF CONFIDENCE

August 2000

By Dan Randle

We sat underneath heat lamps, Alaska-bound through the Inside Passage, bundled in blankets and sleeping bags on the open-backed observatory deck of the Alaska state ferry *Matanuska*. When we'd left the ferry terminal in Bellingham, Wash., the night before, the temperatures were warm and the skies sunny. Now we sat huddled against the cold, but glad we had arrived early enough to find a spot underneath the ship's canopy. On the unprotected deck beyond, one saturated tent after another collapsed in the driving wind and rain.

My friends and I talked with a chatty couple from Soldotna. We told them we were on our way to Denali Park to guide on the Nenana River. They informed us that the Nenana is a very dangerous river—that it kills several people every year. Greg and I shot each other subtle, knowing smiles. You see, we knew better—we'd been guiding on the Nenana a combined 11 years, and had never heard of anyone getting seriously hurt during that time. We gave this couple a condescending "Wow, is that right?" then tuned out of the conversation. My thoughts drifted to the upcoming summer, and I wondered what the hell I was doing going back. I had a classic case of burnout. Guiding on the Nenana had, for me, changed from a fun summer job to a drudgery of herding human cattle down the river for a good paycheck and decent tips. I felt I had lost my love for guiding and my respect for the river. A few weeks later, on May 29, 1999, the Nenana taught me a lesson that will likely haunt me for the rest of my life.

I knew it was going to be a long evening's work. The air temperature was 38 degrees F, and the gusty wind made it feel much chillier. A cold snap had halted run-off into the glacially fed Nenana. The river had lost half its flow overnight, and the water level continued to drop—now lower than it had been at any time since breakup. Most of our passengers were part of a senior citizens' Baptist group from Georgia, on a whirlwind bus tour of Alaska. They were scheduled to arrive in Denali Park at 5 p.m., then go rafting from 6 to 10. Following a late dinner, they would be allowed a few hours of sleep before getting up at 4 a.m. for an eight-hour bus tour into Denali Park, only to hop on another bus and ride five hours to Anchorage. These people had been on a similar schedule for a week and a half now—the sort of experience that makes even the most affable of wives cantankerous and their already cantankerous husbands unbearable. Many of them probably had no idea what they'd be doing next ("Get off the bus now folks. You're going rafting").

Time to put on phony smiles and let out the warmest sounding "howdy" that could be mustered (gotta work those tips). There was a time when that grin wasn't fake—why was it becoming so difficult to be genuine? I was dreading the time ahead—three hours spent with cold, grouchy people—on the relatively boring Wilderness Float, known (not-so-affectionately) by the guides as the Wildee-Bunk.

In spite of my low expectations, my passengers and I were enjoying the trip. The insulated survival suits we had dressed them in were doing their job, and all were staying warm and happy. They were pleasant, talkative people who were interested in the land and waters that I still loved, despite my burnout. I felt guilty for having dreaded the float so much. I even recited "The Cremation of Sam McGee," something I did only for those I genuinely liked.

I had not recited it in a very long time.

About five miles into the 13-mile trip, there is a little section of class II-III rapids, where the river cuts into an ancient lava flow. At normal to high water levels this ledge creates a tricky wave that is popular among kayakers for surfing. At low flow, however, the river drops 2 feet over this lava ledge and creates an ugly, deceptively powerful keeper hole. The normal raft route during low water is a wide, easy-to-find tongue of water that runs between this 40-foot-wide hole and a rocky island. During my six years of guiding on the Nenana, I had seen the river much lower than it was on this night, so I wasn't expecting the dangerous conditions ahead. When we reached the rapids, though, I found the rocky island had shifted left during high water and the tongue of water had disappeared.

I watched the raft ahead of me hit the far right side of the hole, stop for a moment, and then float out down the river—no problem. My raft dropped into the hole and the same thing happened to me. Maybe it wasn't so dangerous after all. The last boat, guided by a trainee, dropped into the middle of the hole, stopped momentarily, and washed downstream about 10 feet. Then the roiling water sucked the raft back into the hole sideways.

I blew my emergency whistle and signaled for the boat ahead of me to pull over. As I reached shore, the stricken raft went vertical, lifting its entire floor out of the water. I tied off, grabbed a throw rope and picked my way upriver as fast as the slippery rocks would let me.

The raft in the hole was locked in a violent swirl: Every 10 seconds, it would go through a cycle of vicious beatings, then three or four spins in the hole, until the water pouring over the ledge caught an edge of the raft and sent it up on its side, to the point of almost flipping, before dropping back down to start all over again.

When I arrived, I was horrified to count only six heads instead of seven. I looked downstream, but saw no bright orange survival suit. I threw a rope to a guide in the raft, and he managed to tie it to the oarlock before the raft went for another near flip. Then the tug-o-war began. After almost 20 minutes of pulling and nearly being pulled in myself, I was exhausted. I could hear, along with screams of panic from the raft, my very own haunting words echoing in my head: "Who needs pulleys and other rescue gear, anyhow—it's only the Wildee-Bunk. What's the worst that can happen—someone will take a short swim. Hell, if someone falls in, it will teach 'em to hang on a little better."

I couldn't pull hard enough as I saw a woman lose consciousness and float face down in the self-bailing raft that wasn't bailing fast enough. I couldn't pull hard enough as that same woman slid into the hole and tossed lifelessly around for 30 seconds before washing out, face down in the cold, fast water. I knew that, if I couldn't pull hard enough to free the raft from the battering hole, others would not be far behind.

I was losing the last of my strength and the last of my hope, when out of nowhere, two men from my raft grabbed the rope and pulled. The three of us inched the raft closer to shore, yet were unable to free it from the hole. Realizing that we needed his help, the guide jumped in the river, using the taut rope to pull himself to the bank.

Despite our exhaustion, the four of us worked together and finally managed to pull the boat out of the hole and then to shore below—two people were missing.

We quickly broke into emergency dry bags filled with warm, dry clothing and treated the remaining five passengers for serious hypothermia. All were on the edge of consciousness and two of them blacked out several times. We spotted campfire smoke a short distance downstream, so we carried the bundled people to the raft and floated them to the fire.

When we reached the fire, we saw frightened people clustered around it, quietly, in a bright mass—watching. I saw my friend and fellow guide outside the huddle of orange, kneeling over something else that was orange—pumping his hands into that something orange. My friend looked up—and I saw an exhausted, frightened, sickened expression on his face—a look that can come only from going mouth-to-mouth with river water, stomach bile . . . and death. I quietly asked if he had recovered a second swimmer, and he shook his head no.

I helped unload and carry my passengers to the fire, then set out for help, wishing I hadn't forgotten the emergency cell phone that, just a couple of hours earlier, I'd been certain I would never need. I rowed downstream as fast as my exhausted body would let me—all the while knowing what I would find, but hoping I wouldn't.

Four miles later I spotted what I'd wished I would not see, snagged face down where the river trickles over a gravel bed. My weakened arms and legs struggled to lift the limp form. After a few minutes of literally wrestling the body into the boat, I started downstream again.

Taking a quick glance back, I noticed that, in my haste, I had left the corpse in an undignified heap. I remembered that, just hours earlier, this was a happy tourist—a sweet, loving woman from Georgia. I took the time to prop her up and at least make her look comfortable. We continued to float and my mind began to race with flashes of scenes from the accident and visions of things to come. Weary, sick-at-heart, my thoughts wandering loose in strange channels, I considered this silent passenger on my boat. I though of how ridiculous it would be if I asked her the typical questions asked of normal passengers, in order to spark a little get-to-know-you chitchat. *Is this your first trip to Alaska? Having a good vacation? Are you comfortable? Are you staying warm back there?* The idea of actually asking these questions almost made me laugh out loud—defense mechanisms starting to kick in. *Where are you from? Why are you here? WHERE HAVE YOU GONE? I'm sorry, I tried as hard as I could.*

I found myself weeping out loud.

The wind had settled down and it became abnormally peaceful and quiet on the water, and I, too, eventually found the peace of the emotionally spent. The artic sunset gave the high clouds and the tip of Mount Fellows a touch of pink. We floated past a mother moose standing protectively over her newborn twin calves. An overwhelming feeling of love for this land and for this river rushed over me with a paralyzing tingle, a renewal of my affection and respect for the dangerous beauty that is Alaska.

Then, just as the sunset reluctantly gave way to the dusky arctic night, that peace was broken by a frenzy of ambulances, rescue-helicopters, screaming police radios, and the beginning of an unending string of questions from owners, state troopers, paramedics, insurance adjusters, risk managers, lawyers.

And the only ones without answers are the questions I still ask myself.

Chapter 55

THE FIRST EVER NOME MOOSE NUGGET DROP

November 2000

By Lew Tobin

The concept for the "First Ever Nome Moose Nugget Drop" came to me after Alaska Airlines offered four gift tickets to help raise money for a local Junior Achievement project. I wrote a proposal suggesting that we number 3,000 moose nuggets, raffle them off and then drop them over a target. The owner of the numbered nugget nearest to the target's center would win the tickets, Junior Achievement would receive the lottery's receipts and all would benefit from the publicity that ensued. To my surprise, the idea was chosen.

When I took this news to the Nome Rotary Club, its members were full of support. The head of the local Correctional Center "volunteered" some inmates to number the nuggets. The local Civil Air Patrol offered to drop the moose poop out of their plane, and the First National Bank of Anchorage agreed to bear the cost of printing the 3,000 raffle tickets. Finally, a woman from the Alaska Mining Association offered to collect moose nuggets near her gold mine.

It all seemed so easy in September—then the problems started. The miner misjudged the number of nuggets she was able to collect by about half. By then, winter had set in, effectively burying our local summer's accumulation. In desperation, I went to the Internet and asked everyone I knew to collect moose poop—from zoos, parks, trails, even their front yards. Alaska Airlines offered free freight for my nuggets. I had friends from California to Michigan scheming and scavenging moose droppings for me. We even considered making artificial nuggets. Soon, I was getting e-mail, not just from my scat scroungers, but from public radio stations and The Associated Press. The AP, however, lost all interest in the story when its reporter discovered what moose nuggets were. The woman on the phone explained that the topic might prove too "controversial" to be heard at meal time. In light of vivid descriptions of the affairs of state from Washington, D.C., in recent years, I found it quaint that these reporters had scruples about discussing moose poop.

We petitioned the Federal Aviation Administration for permission to fly at less than 1,000 feet above the high school parking lot to drop our nuggets on target. That request was approved, but we were told we could not drop anything within 1,000 feet to any side of the school. The parking lot we'd planned to use was too close. We changed sites to a football field about a mile from the school, but the local softball league began voicing concerns over the residue they might have to play in the following spring, so we set our sights on the parking lot next to the field.

Then, the CAP sold its slow-flying Beaver with the trap door in its tail. One of its members offered the use of a Cessna 180 aircraft, instead. We would have to find a way to get the nuggets out the door, however.

By mid-October, moose poop was coming in from all over. Anchorage and Minnesota nuggets arrived first. Alaska Airlines had shipped them frozen to maintain their freshness. Unfortunately, the freezing was hard on the integrity of the droppings and they thawed into a soggy mess. Michigan's offering turned out to consist of summer nuggets from moose feeding on soft swamp grasses. They lacked integrity, as well. Fortunately, Montana's contributions soon followed and they were superb; firm but not brittle, golden brown . . . certainly these nuggets could hold their own against the best that even a real Alaska moose could produce.

The inmates worked through the weekend putting the last numbers on the new nuggets.

Meanwhile, I created an airplane dumping device affectionately christened "the poop chute." It consisted of two 8-inch sections of stovepipe with a damper in the middle and a metal hopper on top. We fastened the contraption between the seats and the open plane door with bungee cords and let the bottom of the stovepipe hang out. Because we had so many extra unnumbered nuggets, we preloaded a test batch of about 1,000 in the chute. We put a plastic bag containing the numbered nuggets in front of the passenger's seat.

Just before noon on "drop day" the ground crew set out with radios, cameras, a target and measuring string while the dumpers headed for the airplane. After trying to power through a snowdrift blocking our path to the drop site, I found myself proving the old adage that four-wheel drive vehicles just get more stuck farther from home. When I ran out of momentum, we could barely get the doors open, the snow was so firm and deep. The three of us unloaded and walked in, struggling through the drifts to keep on schedule. We were joined by the staff of the *Nome Nugget,* our local newspaper, about 15 minutes later. They had wisely parked on the main road.

Even though the camera was frozen, and we couldn't make radio contact with the drop plane when it came into view, we all stood in a line pointing out the wind direction. The test drop went perfectly. All 1,000 unnumbered nuggets left the plane in a tight circle, hung in the air a minute and then fell straight down, in unison. They looked for all the world like a swarm of honey bees. As the plane circled we braced for the real drop. It wasn't as dramatic, but a thin crescent of nuggets floated gently down to the snow. We raced to find the winners as the plane circled overhead. Just as we got to the site, the plane buzzed overhead and released more nuggets. They circled and made a fourth, and finally a fifth drop. It wasn't until the aircraft had completely left the area that we dared venture back into the target zone to pick out the winners. Then we abandoned our truck and hitched a ride with the reporters. Back in town we found out that an operator error had caused a malfunction in the "poop chute."

It seems the co-pilot/nugget bombardier had caught the edge of the hopper with the plastic bag while loading the numbered nuggets. The wind came back up through the crack at the front of the open door and sent nuggets buzzing around the inside of the cabin like a swarm of angry hornets. That problem became moot, however, when he opened the damper and the rest of the 3,000 moose nuggets blew back into the cabin. The pilot likened the experienced to being inside a lotto machine after the blower is turned on. For the next four passes, he and the co-pilot collected as many of the nuggets as they could grab out of the air and off the floor, and threw them out the door as they passed over the target.

The co-pilot was a psychology professor who had to go to work as soon as he left the plane. He said he had nuggets dropping out of his shirt during the class and he continued to find them in his clothes for the rest of the day.

In spite of the technical difficulties, "The First Ever Nome Moose Nugget Drop" was a success. We raised about $1,000 for the Nome Junior Achievement club and brought a laugh to just about everyone who heard about our adventures.

And, with sunlight shrinking by almost an hour a week as we phased into winter, that laughter was great medicine.

Chapter 56

GREEN SEAS, WHITE ICE

March 2001

By Toby Sullivan

The Opilio crab season began in January, and by the end of February we were tired, worn out beyond physical fatigue. We pulled crab pots 20 hours a day and lived on coffee and candy bars and one hot meal gulped between strings of gear. There were times when we worked long past midnight, praying for the last pot of the night, the steam from our breaths blowing away in the black and freezing wind. Exhilarated and exhausted at the same time we winched the pots over the rail hour after hour and shook the crabs out, dripping and golden in the brilliance of the deck lights. And every morning we crawled out of our bunks with four hours of sleep to chop ice off the deck equipment and start another day.

After awhile it showed on our faces in a way that reminded me of those photographs of weary soldiers after a battle, mud-covered men standing in a trench in France in 1917, or those haunting Larry Burrows shots of the Walking Dead Battalion slouching out of the Citadel in Hue in 1968. We had that same thousand-yard stare, that same unfocused dream state with the sunken eyes, an old look with a new name: the Aleutian stare. We'd sit at the galley on the run between strings of gear, so numb with the pleasure of just sitting down it was too much effort to pull our rain pants all the way off over our boots. We would drop the shoulder straps and peel them down around our ankles and collapse onto the bench or the deck around the galley table, curled up against each other like dogs. The ice on our raingear would melt and the water would run back and forth across the galley deck as the boat rolled. I would watch the rivulets, counting the rolls in a hypnotic repetition until the skipper called down the five-minute warning or until somebody let his cigarette burn down between his fingers and started swearing and jerked up back awake.

People would ask us why we worked like that, put up with that kind of misery, even for the sort of money they imagined we were making. It was true, you really could made $50,000 in 10 weeks, but there were loser seasons, too, when we never even made expenses.

And beyond the money, win or lose, people died at a rate far out of proportion to even the best crew shares. "The Russian Front," we called it, "The Most Dangerous Job in America" according to the Discovery Channel. Ten or 20 guys a year (out of a fleet of 1,500 men) were swept overboard, crushed by swinging pots full of crab, or "lost with all hands" when boats sank, or rolled over, or simply disappeared off the radar screen. But we blithely ignored the casualty rate with the sure assumption of the young that we were bulletproof heroes, beaters of any odds. We thought such fates belonged to other people, an unlucky few. Instead, amazed and beholden to the mix of danger and magic that existed in the Bering Sea, we thought ourselves gods. We thought we were lucky just to be there, to get rich (maybe), to live life extremely (for sure), all of it out in the ocean wilderness, a million miles from land.

We were always hearing stories that convinced us we were in a place outside the usual rules of civilization. Like the 20-year-old kid who lucked into a $100,000 crab season his first winter out there. Or the guy who had a fight with his skipper and walked off the boat the night before it went out and rolled over. (One last radio call at 2 in the morning, "Mayday! Mayday! Mayday! We're going over!" and then the slow circling of the Coast Guard plane all the next day over an empty ocean.) Or the Coast Guard helicopter rescues every winter that were almost predictable in their insanity. (The pilot flying blind in a snowstorm, trying to hold a hover over the sinking boat, 50-foot seas and hurricane winds, the crew chief hanging out the door on his safety strap, screaming directions into his headset—"Up! Up! Up!"—as the boat came up at them on a rising wave, the mast aimed like a spear at the belly of the helo.)

But sometimes there was simply a basic, animal joy in just being alive and young and present in the world, in seeing the beauty of the earth after a long night of working in the wind. We would stand in the wheelhouse after pulling pots all night, and the sun would rise out of the sea. In the dawn light the snow-covered volcanoes of the Aleutians were like a row of giant sharks' teeth far away along the southern horizon, sharp and pink and pure.

Seeing that with dry socks and the exquisite pleasure of fresh coffee—such moments were pure redemption. And all of it, the good, the bad, the horrific and the sublime, got mixed up and sucked down in a way that made the rest of your life on land seem like a black-and-white movie. And then just this, one more good thing, maybe the best thing: starting the long run to town with a load full of crabs, knees locked tight against the bin boards to keep from rolling out of our bunks, beginning the soft ecstasy of falling asleep, too tired to dream.

Chapter 57

THE CRUEL CHRONOMETER

July 2001

By Andy Hall

ummer in Alaska is the time when the midnight sun convinces me I can spend an entirely unreasonable amount of time out of bed, usually outside. The season's approach brings feelings of excitement and wariness: excitement for the activities that come with the warm weather and wariness because I feel as if I'm steeling for an endurance test.

I'm talking 18 hours of daylight and a dusk that never completely darkens. It is a breathless time; three months, more or less, when the sun must be cached against the dark winter days ahead. It's common to sit down to dinner at 10 p.m. or to stay up all night fishing, biking, hiking, or just talking with friends when most people are sound asleep.

There is, however, one element of summer I could do without and it's not the bears, the bugs, or the highway-choking RVs.

It's the fireweed.

The tall, reedy stalks waving their magenta petals in the breeze are common throughout much of the state. I can't think of a flower that is more synonymous with Alaska, except, maybe, the forget-me-not. Fireweed is beautiful. In momentary lapses I've even admired the way it tints a field or far hillside in gauzy crimson. Then I remember the flower's insidious little secret and look away.

The thing is, each fireweed is a living, blooming chronometer of summer, brilliantly marking the season's progress. Sometime this month, when the plant reaches a height of a foot or two, the first blossoms will emerge several inches below the tip. As summer progresses, the petals will climb continuously higher. When they reach the tip, summer is all but over.

For me it's like when the villain in a B movie inverts the hourglass and challenges the hero to complete his task before the sands run out. OK, that's a bit of a stretch, but I can't help but think that way. Worse, a patch of fireweed lines my driveway and, every night, whether I am returning from work or a family outing, I gauge the distance between the highest bloom and the top of the plant. It often prompts a moment of reflection: Have I made good use of the day? Can I complete that long to-do list before summer's end?

More than once I've glanced at the shrinking gap between bloom and tip and skipped watching TV in favor of a hike up the valley with Melissa. Or I've forgone dinner and thrown the float tube into the truck to spend an evening casting for trout in a glassy lake.

It is a compelling signal to get out and *do* something, because when bloom reaches tip and the plant goes cottony with seed, I know the wind that will spread next year's crop of fireweed will soon bear winter's first flakes of snow.

Come to think of it, maybe fireweed isn't so bad after all.

Chapter 58

MARY JOYCE'S EXTRAORDINARY ADVENTURE

March 2002

By Joan Pardes

ifty years before Libby Riddles proved that a woman could win the Iditarod and more than a decade before Barbara Washburn became the first woman to summit Denali in 1947, Mary Joyce decided to drive a dog team 1,000 miles from Juneau to Fairbanks just to see if she could do it. Unbelievable as it may seem, this record-setting event was just one of the many unprecedented accomplishments that Joyce enjoyed during her lifetime. In the 1930s—before Rosie the Riveter went to work and a mere 10 years after women were granted the right to vote—Joyce owned and operated a successful wilderness lodge. She also became the first woman radio operator in the territory and one of the few female pilots in the Juneau area. And, although it was certainly the fashion of the time to have a husband, Joyce never married. But from all reports, she never lacked male companionship.

Born in Wisconsin, Joyce's Alaska odyssey began in 1929 when she was working as a nurse in California. Legend has it that a wealthy matron, Mrs. Smith—as in Smith of the Smith-Corona fortune—hired Joyce to tend her alcoholic son while they journeyed to Alaska on their private yacht. During this vacation, Mrs. Smith purchased the Twin Glacier Camp to keep her son, Hack, out of the public eye while the family empire grew. The camp, 40 miles south of Juneau and between two glaciers on the Taku River, consisted of 15 buildings and a boat that would soon be named the 'Mary J.'

Hack Smith and Joyce seemed to thrive in the Alaska wilderness and while Smith developed competent hunting skills, Joyce became adept at handling the 15 dogs that helped haul wood and supplies to the roadless camp. As Smith's private nurse, she also learned to navigate the local waterways to fetch her charge out of the Juneau bars—a three-hour boat ride from camp. In 1934, after Smith died of a heart attack while hunting, the Smith family gave Joyce the lodge. She converted the camp into a tourist resort that could accommodate 30 guests and changed the name to Taku Lodge. The business thrived and along with tending her thriving enterprise, cooking all the meals and entertaining guests, Joyce became the first female radio telephone operator in Alaska when Pacific Alaska Airways (a subsidiary of the airline that is now known as Pan-Am) needed a communications station on the Taku for its twice-a-week run from Juneau to Fairbanks.

Although Joyce was known for handling dogs, boats and guns with a skill that was rare even among men, her plan to drive a dog team to Fairbanks met with skepticism. She was quoted as saying, "When I first got the idea of driving my dog team to Fairbanks, the people in Juneau said it would take me two years to drive to Fairbanks and that I would be pulling the dogs in. They also said that I would eat the dogs or the dogs would eat me."

Fortunately, neither prediction came true.

On December 22, 1935, Joyce hitched five dogs to a sled and headed north toward Fairbanks with a plan to arrive in early March to attend the fledgling Ice Carnival. Though headstrong and confident, Joyce did not make the trip alone. She began her journey with a group of Natives making their annual return to Atlin, British Columbia. At Tulsequah, she parted ways with her friends and set off on the nearly frozen river with a new guide. Her journal reads, "Chocak Lagoose (her guide) scolded his sons and made them put boughs over holes so I could not see water underneath while crossing. 'White lady plenty scared.' Crossed on my hand and knees and dogs followed like soldiers. Crossed upper Taku and another place over rapids on huge cakes of ice three feet apart held by sweepers and snags. Put chain on Tip (her lead dog) and each dog fell into water, pulled them out on another cake of ice. In places, just room for sled on ice cakes with water leaping over and gurgling underneath."

Meeting up with a new guide after traveling the Naxina River, Joyce struggled up Skolo Mountain for three days before reaching the summit, and then dropped down to Morton Hot Springs. "Traveled 20 miles through deep, fluffy snow. I hopped, skipped and jumped to pack snow down so dogs could pull sled up hills," she wrote in her journal. "Finally came to farm. Rapped on window. Two eyes glared out from glass opening and told me, 'Go away, you nobody,' a fact that I knew but hoped no one suspected. I was furious, but fear followed indignation and I got away in a hurry. After I got out of rifle range, I laughed heartily and mushed on. Trees beautiful as any trail of fairyland with each twig on every branch covered with frost and snow. Every tree an artist's model."

Joyce rested in Atlin for six days, then forged on with another guide following the Portage Trail into Yukon Territory and across Tagish Lake. They took the White Tail Pass rail route from Carcross to Whitehorse, where they restocked their food and changed sleds. A lack of shelter and temperatures that dropped to 60 degrees below zero made the next 300 miles, from Burwash Landing to Tanana Crossing, the most hazardous stretch of the expedition. Joyce and yet another companion followed the Kluane River and slept in a silk tent heated with a wood-burning stove while her dogs burrowed in the snow. On February 24, they reached the Alaska border and forged through deep snow for the next 25 miles to Tetlin and on toward Tanana Crossing in a blizzard.

Upon reaching the crossing, Joyce learned that several newspapers were tracking her progress and that her journey was attracting national attention. "Eastern cities are anxious over Mary Joyce's safety and have been making repeated requests for information," read one of the telegraphs that the *Fairbanks Daily News-Miner* received from The Associated Press office in Seattle. It also became apparent to the young musher that she would not reach Fairbanks in time for the Ice Carnival. Vowing to return to continue her journey with her dogs, she arranged for a pilot who happened to be at Tanana Crossing to fly her to the Interior city so she could take part in the festivities that included a 50-float parade, dog derby, ice pageant, skiing, snowshoe races and the coronation of Miss Alaska.

After arriving in Fairbanks, Joyce was met with a warm reception and the news that the people of Juneau had entered her in the state's beauty contest. She declined the opportunity to compete for the Miss Alaska title but gladly accepted an honorary membership from the Pioneer Women of Alaska. But as soon as the carnival ended and the weather cleared, Joyce flew back to her dogs to finish the remaining 250 miles of her journey.

On March 26, 1936, three months after leaving her home on the Taku River, Mary Joyce and her five dogs mushed into Fairbanks via the Richardson Highway. The *News-Miner* described the scene, "Bronzed by blazing spring sun reflected from measureless realms of snow, tanned by winds and weathers of all sorts, yet with light heart and buoyant step Mary Joyce, courageous 27-year-old musher, made her triumphant entry into Fairbanks completing a journey of some 1,000 miles by dog team and hanging up a record seldom if ever before reached in woman's world of achievement."

Known for her good judgment, poise and equanimity, Joyce reportedly seemed pleased but unfazed by the kind words and said, "It was a gorgeous trip. I just wanted to see the country and experience some of the things the old-timers did. I didn't hurry through it so I wouldn't get too tired. I just wanted to see if I could do it."

After her famous journey, Joyce returned to her life on the Taku River and shared her newfound celebrity with her salmon-eating cow. "That cow is the sweetest thing," Joyce told the local paper. "Why, when I feed the dogs, she just follows me around until I give her some fish. And if I don't, then she tries to drive the dogs away for theirs. She's just crazy about salmon." The following summer the cow became even more famous when it reportedly attracted the amorous attentions of a moose.

Regardless of her cow's fame, Joyce's legacy continued to grow when she took up flying and became one of the first female pilots in Juneau. Although she soloed after five hours, another record-setting event for an Alaska woman, she hung up her wings after a minor collision with a boat in the Gastineau Channel. She then rerouted her interest in aviation into a career as a stewardess for Pan-Am and Northwest Air. Joyce loved to travel, but she remained loyal to her home on the Taku ". . . where the most beautiful scenery in the world lies," she said after returning from a coast-to-coast trip. "Let me tell you that 'dog teaming' 1,000 miles was child's play compared with crossing one of New York's streets."

During the 1940s, Joyce and her dogs hauled radio equipment for the U. S. Navy, and entertained tourists in Sun Valley, Idaho, for a season or two.

During World War II, when the threat of a Japanese invasion seemed plausible, Joyce left her beloved Taku and moved to Juneau. She worked as a nurse at St. Ann's Hospital before buying the Top Hat Bar. From behind the bar of her popular drinking establishment, Joyce enthralled friends and visitors over the next several decades with the stories of her adventures. In 1976, in the home of friends, Mary Joyce died of a heart ailment.

Today, the back wall of the Lucky Lady, her former bar, is a shrine, complete with photographs, clippings and maps documenting her adventurous exploits. And, 40 miles south of Juneau, the Taku Glacier Lodge attracts more than 14,000 visitors each summer to Joyce's former home that still contains her sleds and other memorabilia.

But, after all that has been written about her, it was one of Joyce's pals that said it best: "Mary Joyce was one hell of a woman and lived a life that any man could envy." And, I might add, she lived that life 30 years before the feminist movement got their act together and without polypropylene or Gore-Tex. Now, that's tough.

Index